Labour Party Defence Policy Since 1945

Labour Party Defence Policy Since 1945

Dan Keohane

Leicester University Press
Leicester and London

*Distributed exclusively in the USA and Canada by
St. Martin's Press, New York*

Leicester University Press
(a division of Pinter Publishers)

First published in 1993

© Dan Keohane 1993

Editorial offices
Fielding Johnson Building, University of Leicester,
Leicester, LE1 7RH, England

Trade and other enquiries
25 Floral Street, London, WC2E 9DS *and*
Room 400, 175 Fifth Avenue, New York, NY 10010, USA

Dan Keohane is hereby identified as the author of this work as provided under Section 77 of the Copyright, Designs and Patents Act, 1988.

British Library Cataloguing in Publication Data

A CIP catalogue record for this book is available from the British Library

ISBN 0 7185 1467 X

Library of Congress Cataloging-in-Publication Data
Keohane, Dan, 1941–
    The Labour Party's defence policy since 1945 / Dan Keohane.
        p. cm.
    Includes bibliographical references and index.
    ISBN 0-7185-1467-X
    1. Great Britain—Military policy.   2. Labour Party (Great
Britain)   3. Nuclear weapons—Great Britain.   I. Title.
UA647.K43   1993
355′.0335′41—dc20   92-24749
                                                                                    CIP

Typeset by Florencetype Ltd, Kewstoke, Avon
Printed and bound in Great Britain by Biddles

Contents

Preface

In the period from the late 1940s until the end of the 1970s, successive British governments identified the Soviet Union as the principal potential military threat to the security of the United Kingdom and Western Europe. This view was shared by the leadership of the main British political parties and by the majority of public opinion. They agreed also that the appropriate response to this perceived threat was to maintain a balance of power in Europe. To this end it was essential to have US military forces, ultimately supported by that country's strategic nuclear capability, involved in the defence of Western Europe. Likewise, it was indispensable for Britain to participate whole-heartedly in the North Atlantic Treaty Organisation and to accept, or at least acquiesce in, the nuclear strategy of the alliance. It was well understood among Britain's political élite that a price had to be paid for retaining the US commitment. Part of the price was that Britain and Western Europe assented to Washington having a dominant role in determining NATO's strategy and direction.

In the half decade from 1979 to 1983, the general consensus on UK defence policy, between and within the main political parties, collapsed in the most unambiguous fashion. The breakdown of the national accord was expressed in fierce inter-party controversy, and in the near leading role of defence in the General Election of 1983. The Labour Party, which had established the consensus when in government after the Second World War (1945–51), broke with it on two related issues, namely nuclear weapons and the US role in NATO.

Spurred by the passionate revulsion of the British peace movement against nuclear weapons in the early 1980s, Labour repudiated any role for, or any reliance upon such weapons. Thus Labour judged that the risks of nuclear war between the hostile alliances of NATO and the Warsaw Pact were a greater peril than the improbable chances of Soviet military aggression in Central Europe. Accordingly, the Labour Party demanded the earliest unconditional removal of all US nuclear weapons from Britain, the unilateral renunciation of Britain's nuclear force, and the shift of NATO's strategy towards a non-nuclear policy. Labour's insistence upon the eviction of UK-based US nuclear arms was not only a rejection of those weapons. It was also a fundamental challenge to the US role in NATO and to a central tenet of the alliance. That tenet assumed that the member states accept the risks as well as the benefits deriving from participating in NATO.

Labour's repudiation of the Atlanticist defence consensus reflected deep cleavages within the Party. Along with other contentious issues, it led in 1981 to the departure of senior politicians to form the Social Democratic Party. In turn these divisions and splits, together with the unpopularity of some of the Party's policies, resulted in 1983 in Labour's worst election defeat for half a century.

Following another overwhelming election defeat in 1987, the Labour Party established a policy review process. It produced substantially revised policies, including a reformed defence policy in 1989. This modified policy narrowed the gap between Labour's approach to defence and that of other major British parties, mainly as a result of a disavowal of unilateral action regarding nuclear weapons and NATO. That gap was further reduced in 1990 and 1991, as NATO diminished its reliance upon nuclear weapons (in response to the transformation of politics in the Soviet Union and in Central and Eastern Europe), and Labour edged closer towards the consensus on nuclear weapons and NATO.

This book traces the evolution of Labour's perception of the Soviet threat and its approach to NATO and nuclear weapons until the mid-1970s. It goes on to elucidate the various domestic and international events and anxieties which produced the Party's profound alienation from the North Atlantic Treaty Organisation in the early 1980s. The study provides a detailed survey of the development of the Party's non-nuclear defence policy in the 1980s and it accounts for the Party's return to multilateralism by the end of the decade. Thereafter, Labour's response to the changed strategic environment of the 1990s is examined, and the book concludes with an assessment of the Party's defence policy up to 1992.

This study contends that in a complex and uncertain international context, Labour's defence policy often displayed a reactive and inconsistent character. Instead of identifying and then pursuing a coherent plan to shape Britain's strategic environment, Labour's policy reflected the strongest pressures experienced by the Party at specific times. From 1974 to 1979, Labour pursued a divided defence policy. In line with other NATO members, the Labour government supported both a nuclear dependent policy and the alliance decision to increase resources for military purposes. At the same time, the Party (i.e. the National Executive Committee and Annual Conference) took a contrary view on those issues. Such contradictions generated intense recriminations after Labour lost the General Election of 1979.

In the early 1980s, when the peace movement was at its zenith, Labour's defence policy centred upon the commitment to early unilateral nuclear disarmament by the United Kingdom. But the Party did not discover how to make the policy feasible nor how to persuade other nuclear powers to eliminate their nuclear capability. Towards the end of the decade, electoral and international pressures forced the Party to retreat from unilateralism. Then the Party's non-nuclear commitment was seriously weakened, and Labour did not quite succeed in mapping out a credible route to advance that objective.

In the early 1990s, at a time when the strategic environment has been transformed, Labour has not come forward with a full analysis of the options for Europe's defence. This reticence is associated with Labour's extremely negative electoral experience with its defence policy in the 1980s. Consequently, the Party decided against any major initiative on the subject and thus Labour lost an opportunity to influence thinking on Britain's defence relationship in the years ahead.

Turning to the structure of this book, the sequence is as follows. Chapter 1, covering 1945 to 1974, examines the values and principles of the Party as they related to foreign policy and defence. It goes on to explain how the different Labour tendencies viewed the Soviet Union (i.e. politics, ideology, capabilities, behaviour and intentions), and to indicate how those perceptions influenced their attitudes to the Atlantic Alliance. The final section of the chapter deals with Labour's cyclical approach to atomic-nuclear weapons over the years 1945–74.

Chapter 2, embracing the period 1975 to 1981, discusses the major change in Labour's approach to defence, which derived in part from the shift in the Party's leadership (i.e. in the National Executive Committee). It focuses upon the growing hostility of the Party to any reliance upon nuclear weapons and thus to NATO's strategy, and it explains how Labour came to reject the view that the Soviet Union was the primary military threat to Western Europe. The chapter also explores the divisions on defence between the Labour government and the Party in 1974–9, and within the Party in 1979–81.

In Chapter 3, which covers the period 1982–7, Labour's response to the perceived threat of nuclear war is delineated. Thus the chapter examines Labour's adoption of the concepts of common security and defensive deterrence, and it considers the implications for Britain and NATO were these notions to be accepted. In addition, the chapter reviews the evolution of Labour's defence policy in relation to domestic British politics, and it discusses the Party's view on how the country's defence role should be adjusted to match the UK's capabilities.

Chapter 4 is also set in the period 1982–7, but it concentrates on the consequences of Labour's non-nuclear policy for Britain's relations with the United States, Western Europe and the Soviet Union. The implications of the policy for Anglo-American ties could be especially significant as they impinged upon the US role in the NATO alliance.

The subject of Chapter 5 is the review of Labour's defence policy, which was part of the wider Policy Review process of 1987–9. It centres on the efforts of the Party leadership, within and apart from the Policy Review, to shift Labour to an unequivocal multilateral posture. This chapter examines the debate between Labour unilateralists and multilateralists and it concludes with an analysis of the rationale for the revised policy issued in 1989.

Most of Chapter 6 is concerned with the period 1989–92, but in addition it embraces international events which occurred in 1987–8. It starts with a review of the immense changes in the (then) Soviet Union and in Central and Eastern Europe. This is followed by a discussion of NATO's response to the new circumstances in Europe, and by an exploration of Labour's perspective on NATO and an EC-based defence system. The last part of the chapter provides a summary of Labour's perception of the Soviet Union at the start of the 1990s and an examination of the Party's view on Britain's defence role and expenditure at that time.

In the seventh and final chapter, there is an assessment of the coherence and feasibility of Labour's defence policy and of the role of the Party leadership in shaping it. The chapter concludes with an analysis of the prospects for Labour's defence policy in the changed strategic context of the 1990s.

Dan Keohane
Keele, August 1992

Acknowledgements

This book developed out of a NATO Fellowship project on the Labour Party's defence policy and its perception of the Soviet Union. As the project took shape, it became clear that a fuller treatment of the subject would be desirable.

Many persons have contributed, in various ways, to the writing of the book. At Keele, I am grateful for the advice of colleagues, and especially Alan James, for his sustained support and encouragement. Beyond Keele, I would like to record my appreciation to Adam Roberts and William Wallace for their counsel and support.

My knowledge of Labour's defence policy was much improved by interviews with the following Labour Members of Parliament: Robin Cook, the Rt. Hon. Denzil Davies, Sir Patrick Duffy (MP until 1992), Bruce George, George Robertson, Gavin Strang, and with the late Lord (Michael) Stewart. I also benefited greatly from interviews with Mike Gapes (Senior International Officer of the Labour Party until 1992, elected to the House of Commons in April 1992), Mary Kaldor (former adviser on defence to the Labour Party), and Len Scott (former adviser to Denis Healey). I am grateful also for valuable discussions with Eric Shaw and Karsten D. Voigt, Member of the West German Bundestag and SPD defence spokesperson, and for written communications from Labour MP David Winnick.

My grasp of US perspectives on Labour's defence policy was much improved by meetings (mainly in Washington, DC) with Peter Abbruzzese, Bob Bell, Richard Betts, Lynn Davis, Bill Hoehn, Robert Hunter, Charles M. Lichenstein, Robert Schaffer, Stanley R. Sloan, Walter Slocombe, James Woolsey, and James Steinberg.

I should mention as well that I learned a lot about Labour's approach to defence by attending fringe meetings at the Party's annual Conferences and discussion meetings organised by the Fabian Society and by the Labour Coordinating Committee.

My travel to the United States and elsewhere was facilitated by a NATO Fellowship, for which I am most grateful. I am very pleased to acknowledge my debt to Maureen Groppe and Pauline Weston for typing the manuscript. Finally, I am especially grateful to my wife Modesta for her support and understanding while I was writing this book.

1 Labour's perception of the Soviet Union and Britain's commitment to NATO, 1945–74

It is appropriate to start this study by outlining the Labour Party debate after the Second World War on whether the government should pursue a socialist or bipartisan foreign policy. In turn, that debate involved an assessment of the values and principles that should condition the outlook of a Labour administration in its conduct of foreign policy. It leads on to the central theme of this chapter, namely how Labour perceived the Soviet Union and the conclusions the Party drew from its perception.

Within the post-war Labour Party, there were differing perceptions of the Soviet Union, that is of Soviet politics and ideology, and Soviet military and economic capabilities. The basic issue was how the Labour government interpreted Soviet behaviour and intentions, because that judgement would decide the response of the United Kingdom.

From 1947, the Attlee administration concluded that Britain and Western Europe required a collective defence organisation embracing the United States to counter the Soviet Union. Labour Foreign Secretary Ernest Bevin played a central part in establishing the North Atlantic Treaty Organisation (in 1949), which provided the framework for Britain's defence policy for decades thereafter. The final part of the chapter examines Labour's approach to nuclear weapons, which in the early 1960s became a very contentious issue within the Party.

A socialist or bipartisan Labour foreign policy?

There is a deep difference of opinion between the Labour Party and the Capitalist parties on foreign as well as on home policy, because the two cannot be separated. The foreign policy of a Government is the reflection of its internal policy.[1]

This affirmation by Labour leader Clement Attlee in 1937 can be set against his view as expressed in the years after 1945. Then he noted: 'It is desirable, wherever possible, that, in foreign affairs particularly, Government policy should have the support of all. It strengthens us in giving what I believe is a necessary lead in international relations.'[2] This reversal in the approach of Labour's most enduring and successful leader marked his experience during and after the Second World War. It can also be found among many of his successors and it points to a persistent tension in the Party's handling of foreign policy.

The main issues of contention in this debate concern, first, the nature of the state, the international system, and how best to prevent war, second, the identity of Britain's adversaries and allies, and, third, the range of what Britain could achieve in its foreign policy. Those on the left of the Labour Party who regarded themselves as its 'socialist conscience' deeply distrusted the attitudes and outlook of the ruling establishment. In their view, a Labour government could not unreservedly espouse the traditional notion of pursuing the national interest. According to their perspective, which was widely accepted by the Party in the 1930s, adherence to the national interest would involve placing the narrow parochial interests of a particular state above the general interests of the international community. Moreover such a course would imply subordinating Labour's proclaimed commitment to, and solidarity with, working people and oppressed groups in other countries (with whom it had common interests) to appeasing the 'exploiting classes' in the United Kingdom. However, by joining the Churchill-led wartime coalition:

> Labour leaders had recognized that for them, as much as for Churchill and the Tories, there was an overriding national interest, a concept which many in the Labour Party had traditionally rejected in theory at least as incompatible with loyalty to internationalism and irreconcilable with the class war.[3]

They acknowledged also that Labour's deep repugnance for arms and for the use of force, a view which the pacifists in the Party greatly valued, could not survive in times of war or international tension.

With regard to the international system, the left of the Labour Party did not deny that the international scene was a very competitive and often a hostile environment, partly due to the rivalry and conflict among capitalist powers and between capitalist and non-capitalist states like the Soviet Union. Similarly, it recognised that in the anarchy of the international system a state which failed to demonstrate a willingness and a capacity to defend itself might be subjected to foreign domination. More positively, the Labour left stressed the need to diminish the role of force and of power in international politics, which it saw as a reflection of relationships of domination and oppression within states. It also favoured the transformation of the international system. This objective could be advanced by increasing the role of non-state actors such as trade unions, 'peace' organisations and professional and cultural groups.

In pursuit of changing the nature of the international system, it was contended that a Labour-ruled Britain should, in cooperation with like-minded governments and movements, endeavour to reduce the factors of mistrust, hostility and arms competition which produce international conflict and war. Until the 1970s, the United Nations was perceived by many Labour politicians as 'the chosen instrument by which the world can move away from the anarchy of power politics towards the creation of a genuine world community and the rule of law.'[4] Such a world community would, it was hoped, embody socialist values of social justice, cooperation and solidarity. Thus UN specialised agencies could be vital instruments whereby rich states could assist developing countries and simultaneously benefit the entire international community, without the donor states dictating to the recipient nations.

For many left-wing socialists, within and outside the Parliamentary Labour Party, the branding of the Soviet Union as Britain's adversary in the early post-war years was very difficult to accept. They regarded the Soviet Union as a socialist society with which they had significant affinities. It was even more unpalatable for them to acquiesce in a strong and close alliance with the United States, itself a country where socialist ideas and organisations were pitiably weak, and which epitomised the uncaring, materialistic, and untamed variety of capitalism. In contrast, many Labour Atlanticists admired the outlook, attitudes and policies of the liberal wing of the US Democratic Party. They felt themselves immeasurably closer to Roosevelt and Truman than to Stalin.

Atlanticists or centre-right Labour politicians like Attlee and Gaitskell did not differ greatly from their left-wing colleagues about the desirability of adhering to socialist values and principles. Rather they contended that power and force were inescapable realities of international politics which could not be wished away by fidelity to socialist norms of any state, including Britain. In their view, governments, especially socialist ones, should make the fullest use of diplomatic and other means to manage conflict. They believed that in the final analysis the possession of a strong defence was the essential and most effective way to prevent war. Thus many Atlanticists endorsed Attlee's comment that:

> There is always a tendency on the part of some people in the Labour Party to over-simplify foreign affairs. It's partly due to a certain woolly idealism, seeing everything black and white when in fact there are all sorts of shades of grey. They mean well but they don't like looking at unpleasant facts.[5]

According to the Labour Atlanticists, after 1945 two unpleasant facts left an especially deep imprint upon those responsible for the conduct of Britain's foreign policy. The one referred to the uninterrupted and grave relative economic decline of the United Kingdom, and the other related to the emergence of an apparently hostile superpower, namely the Soviet Union. These two elements combined to limit decisively Britain's freedom of manœuvre and to reduce its influence on the international stage after the Second World War.

Substantially due to the straitened and vulnerable position of Britain, a chasm opened up between the declaratory policy of the Party and the operational foreign policy of post-1945 Labour governments. To many, the latter seemed virtually indistinguishable from the course of Conservative administrations. For example, the Labour leadership committed itself to a series of highly controversial positions, mainly because of Britain's close ties with and heavy military and financial dependence upon the United States. Thus issues like the size and financing of the British rearmament programme in the early 1950s, German rearmament in the mid-1950s, and UK support for US policy in Vietnam in the 1960s produced convulsions within the Labour Party. These conflicts occurred because for many such British policies and obligations violated the very principles for which the Party stood. Likewise, the question of British possession of nuclear weapons caused deep divisions in the Party around 1960.

In the eyes of Labour realists, some left-wing Labour politicians preferred to proclaim their socialist commitment from the opposition front benches or the government back benches (in Parliament) than to run the risk of failure in office. The Atlanticists who monopolised senior posts in foreign and defence portfolios in Labour governments from 1945 to 1970 recognised that when in office leading politicians 'have both party and Government roles, and the claims of these roles are not always identical.'[6]

Thus when senior Labour politicians moved from opposition to government posts they were increasingly subject to the pressures of office. These included the demands of foreign governments, the obligation to respect the norms of collective cabinet responsibility and of official secrecy, and the continuous exposure to the advice and influence of experienced senior civil servants. In this way, the extent to which Labour leaders were in contact with and influenced by rank-and-file Party members greatly diminished.

For politicians holding senior office, whether they were Labour or another party affiliation, the attractions of pursuing a bipartisan foreign policy were very considerable. First, it was advantageous for a government to maximise domestic support for its foreign policy where this could be secured without sacrificing essential elements of its policy. Labour governments have felt vulnerable to Conservative Party charges that they (in contrast with Conservative governments) were not reliable defenders of the national interest. Accordingly, Prime Minister Harold Wilson found it necessary and beneficial, at least at the rhetorical level, to stress his devotion to promoting Britain's interests. With the exception of the late 1960s, when the Labour administration violated Party commitments by introducing immigration laws based upon racist sentiment, and reduced the level of overseas aid, Labour governments could claim to be reconciling their socialist values with the pursuit of the national interest.

Second, a British administration could play a more effective international role if it was evident that the agreements and commitments it undertook would not be dishonoured by its successors. This latter consideration also discouraged a Labour government from making radical departures in Britain's foreign policy. Consequently, left-wing members of the Parliamentary Labour Party found convincing reasons for their suspicions that Labour ministers' management of Britain's foreign policy reflected priorities and attitudes which too often were closer to those of Conservative administrations than to their own concerns.

Labour perceptions of the Soviet Union, 1945–74

This chapter does not, for the most part aim to examine why the British Labour Party subscribed to a particular perception of the Soviet Union. Rather it seeks to specify clearly the elements which constituted the Party's perception of that country. To this end it starts with an outline of Labour's view of the Soviet Union in the years following the Russian Revolution. Thereafter the study focuses upon Labour Atlanticists and left-wing assessment of the internal politics of the Soviet Union and of its military, economic, political, and external capabilities. It goes on to examine differing Labour interpretations of Soviet behaviour on the international stage.

The historical dimension

Due to a conjunction of circumstances, the British Labour Party regarded the Soviet Union with sympathetic if ambivalent concern in the early years after 1917. In the Party's view, the overthrow of the Tsarist regime was an occasion for celebration and the advent of Bolshevik power gave promise of advance in a socialist direction.

Although the Bolsheviks were unsparing in their condemnation of democratic socialist figures such as the leaders of the Labour Party, one factor was especially important in fostering Labour feelings of goodwill towards the emerging Soviet state. This was the Labour perception 'that the new Soviet state and itself suffered the implacable enmity of a common foe: international capitalism, especially in its virulent British form at the time.'[7] Specifically, the British Labour movement vehemently opposed British and other Western military intervention, 'more from dislike of further war than from any love of the Bolsheviks',[8] many of whose attitudes and policies were deeply repugnant to socialists in the United Kingdom. Because threats of a general strike by British trade unions were believed by Labour leaders, perhaps inaccurately, to have rescued 'the Russian Revolution from destruction',[9] the Party came to view the new Soviet state in a protective way. In 1924, the first Labour government, under Ramsay MacDonald, gave formal *de jure* recognition to the Soviet Union.

For decades after the Bolshevik Revolution, many Labour politicians and activists viewed the Soviet Union quite differently from those on the right of the British political spectrum. These Labour observers did not for the most part form their perception of the Soviet Union upon the basis of first-hand knowledge and experience. Rather in judging the Soviet Union in the 1920s and 1930s they stressed the cumulation of overwhelming problems which shaped the Soviet Union's polity and economy. These factors included revolution and civil war, Western military intervention, sustained hostility by the capitalist powers, the disruption following the First World War, and the economic backwardness of the economy. Labour analysts contended that in such particularly unfavourable circumstances the efforts of the Communist Party of the Soviet Union to establish a new non-capitalist order deserved recognition and critical support.

In the early period after 1917, it appeared to many in the Labour Party that the new Soviet state (which was gravely threatened from within and without by implacable enemies) could not be expected to demonstrate comparable respect for basic rights and legal processes as a secure and stable polity. The fact that the most intransigent domestic opponents of the Labour Party were also the sharpest critics of oppression in the Soviet Union did much to discourage Labour sympathy for such censure. At the same time, socialists who offered even mild criticisms of the Soviet Union were aware that they would thereby be branded as 'lackeys of capitalism' and the like by the Soviet Union and by British communists and fellow travellers. Labour observers appreciated also that some of those who stressed the failures and the inhumanities in the Soviet Union and denied its significant positive achievements used anti-communist sentiment to attack and weaken the appeal of socialist ideas in Western countries.[10]

In the 1930s many younger British socialists tended to view the Soviet Union in a favourable light, not so much due to events and developments there, but because of the apparent failure of Western political parties (whether of the left, centre or right) to resolve the daunting economic problems of the time. Moreover, these parties seemed unable to halt the advance of fascist movements in a number of European countries.

Despite the strong current of sympathy and admiration for the Soviet Union among British socialists in the inter-war years, 'the majority of Labour Party leaders' and the Trades Union Congress regarded the Soviet Union as a 'dictatorship of the Left as inimical to freedom as any dictatorship of the Right'.[11] They rejected contentions that in Western capitalist states there was no freedom worth defending.

Perceptions of the Soviet polity

In the years after 1945, three relatively distinct strands of opinion on the Soviet Union emerged in the Labour Party. In the view of the right-wing of the Party, the Soviet Union was 'a denial of everything Labour stood for and a travesty of socialism'.[12] Specifically it lacked democratic rights and the state controlled Soviet trade unions. Therefore for leaders such as Bevin, Gaitskell and Callaghan, and for many Labour trade unionists, the Soviet Union was anything but a model socialist society.

This perspective judged the Soviet Union largely by the standards of Western democracy. Adherents of that view welcomed the ending of the mass terror of the Stalin era as a positive development. Yet they regarded the repression of dissidents and the extensive violation of human rights, even as late as the 1970s, as proof that Soviet practice was still deeply repugnant to the values of democratic socialists. Neither could the Marxist–Leninist claim to possess a unique insight into the nature of socio-economic change and development find much credibility when the growth rate of the Soviet economy fell in the 1970s and the Soviet Union became increasingly reliant upon Western technology and grain imports.

For a large segment of the Labour left, the appropriate criteria for evaluating the Soviet polity were not identical with those applicable to societies with long traditions of democratic rights and freedom. Instead, due account should be taken of the absence of such traditions in the Soviet Union and the Russian Empire. Moreover, this view contended that the Soviet experience of Western pressures to 'strangle the Soviet revolution of 1917 in its cradle' [13] and the Soviet perception of external hostility and encirclement for most of its existence reinforced 'the Tzarist tradition of tolerating scant political or intellectual dissent'.[14] Thus Western intervention in, and unrelenting ostracism of the Soviet Union helped to produce Stalinism. It 'had contributed to making a nationalist caricature of a great international doctrine.'[15]

Labour politicians like Aneurin Bevan, Richard Crossman and Michael Foot rejected an anti-communist posture and this was an important element in distinguishing their approach from that of Atlanticists in the Party. But they still considered the Soviet polity as fundamentally incompatible with their concept of a socialist society. For them the 'autocrats of the Kremlin had betrayed the democratic principle without which socialism was not worth having.'[16] The unbridgeable gulf they perceived between Soviet society and a genuine socialist order had much to do with differences of outlook and tradition between the Soviet Union and the United Kingdom. In particular it had to do with the British commitment to reliance upon democratic means and Soviet espousal of oppressive methods. Moreover, in the decade after 1945 some British socialists believed that the Soviet leadership 'wanted democratic socialism in Britain to fail because otherwise it would present too formidable a rival.'[17]

The third strand in Labour perspectives on the Soviet Union internal order in the post-war years comprised those who found much to admire in the Soviet Union. These left-wing figures (e.g. MPs Konni Zilliacus, Tom Driberg, John Platts-Mills, James Lamond and William Warbey)[18] viewed the Soviet Union as a socialist–communist movement, which in the face of intense external and some internal pressure had secured major advances. They saw the Soviet Union as 'a Socialist country' and given a chance it 'might develop towards democracy'.[19] Many of this group did not deny that great crimes and purges occurred under Stalin's rule, the victims often being dedicated communists. Nor did they assert that the Soviet Union was free from serious defect either in its observance of human rights or in its economic organisation. At the same time they noted that in the West 'political democracy, as we understand it, free public debate' existed 'side by side with all the abuses of free enterprise', while 'in the East is found no unemployment . . . a vigorous attempt to plan society for the benefit of all: but no real freedom to criticize in speech or in print those in power.'[20] These Labour left-wingers believed that British socialists should be reluctant to criticise publicly the Soviet Union. They accepted that wherever possible in Europe (as in the case of the Nenni Socialists and Communists in Italy in 1948)[21] socialists should cooperate with communists to gain maximum influence for left-wing forces and objectives.

After 1945, certain events and developments produced major changes in the relative strength of the three Labour perspectives on the Soviet Union. In the aftermath of the Second World War, Labour's gratitude to and admiration for the Soviet contribution in winning that conflict was intense. Within two years, the Cold War confrontation between the Soviet Union and the Western Powers seriously tarnished the favourable image of the Soviet regime, if not of the Soviet people.[22] Over the following two decades, Khrushchev's denunciation of Stalin's rule, together with the Soviet invasion of Hungary in 1956 and Czechoslovakia in 1968, and the Sino-Soviet split, greatly weakened Soviet claims to be either a model for socialists–communists, or the leader of a united international communist movement.

Despite its ascent to superpower status by the early 1970s, the Soviet Union did not permit the development of democratic rights and freedoms nor did it offer acceptable solutions to problems which then concerned British socialists. Such issues included environmental protection, gender discrimination, and rising unemployment. Although the Soviet Union was believed to be comparatively successful in providing jobs for most of its work force, Labour observers (who were acutely aware of the relatively poor performance of the UK economy) looked to countries like Austria, Sweden and Japan for insights on the way to achieve prosperity. For these and for other reasons, the strength and influence of the pro-Soviet element within the Labour Party shrivelled to a minor force by the mid-1970s.

By that time, there was a great degree of consensus within the Labour Party regarding the internal order of the Soviet Union. Except for the remnants of the pro-Soviet left (e.g. MP James Lamond), many on the Atlanticist right and on the left of the Party would agree with Robin Cook's assessment that the Soviet leadership 'find it convenient to retain mass conscription and to promote a siege mentality towards external threats as part of their armoury of devices for manipulating the population.'[23]

Perceptions of Soviet military strength

In forming its perception of Soviet military capability after 1945, the Attlee government placed great emphasis on the imbalance between the Soviet Union on the one side and the countries of Western Europe on the other. The starting point of this approach was that at the end of the war 'The magnificent record . . . [of Soviet armies] . . . gave her immense prestige and popularity in all countries; for the first time since the revolution [the USSR was] . . . everywhere accepted as a major world power whose agreement was indispensable to the settlement of any world problem.'[24] At that time (1947), and for decades thereafter, Soviet forces controlled Eastern Europe and much of Central Europe, including part of Germany.

Compared to the immense military strength of the Soviet Union, the West European countries were extremely weak and vulnerable in the second part of the 1940s according to Foreign Secretary Bevin. Those societies had experienced defeat, occupation and humiliation during the war, and their economies remained close to collapse in the aftermath of the conflict. Moreover, Mr Bevin feared that economic and political weakness in France and Italy could enable the strong pro-Moscow Communist Parties to take power in those countries.

The 1945–50 Labour government believed that no single West European country could withstand determined Soviet military pressure. Even if those states combined, there was 'little chance of stopping the Red Army from occupying Western Europe.'[25] But lack of confidence in themselves and mistrust between the West Europeans reduced their capacity to act collectively in their own defence.

Like the Attlee government, Labour's left wing and like-minded analysts stressed the context of Soviet military capability. But unlike Labour Atlanticists, the latter group concentrated upon the context as viewed by Soviet decision-makers and how the West contributed to those Soviet perceptions. Left-wing observers[26] contended that Western interpretations of Soviet capabilities often neglected the factors which led to Moscow maintaining its military strength.

After 1945, it was argued that the recurring experience of external invasion and occupation induced the Soviet Union to overinsure in assessing the appropriate level of military strength. Following the uprisings in Eastern and Central Europe (East Berlin in 1953, Hungary in 1956), it became evident that the Soviet Union also had reason for much anxiety regarding the stability of regimes in those countries. That point was emphasised by the Soviet invasion of Czechoslovakia in 1968.

Second, left-wing analysts judged that viewed from Moscow the external environment appeared hostile and threatening. Thus the failure by the United States during the war to inform the Soviet Union about its construction of atomic weapons, together with the use of those arms against Japan, strengthened Stalin's feelings of vulnerability and technological weakness. Such perceptions were thought to be deepened by 'the establishment of American bases from Japan through the Middle East to Iceland'[27] in the years after 1945.

From the late 1940s, Western plans to rearm West Germany, the country especially feared in the Soviet Union, were likewise considered to exacerbate Soviet feelings of insecurity. Thus in the two decades after 1945, the Soviet Union was believed to be sustaining a major lead (over the West) in conventional capabilities, partly to offset American nuclear superiority.

The issue of Soviet military strength came to the forefront of Labour debates following the outbreak of the Korean War in June 1950. The Labour government accepted that the West Europeans, including the United Kingdom, should take measures to counter the immense Soviet military capability. At that time the UK government assumed that the Soviet Union possessed 175 combat-ready divisions. Under the intense promptings of, and largely to impress the United States, the Attlee administration announced a heavy rearmament programme in mid-1950.

By April 1951, Health Minister Aneurin Bevan (and others) resigned from the Labour government in protest against what they regarded as an unsustainable rearmament burden. Among other things, Bevan (who led the left wing of the Party for much of the 1950s), argued that the government had misjudged Soviet military strength. He accepted that the Soviet Union 'has at its command huge armies, masses of tanks, masses of aeroplanes and more submarines than the Germans possessed in 1939.'[28] But he agreed with the conclusion that 'The American superiority in atomic weapons is overwhelming' and the 'policies of the West are based on a gross overestimate of Soviet strength.'[29] For many years after 1951, Labour's left wing concurred with that view.

While perceptions of Soviet military strength did not attract particular attention within the Labour Party in the 1960s (Soviet forces were reduced substantially in the late 1950s), that situation changed in the 1970s. Then the issue of the relationship between NATO and Warsaw Pact military capabilities became a matter of keen contention within the Party.[30] The Atlanticist section of Party identified reasons for deep concern regarding the size, disposition, quality and strategic doctrine of the Pact's forces. Without specifying explicitly the criteria for their assessment, they argued that 'the size of these forces is beyond anything that the Warsaw Pact could conceivably need for its own defence.'[31] These observers noted that in numerical terms Warsaw Pact forces exceeded those of NATO by a large margin. In main battle tanks, artillery and fixed-wing tactical aircraft the Warsaw Pact was believed to enjoy a ratio of more than 2 to 1 over NATO while it possessed a lesser advantage in anti-tank guided missiles and in military personnel. These ratios added up to a highly unsatisfactory imbalance of forces.

Two other factors were perceived to exacerbate the unfavourable balance of forces between NATO and the Warsaw Pact. 'In particular the proximity of the Soviet Union to the central region would clearly favour the East should a period of heightened tension necessitate the reinforcement of those forces already on the ground.'[32] Thus, while the leading country of NATO, namely the United States, would have to transport reinforcements thousands of miles across the Atlantic, the Soviet Union could rapidly shift a substantial number of combat divisions and heavy equipment in the western district of the Soviet Union to the central front. Second, Atlanticists considered that since the late 1960s the major enhancement of Warsaw Pact naval forces in the Atlantic (such as Soviet submarines and naval aircraft possessing extensive range) intensified the threat to NATO's reinforcement capability.

With regard to trends in the NATO–Warsaw Pact balance of forces, Atlanticists identified three disturbing developments and responses. One of these referred to the perceived reaction of the Warsaw Pact to NATO efforts to diminish the advantage of the Pact which was 'to build up its conventional forces yet further, thereby fuelling the arms build up and making impossible the establishment of a relatively stable balance of forces in Europe.'[33] A second unwelcome development for Labour Atlanticists was that the long-established technological advantage in conventional arms held by NATO over the Warsaw Pact was being eliminated from the mid-1970s as the Soviet bloc introduced new tanks, artillery, helicopters and aircraft. Third, the deployment from the mid-1970s of new Soviet intermediate-range missiles (targeted upon Western Europe) exacerbated European perceptions of vulnerability to potential Soviet predominance.

In the view of Labour Atlanticists the advent of Soviet SS-20s (in the mid-1970s) became an issue of much concern when set alongside the other elements in the NATO–Warsaw Pact military balance. For decades the Warsaw Pact's perceived superiority over NATO in conventional capabilities was offset by the US lead in nuclear weapons, but from the end of the 1960s the Soviet Union had reached parity with the United States in strategic nuclear arms. Thus from the mid- to late 1970s the Soviet bloc was believed to hold an advantage over NATO in both conventional and intermediate nuclear capability, an advantage without mitigating or compensatory factors.

Analysts on the left of the Labour Party questioned the reliability of NATO data on Warsaw Pact military strength and they challenged interpretations based upon worst-case assumptions. Largely due to the obsessive secrecy and suspicion of the Soviet regime, the principal sources of data on Soviet military capability were US intelligence agencies. Accordingly, many Labour observers judged that it was prudent to be somewhat sceptical about the objectivity of information produced by those organisations.

Left-wing analysts suggested that the reliability of East European forces might be doubtful in some circumstances, noting that these countries had been the main victims of Soviet military might since 1945. While those forces would probably be entirely loyal in defence of their homeland, this might well change if they were used for aggressive purposes far from home. Therefore in certain situations, 'it is appropriate to deduct army divisions of her Warsaw Pact colonies from the army divisions of the Soviet Union, rather than adding them together, when calculating the potential military strength with which the Warsaw Pact might attack NATO.'[34] In addition, 'at least some part of the Soviet armed forces should be treated as garrison troops and possibly even subtracted from the total available for invasion of Western Europe.'[35] If such calculations were made for the Warsaw Pact, the Pact could be decidedly inferior to NATO in conventional strength. This Warsaw Pact disadvantage would be even greater if, as some left-wing (and other) observers suggested, the military strength of France were to be added to the NATO totals in the event of war in Europe.

The point of this questioning of orthodox Western interpretations was not to claim that alternative calculations were entirely correct. Rather it sought to illustrate the point that it was gravely misleading to claim that numbers which were 'alarming to the West and others like it, are bandied about every day as if they represented the true positions.'[36] Moreover, it was alleged that, not surprisingly, NATO and US spokespersons highlighted categories where the Warsaw Pact was ahead, while remaining circumspect about areas of Western superiority, such as the quality of aircraft.

Towards the end of the 1960s, the Soviet Union harboured fears of being attacked from two directions, namely China and the West. Those fears were exacerbated in the early 1970s as Sino-American military cooperation developed. From Moscow's perspective that development was a dangerous military encirclement and it indicated a potentially sharp deterioration in the world correlation of forces.

Left-wing analysts also contended that NATO and Western assessments, which emphasised states' quantitative and measurable elements of military capability, were of more limited value than appeared to be the case. One reason for this acknowledged limitation was the long-established Soviet tendency 'to hang on to equipment which NATO would long since have been scrapped (or sold to a poorer state).'[37] As a consequence, the apparent military strength of the Warsaw Pact was inflated. Likewise, observers argued that just as NATO tanks 'surpass Soviet tanks in number of rounds carried, rate of fire, long-range accuracy and degree of armour protection',[38] the Western alliance possessed a clear edge in the overall quality of its conventional weapons system. Moreover, it was noted that, given that

NATO divisions included significantly more personnel than Soviet-bloc divisions, a simple count of divisions gave a misleading picture of the relative strength of the two alliances.

According to left-wing analysts, NATO enjoyed a significant qualitative edge over the Warsaw Pact not only in weapons systems but probably also in military personnel. They argued that societies such as the NATO countries, which systematically rewarded initiative and enterprise, were more likely to produce fighting men and women who would respond effectively to the unpredictable conditions of war than relatively controlled and regimented polities. The Warsaw Pact might also suffer the disadvantage that its forces utilised a much higher proportion of 'short term conscripts with insufficient training'.[39] Thus, it was contended that NATO representatives had no need to mislead and persuade their populations and politicians with 'bean counts' of carefully selected indices of military strength. Most analysts, of whatever political outlook, accepted that the course of armed conflict was heavily influenced by factors other than those that could be easily quantified. These included matters like the morale, leadership, sustainability and training of forces, the cohesion, organisation and structure of personnel, and the nature of the terrain. Likewise, the length of warning time of an attack, and the time required to mobilise forces could have a big impact on the outcome of a war.

Perceptions of Soviet economic and technological capabilities

In the period of the Attlee government (1945–51), the major tendencies in the Labour Party made quite similar assessments of Soviet economic and techno-logical capacities. In 1947, Denis Healey, then International Secretary of the Party, suggested the immense costs of the war had set back the development of the Soviet Union by ten years. Mr Healey, who supported the outlook and policy of Foreign Secretary Ernest Bevin, contended that the destruction of 'a third of European Russia', along with the deaths of seven million and the homelessness of about thirty million, had left the Soviet Union in a very weak state.[40] This reality was hidden from the outside world because 'the Russians themselves preferred to minimise their crippling losses.'[41]

A few years later, in 1951, Aneurin Bevan contributed to a *Tribune* (newspaper) pamphlet, which argued that in any long war between the Soviet Union and the West the 'strength of the Western powers is overwhelming.'[42] It went on to note that the NATO countries 'produce six times as much steel as the countries of the Soviet bloc, three times as much coal, eight times as much petroleum, five times as much pig iron.'[43] In addition, the pamphlet called attention to the very low levels of productivity in the Soviet Union, which were said to be far inferior to those obtaining in the West.

In the late 1950s and early 1960s, the international image of Soviet technology was enhanced after the flight of Sputnik (1957) and the launching of the first person into space (1961). But those achievements did not translate into a serious economic or technological challenge to the West. By the 1970s, it was recognised in Britain and in the Labour Party that the Soviet economy faced grave problems of declining rates of growth in both capital and labour productivity. Thus, the claim made by Mr Khruschev (in the early 1960s) that the Soviet Union would surpass the United States in per capita output by 1970 remained unfulfilled. Agreement among Labour observers and other analysts regarding the relative inferiority of Soviet civilian technology *vis-à-vis* the West was coupled with a consensus that in 'the Soviet Union military technology is at a higher level than civilian technology.'[44] The advantageous position of Soviet military technology owed much to being the 'highest priority sector in Soviet industry',[45] and, as a result of receiving the best machinery and personnel, being largely protected 'from the shortcomings in the rest of the economy'.[46]

But the privileged position of Soviet military technology did not indicate that Labour analysts believed Soviet weaponry to be superior to those of the West. In fact, Labour observers, and especially those on the left of the Party, broadly agreed with the assessment that 'All the technological innovations the Soviet Union makes tend to follow the American lines: albeit at a slower rate, albeit with much greater emphasis on simplicity and quantity as befits the nature of their enterprises.'[47]

A further significant strand in Labour perceptions of Soviet material resources concerned the alleged distorted depiction of Soviet capability. This referred to Western estimates that the Soviet Union had allocated about twice the proportion of its gross domestic product (i.e. 12–17 per cent) for military purposes as did the United States. This assessment fuelled the conclusion that the Soviet Union constituted an immensely powerful military challenge to the West. It also supported the insinuation that the Soviet Union already harboured, or might come to adopt highly dangerous intentions about the possible external use of its very strong military forces. But in the view of many Labour analysts it was erroneous to associate security too closely with military capability because 'security is created by economic strength and political will as well as military power.'[48] In addition, Labour observers held the view that states were unlikely to enjoy sustained peace until just relations were established within and between countries.

When the economic strength of the Soviet Union was compared with that of the United States in the 1970s, it was noted that the latter's output was about twice that of the Soviet Union. Therefore in the view of Labour observers the high percentage of Soviet resources devoted to the military budget was comparable with the lower proportion of a much greater output allocated by the United States. These analysts contended that any exact assessment of the absolute or relative level of Soviet military spending was quite problematic for a number of reasons. That was because verifiable data regarding the Soviet military budget were lacking, Soviet prices did not necessarily reflect scarcity values, and the Soviet armed forces included a high proportion of conscripts. Moreover, there were formidable obstacles to converting expenditure in one country into resource costs of a quite disparate economy.

What Labour observers (who typically perceived high military spending as a severe handicap for the British economy) seemed quite sure about, was that Soviet military allocations constituted a grave handicap in achieving domestic growth, and in catching up with the more technologically advanced Western societies. In their view the Soviet Union possessed the attributes of a military superpower, but was relatively backward in the level of its technology.

Labour interpretations of Soviet behaviour and intentions

When the Labour Party came to interpret Soviet behaviour and intentions after 1945, it did so in a context of considerable familiarity with the behaviour of British communists and fellow travellers. For example, Foreign Secretary Bevin's view of the Soviet Union was influenced 'by long experience of the persistent attempts of the Communist Party, faithfully following the Moscow line on tactics, to penetrate and capture the British Labour Movement.'[49]

Labour believed that the Communist Party of Great Britain (CPGB) was a revolutionary group which took its orders from Moscow. The Party judged that if it did not maintain and be seen to sustain constant vigilance, the CPGB would subvert its organisation, policy and candidate selection, thereby inflicting fatal damage upon Labour. This would occur because the British electorate would reject any party which was believed to be closely associated with and infiltrated by the Communist Party.

In 1945 Labour refused an application to affiliate from the Communist Party. Subsequently the Attlee government enacted measures to exclude communists from sensitive posts (i.e. those related to national security), and the Transport and General Workers' Union banned communists from holding office. Yet in 1952, the future leader of the Party, Hugh Gaitskell, warned against the infiltration of Labour by communists, whereby a sizeable section of delegates to annual Conferences were communists.[50] Similarly, Labour leaders expressed concern about communist influence in major trade unions, and the Party prohibited its members from participating in or associating with communist-front organisations (i.e. World Peace Council).

By 1973–4, Labour's National Executive Committee followed a tolerant attitude towards British communists. By then, a left-wing and more liberal-minded majority led the National Executive Committee, disciplinary-minded anti-Communist Party officials had retired,[51] and coalitions of left wingers and communists held leading positions in major trade unions affiliated to the Labour Party. Moreover, the CPGB had become increasingly critical of the Soviet Union and it espoused policies and approaches quite akin to those of Labour's left wing.

Turning to the evolution of Labour's approach to and interpretation of Soviet behaviour and intentions in the post-war era, the years 1945–9 were especially significant. Starting with the perspective of Foreign Secretary Bevin and the right wing of the Party, three factors shaped their approach. First, with the elimination of states like Germany, Italy and Japan, only three world powers survived in 1945, namely the United States, the Soviet Union and the United Kingdom. Because of the immense advances in military technology, the 'frontiers of territorial influence of the Big Three ran everywhere together.'[52] Thus they were like 'three elephants in a boat'.[53]

Second, while Britain was determined to retain its world role, because of the war its exhausted and distorted economy was no longer capable of supporting such commitments. Britain's military strength was far inferior to that of the Soviet Union (and the United States), and the Soviet Union now occupied a dominant position in Europe.

Third, the long experience of Ernest Bevin with British communists, together with his negative view of Soviet leaders (a view which was fully reciprocated), infected Anglo-Soviet relations with a strong element of mistrust. Related thereto, Labour analysts considered the Soviet government enjoyed one 'inestimable advantage'.[54] Unlike democratic rulers, it could, without warning, completely reverse its policy (e.g. the Nazi–Soviet Pact of 1939) as it was not accountable to Soviet public opinion or the Communist Party.

In such difficult international and domestic circumstances, the Labour government had three possible options in its relations with the Soviet Union. If the Soviet Union was content not to exploit its strong position *vis-à-vis* the United Kingdom in Europe and elsewhere (and the United States did not exacerbate Soviet feelings of vulnerability), then the three world powers could continue their wartime alliance. That would be on the basis of accommodating each other's interests and cooperating in the reconstruction of a war-torn Europe. If, however, the Soviet Union sought 'the elimination of Britain as a European and Middle Eastern power,'[55] the United Kingdom had two choices. In principle, it could acquiesce in Soviet hegemony and follow a policy of appeasing Soviet demands. Such a course would be entirely contrary to the traditions of British foreign policy and could be seen as akin to the reviled appeasement policy of the pre-war Chamberlain government. Alternatively, it could seek to offset Soviet dominance and contain its perceived expansionism by seeking external support.

From mid-1945 to early 1947, the UK government identified what it considered incontrovertible evidence of Soviet hostility. Soviet encroachments against Iran and Turkey, which could be viewed as a great power's efforts to secure recognition of its legitimate interests, were seen by Mr Bevin as manifestations of an expansionist approach. The heavy Soviet reparations from its zone in Germany (themselves a product of Soviet economic weakness) placed a heavy and unsustainable burden upon Britain (in its German zone). Thereby, those Soviet impositions contributed immensely to the subsequent division of Germany into rival states. Labour leaders also perceived overwhelming evidence of Soviet intransigence and hostility in the negotiations between the Soviet Union, the United Kingdom and the United States, and at the United Nations.

From 1946 to 1948, the treatment of democratic parties and politicians in Eastern and Central Europe left a deep imprint upon Labour politicians. They knew that the leaders of the peasant parties in countries such as Poland and Hungary had been arrested and imprisoned while some were executed. In those countries the socialist parties were destroyed. This occurred because the Communists found

> socialist allies within the party, who were prepared (with Communist support) to force a split on the issue of working-class unity, set up a United Workers Party with the Communists and carry out a purge of those who refused to join.[56]

These events and the communist seizure of power in Czechoslovakia (1948) indicated to Labour politicians that a deep chasm separated them from communists on the issue of acceptable methods in politics.

The Soviet Union and its accomplices and supporters were seen to have no respect for free elections and democratic rights in Eastern and Central Europe. They were perceived to have used brutal and coercive means to destroy socialists and other political rivals, and their willingness to employ force was demonstrated further when the Soviet Union blockaded Berlin in 1948–9. Foreign Secretary Bevin played a key part in devising arrangements to balance and contain Soviet power by encouraging the United States to make a commitment in support of Europe and by translating the US offers into specific plans. Thus US economic assistance was embodied in the Marshall Plan of 1947 and the military security pledge was enshrined in the North Atlantic Treaty Organisation of 1949.

According to the Atlanticist right wing of the Labour Party, the behaviour of the Soviet Union, and of like-minded communists in the second part of the 1940s, conveyed a clear message. Within the Soviet Union, the Communist Party maintained a monopoly of power. Similarly, only communists who supported or accepted Moscow's direction were allowed to operate in the Soviet-controlled states of Eastern and Central Europe. Therefore democratic socialists like the British Labour Party 'are committed to the "anti-communist" camp not as a matter of choice, but by their very nature',[57] because they belonged to the Western democratic camp. It followed that, even if there was no military issue between the Soviet Union and the West, the existence of free European countries would endanger the Soviet bloc countries. That was illustrated by the construction of the Berlin Wall in 1961.

While the Korean War of 1950 increased greatly Western and British fears of Soviet expansionism (thereby accelerating the development of NATO), such anxieties were mitigated with the passage of time. But for the most part Labour Atlanticists accepted there were compelling reasons for accepting a sober and pessimistic assessment of the Soviet Union. Among these reasons were the perceived willingness of Moscow to resort to force and coercion in its relations with other states (Hungary in 1956, Czechoslovakia in 1968), the continuing ideological hostility between East and West, and the accession of the Soviet Union to the status of a military superpower. They also referred to the offensive character of Soviet military doctrine including the Soviet plans to take the initiative if war seemed unavoidable. In the judgement of Labour Atlanticists, if the NATO alliance experienced collapse or rapid fragmentation it might well produce a situation where the individual countries of Western Europe found themselves having to accommodate their behaviour to Moscow's wishes. It was thought that the Soviet Union was much more interested in seeking such dominance over Western Europe than in risking a catastrophic war in Europe.

The assumption that the West must maintain a guarded posture *vis-à-vis* the Soviet Union rested not only upon a reading of Soviet behaviour in the late 1940s. It was based also upon an expectation that any Soviet leadership was likely to sustain the ideological competition with the West. In addition, Atlanticists perceived that the West would be unable to maintain the confidence to reject Soviet pressures unless NATO sustained a credible military strength. This perception coexisted with a clear recognition that East and West shared the risk of catastrophic conflict. Accordingly, Labour Atlanticists acknowledged that they had a common interest with the Soviet Union in seeking to mitigate these risks, in reducing the burdens of military rivalry, and in increasing mutually beneficial contacts like trade.

In July 1945, Labour's left wing hoped for the continuation of Britain's wartime alliance with the Soviet Union, and it demanded that the Labour government pursue a socialist foreign policy. It was soon to be disappointed on both counts. Initially, much of the left criticised the belligerent tone of Foreign Secretary Bevin in his dealings with the Soviet Union. Gradually, however, it grew disillusioned with Soviet behaviour, such as Moscow's hostile attitude towards the Attlee government and the intimidation and persecution of socialists in the Soviet-controlled countries of Eastern Europe.

For about two years from 1946, much of Labour's left wing, such as Michael Foot and Richard Crossman, sought to define a course which was distinct from the Atlanticist perspective on the one side and the pro-Soviet fellow travellers on the other. They proposed a socialist Third Force of European countries between the 'extremes' of the capitalist United States and the communist Soviet Union. Such a force would be consistent with domestic UK policies which was neither capitalist nor communist. They hoped the Third Force would reduce the risk of war by mediating between the Soviet Union and the United States. In contrast, it seemed to Labour's left wing that Foreign Secretary Bevin's policy was contributing to the division of Europe into hostile camps and making Britain subservient to US capitalism.

By 1947-8, a major part of the Labour left concluded it could no longer stand aside from the deepening split between East and West. The Third Force option had ceased to be, if ever it was, a viable option and Britain had to participate fully in the Western bloc. Three developments produced that change of perspective among much of Labour's left wing. First, the United States offer of Marshall Aid (1947) was perceived to be essential for Britain's economic advance and for the recovery of Western Europe. Second, the refusal of the Soviet Union to participate in the Marshall Plan and, third, Moscow's insistence that its East European allies do likewise were perceived as extremely obstructive and divisive responses. Thus, Labour's image of the United States shifted in a favourable direction while its perception of the Soviet Union deteriorated further. That deterioration was reinforced greatly by the communist seizure of power in Czechoslovakia in 1948. Cumulatively these events convinced many left-wing Labour Members of Parliament that the Soviet Union had to be contained even if it involved an alliance with the leading capitalist country, namely the United States. Thus in the House of Commons vote on the North Atlantic Treaty (1949), very few Labour MPs voted against approval, although a large number abstained.

The developments of 1947-8, which shifted decisively the attitudes of many in the Labour Party towards the United States and the Soviet Union, also marginalised the influence of the pro-Soviet section of the Party. That element was critical of many aspects of the Marshall Plan. It seemed improbable to them that the US Congress would vote in support of economic aid for the Soviet Union. In reality, the Plan appeared designed to entrench an anti-communist bloc in Western Europe and to increase UK and European dependence on the United States. Moreover, Labour's fellow travellers could not envisage circumstances where a socialist country would ally itself with the aggressive capitalism of the United States against the Soviet Union.

At the start of the 1950s, the outbreak of the Korean War reopened Labour's debate on the nature of the Soviet and communist threat and how Britain and NATO should meet that challenge. The core of the left's argument was that the main element of the Soviet attack was on 'the social, political and economic fronts'.[58] Therefore it was erroneous for NATO and Britain to undertake an excessive rearmament programme, while neglecting the vital domains of economic and political development. Such neglect was believed to account for the immense advances by communist parties in France and Italy.

In the 1950s and thereafter, Labour's left wing focused upon the interaction of East and West in explaining Soviet foreign and defence policy. Unlike Labour's Atlanticists, it did not identify a strong link between Soviet ideology and foreign policy. It accepted that a spiral of hostility set the scene for a sequence of mutual fear, occasional crises (Berlin, Cuba), and a relentless arms race.

According to left-wing observers in the 1960s and early 1970s, the East–West military competition had been sustained by various factors. These included the Soviet determination to respond to and catch up 'with military developments in the West'[59] (which, it was believed, led in military innovations) and especially Moscow's anxiety to achieve nuclear parity with the United States. In addition, the Soviet Union was committed to minimising its security vulnerability upon its adversary. At the same time it was contended that Western investment in new generations of weaponry were fuelled partly by US and NATO assessments, which greatly exaggerated Soviet military capabilities.

With respect to Soviet intentions towards the West, Labour left-wingers considered that there was no Soviet interest in seeking to occupy Western Europe, still less in risking the forbidding dangers in any use of force against NATO. Rather, left-wing observers viewed the Soviet Union as a *status quo* power in Europe, anxious to maintain and enjoy the benefits of the post-war division of the continent. They suggested that Western fears of Soviet military coercion were greatly exaggerated. Instead, these analysts stressed the common interest of East and West in reducing confrontation and in promoting trade, technology and other exchanges between the blocs. Accordingly, they were keenly critical of some of the obstacles to the expansion of Fast–West trade, especially the decisions of the fifteen-nation Coordinating Committee for Multilateral Export Controls (COCOM).

Labour, Britain and NATO

From the early months of 1947, Foreign Secretary Bevin made a determined effort to secure American economic and military support for Europe. By itself, neither economic assistance nor a military alliance could meet Europe's requirements. Thus US economic aid could not counter Soviet military dominance, while a military guarantee could not deflect potential economic collapse and domestic turmoil in Western Europe. The Labour government realised also that the United States would not make a commitment to Europe's defence unless the Europeans coordinated their own defence plans first.

In 1947, the Marshall Plan was a major step towards restoring European economic stability and political confidence. Within a year, Britain, France and the three Benelux countries signed the Brussels Treaty committing them to assist each other in the event of aggression in Europe. Mr Bevin's hopes for US involvement in Europe's defence were accomplished with the formation of the North Atlantic Treaty Organisation in April 1949. Thus Britain's objectives of establishing strong transatlantic ties and of making the United States into a European power came to fruition in the period from early 1947 to early 1949.

The key elements of the defence structure established by the Attlee government were supported by successive governments for four decades and to a large extent by the Labour Party until the mid- to late 1970s. These elements were that the collective defence of Western Europe should be based upon the combined military efforts (including a nuclear element) of the said countries and upon the promise of both the United States and the United Kingdom to defend continental Europe. This British approach rested upon two assumptions, namely that the United Kingdom's independence would be in mortal peril if Europe were controlled by a hostile power. Second, it was assumed that Britain had an overriding interest in fostering the maintenance of the US commitment to the defence of Western Europe.

The logic of these assumptions had compelling implications for Britain's defence policy. One deduction was that as the United States possessed immense military–technological capabilities and was perceived to be indispensable for Europe's defence, its leadership of NATO (in settling military strategy and other priorities) had to be accepted and supported. Successive British governments also drew the conclusion that the United Kingdom should seek the closest military collaboration with the United States. Likewise, Britain should endeavour to attain the maximum influence upon US military and diplomatic policy in Europe and elsewhere.

Another deduction made from Britain's approach to defence was that the United Kingdom must endeavour to cement military cooperation among the West European states and to avoid initiatives which might undermine the trust of the Europeans and particularly of the Federal Republic of Germany (after it joined NATO in 1955). Specifically, this meant that NATO's strategy (of forward defence) had to be particularly responsive to the anxieties of West Germany, and Britain could not withdraw its military presence on the continent without damaging confidence among the countries of Western Europe.

Another consequence of those assumptions, and one that received little public attention, concerned the central symbolic role of atomic-nuclear weapons in NATO. These weapons were seen both as a means and as an expression of US leadership in the alliance, not least because that country's nuclear guarantee was at the core of NATO's defence relations. But beyond that, the possession of nuclear artillery by many members of the alliance and the expectation that any nuclear war in Europe would be disastrous for virtually all NATO states tended to spread the feelings of shared risk.[60] For a country like West Germany this sharing of danger was a matter of profound importance. In addition, from NATO's early years, the alliance perceived atomic and nuclear weapons to be the means to reduce the forbidding costs and the conflicts which heavy reliance upon conventional capabilities would produce.

The closeness of Britain's military cooperation with the United States was expressed in diverse ways. It was largely a product of a strong affinity, of language, ideas, values, and outlook on the international relations of the political élites in the two countries. For example, the United States utilised more than one hundred military bases and facilities in the United Kingdom and benefited from British bases in the Middle East and elsewhere (e.g. Diego Garcia, Ascension Island, Bermuda). These bases were used to locate military forces and equipment and for the stationing of aircraft (e.g. F111), submarines (Poseidon, Polaris), missiles (Thor missiles), ammunition, communications and early warning systems.

More importantly, from the late 1950s the United States supplied Britain with vital elements of its strategic nuclear force including both delivery and launching systems, nuclear materials, targeting information and facilities to test UK nuclear warheads. In addition, the two countries cooperated across the world on the collection and interpretation of intelligence data, on NATO's nuclear strategy and on the assessment of Soviet capabilities. Anglo-American military cooperation embraced as well the exchange of technical information on such sensitive matters as anti-submarine warfare, the operation of nuclear submarines, and the design of nuclear warheads. The close coordination of US forces based in Britain with their sister UK service, together with the training of some British service personnel in the United States, generated especially strong ties between the armed forces of the two countries.[61]

For much of the period since 1945, US support enabled Britain to sustain elements of its role as a great power beyond its own capacity. Thus the US financial loan to Britain in 1946 together with Marshall Aid in 1947–8 cushioned the intense pressure of resources on London to curtail or end its involvement in colonial areas and in other states (as it was, Britain was forced to end its involvement in the Greek Civil War by 1947). Conversely, at Suez (1956), Britain was sharply reminded of its dependence on the United States when Washington used its financial strength to bring the British use of force in Egypt to a halt.

Without US assistance it is unlikely that in the 1970s Britain could sustain a nuclear force unquestionably capable of threatening the second super-power, the Soviet Union. For some in the United Kingdom, the separate nuclear force was one of the few symbols of past eminence that the country maintained into the 1970s (and beyond). For others, including many Labour Party members and supporters, Britain's retention of nuclear weapons was one more example of how the country's ruling élite were unable and unwilling to accept the country's situation as a middle-range European power.

Labour and nuclear weapons

In the quarter of a century from the late 1940s until the mid-1970s, Labour's debates on defence centred on two main issues—the level of military expenditure and the role of atomic and nuclear arms. Before the issue of nuclear weapons is reviewed, it is in order to consider briefly the topic of military spending.

The pacifist members of the Party had long opposed the allocation of resources for military purposes. However, after the Second World War, the great majority of Labour Members of Parliament accepted that the United Kingdom had to possess adequate military strength. In the early 1950s, following the outbreak of the Korean War, the Party conducted a bitter and divisive debate on the rearmament programme. The Labour leadership judged it essential for Britain to undertake a crushing rearmament effort. But most on the left of the Party believed that policy would destabilise the economy and displace essential social programmes. In the event, the Conservative government of 1951–5 did not carry forward the planned defence spending.

When Labour regained office in 1964, it resumed its wrestling with defence expenditure. In an effort to contain the strong upward pressures on defence spending, the Wilson government set an arbitrary limit (i.e. £2,000 million at 1964 prices) to the defence budget. But the devaluation of the pound sterling in 1967 obliged the government to accept that Britain was no longer a world power. Accordingly, the United Kingdom decided in early 1968 to wind up the military role East of Suez.

Turning to weapons of mass destruction, the Labour government's secret decision in 1947 to manufacture atomic weapons was largely a product of Britain's anxiety about its status, security and influence, and especially its influence with the United States. The United States had just abruptly terminated the wartime collaboration with the United Kingdom on atomic weapons, and it appeared as if it might be retreating into an isolationist stance. At the same time, fears were increasing in Western Europe about the deepening Cold War with Moscow which was imposing Soviet-type regimes in Eastern Europe. Moreover, the small number of senior scientists, civil servants and politicians involved in the 1947 UK decision assumed that a great power such as Britain was entitled to, and indeed required the most advanced weapons. In part this view about Britain's right to have atomic arms was based on the fact that the United Kingdom had participated in atomic weapons research and development from the start. Therefore in 1946–7, the issue was seen as one of whether Britain should continue with its development of atomic weapons.

When the seminal choice about Britain's atomic weapons was made, it evoked neither the support nor the opposition nor the acquiescence of the Labour Party. This was due to the fact that neither the Cabinet nor any organ of the Party, such as the National Executive Committee or the Annual Conference was told about the decision. Thus a pattern was set whereby Labour leaders in office followed policies on nuclear weapons quite independent of, and sometimes sharply incompatible with the wishes of the Party as expressed in the resolutions of the Annual Conference.

It is not being suggested here that in the period 1947–74, Labour governments were consistently in favour of nuclear arms while the Labour Party was unambiguously hostile to such weapons. Rather it is contended that when in office Labour politicians did not differ fundamentally on nuclear weapons from their Conservative counterparts, although the former tended to place greater reliance upon conventional military capabilities.

In the decade after 1945, and again in the latter part of the 1960s, the issue of atomic or nuclear weapons attracted relatively little attention in the Labour Party. But from the mid-1950s onwards, as fears about atmospheric nuclear tests and nuclear blackmail grew, it became a vital question of principle for a sizeable section of Party members. This anti-nuclear segment was influenced strongly by and connected with the Campaign for Nuclear Disarmament. It won a notable but short-lived victory over the Gaitskell leadership at the Party Conference in 1960. Following that victory, the Campaign for Democratic Socialism and others were instrumental in ensuring the restoration of the leadership's position at the 1961 Party Conference. This recovery of a more orthodox perspective on nuclear weapons and defence was a reflection of the fact that the anti-nuclear element in the Party was considerably weaker than the 1960 Conference decision indicated. At that time, the great majority of Labour Members of Parliament and of the Party's National Executive Committee maintained support for NATO's strategy involving reliance upon nuclear arms. Likewise, it is probable that a majority of Labour voters and of members of the Party were in general agreement with Gaitskell's stance on nuclear weapons. In his view, Britain could give up nuclear weapons for practical reasons (i.e. cost) but NATO must retain such weapons so long as the Soviet Union had them.

By the mid-1960s the issue of nuclear arms, which at the start of the decade threatened to sunder the Party, had faded into the background following the Cuban Missile Crisis (1962), the signing of the Partial Test Ban Treaty (1963) and the election of a Labour government (1964).

For some Labour supporters of British nuclear disarmament, the apparent irrelevance of protests about the nuclear confrontation in Cuba (1962) called into question the value of seeking to influence superpower or other countries' behaviour. For others the achievement of the Partial Test Ban Treaty owed a considerable amount to the efforts of anti-nuclear movements. By the same token the Treaty sharply reduced public concern about nuclear arms.

The Labour government elected in October 1964 promised to renegotiate the purchase of Polaris nuclear submarines from the United States, that is the Nassau Agreement of 1962. In the event, the Wilson administration reneged on its promise. It acquired the nuclear force for the United Kingdom and on so doing cooperated very fully with the United States in constructing the Polaris force. Towards the end of the decade, the Labour government agreed that US F111 aircraft deploying nuclear bombs could be stationed in the

United Kingdom. Given the intense controversy within the Labour Party about nuclear weapons at the start of the 1960s, it seemed remarkable that the Wilson government's espousal of nuclear arms attracted little explicit opposition from anti-nuclear elements of the Party. This absence of vehement dissent can be attributed to two factors. First, the issue of Britain's refusal to condemn the US role in the Vietnam War absorbed much of the energy of the radical left-wing section of the Party in the second half of the 1960s. At the same time, Prime Minister Wilson employed his expertise in obfuscating issues to obscure Britain's continuing adherence to nuclear arms.

With the defeat of the Wilson government in the General Election of 1970, the initiative within the Party passed to radical left-wing critics of the Atlanticist leadership. Thus at the Party Conferences in 1972 and 1973, resolutions were passed demanding the removal of the US nuclear Polaris bases from the United Kingdom. It seems then rather paradoxical that when in opposition the Labour Party devoted much energy to deciding its posture on nuclear arms, but lost interest in the subject when it came to power.

Notes and references

1 C.R. Attlee, *The Labour Party in Perspective* (London, Gollancz, 1937), pp. 226–7.
2 *Hansard, House of Commons*, 12 May 1953, vol. 515, col. 1062.
3 Alan Bullock, *Ernest Bevin: Foreign Secretary 1945–1951* (Oxford, Oxford University Press, 1985), p. 64.
4 Rodney Fielding, *A Socialist Foreign Policy?* Fabian Tract no. 401 (London, Fabian Society, 1970), p. 9. Fielding's extract from Labour's manifesto for the General Election of 1964 is similar in tone to Attlee's commitment of 1945. He stated it was his government's intention 'to make the success of the United Nations the primary objective' of its policy. K. Harris, *Attlee* (London, Weidenfeld & Nicolson, 1982), p. 294.
5 K. Harris, *Attlee*, op. cit., p. 295.
6 Richard Rose, 'Parties, factions and tendencies in Britain', in Richard Rose (ed.), *Studies in British Politics: A Reader in Political Sociology* (London, Macmillan, 1966), p. 315.
7 M. R. Gordon, *Conflict and Consensus in Labour's Foreign Policy 1914–1965* (Stanford, Calif., Stanford University Press, 1969), p. 127.
8 A.J.P. Taylor, *The Trouble Makers: Dissent over Foreign Policy 1792–1939* (Harmondsworth, Penguin Books, 1985), p. 162.
9 M.R. Gordon, *Conflict and Consensus . . .* op. cit., p. 29.
10 See Ralph Miliband and Marcel Liebman, 'Reflections on Anti-Communism', in (eds) Ralph Miliband, John Saville and Marcel Liebman, *The Socialist Register 1984* (London, Merlin Press, 1984), pp. 1–22.
11 Alan Bullock, *Ernest Bevin*, op. cit., p. 105.
12 ibid., p. 106.
13 Michael Foot, *Aneurin Bevan 1945–1960*: Vol. 2 (London, Paladin/Granada Publishing, 1975), p. 303.
14 Robin Cook and Dan Smith, *What Future in NATO?* (Fabian Research Series, no. 337, London, Fabian Society, 1978), p. 7.
15 Michael Foot, *Aneurin Bevan*, op. cit., p. 303.
16 Jonathan Schneer, 'Hopes deferred or shattered: the British Labour left and the

Third Force Movement, 1945–49', *Journal of Modern History*, vol. 56 (June 1984), pp. 197–226, 215.

17   ibid., p. 216.

18   Konni Zilliacus, Tom Driberg and John Platts-Mills were prominent MPs in the House of Commons of 1945–50. Tom Driberg was a leading member of the National Executive Committee of the Labour Party in the 1950s and 1960s, while Platts-Mills was regarded as a crypto-communist and was expelled from the Party in 1948–9. James Lamond was an MP from 1970 to 1992. He was not especially prominent in Parliament. He sponsored many Soviet-supported organisations like the World Peace Council. William Warbey, an MP for most of the period 1945–66, was prominent in protests against the Vietnam War.

19   M.R. Gordon, *Conflict and Consensus*, op. cit., p. 161.

20   Jonathan Schneer, 'Hopes deferred or shattered', op. cit., p. 215.

21   Before the Italian election of April 1948, close to forty British Labour MPs sent a telegram of good wishes to the Italian Socialist Party (led by Nenni) which had an electoral pact with the Italian Communist Party. Those sending the telegram were disciplined by the Labour leadership. See Mark Jenkins, *Bevanism: Labour's High Tide* (Nottingham, Spokesman Books, 1979), pp. 52–4.

22   See Alan Bullock, *Ernest Bevin*, op. cit. , and Mark Jenkins, *Bevanism*, op. cit.

23   Cook and Smith, *What future in NATO?* op. cit., p. 7.

24   Denis Healey, *Cards on the Table: An Interpretation of Labour's Foreign Policy* (London, Labour Party, 1947), p. 10. Foreign Secretary Bevin regarded the pamphlet as a defence of his policy. See Alan Bullock, *Ernest Bevin*, op. cit., p. 79. Note Mr Healey's name does not appear on the pamphlet.

25   Alan Bullock, *Ernest Bevin*, op. cit., p. 583.

26   In 1951, the *Tribune* newspaper published a pamphlet, written by Michael Foot and Jennie Lee, called *One Way Only*. The foreword was written by Aneurin Bevan, Harold Wilson and John Freeman. It notes they were in full agreement with its contents. The pamphlet was strongly critical of what was perceived as the near-hysterical anti-communist attitude of US politicians. For an account of left-wing Labour perspectives on defence and the Soviet Union in the 1970s, see Mary Kaldor, Dan Smith and Steve Vines (eds), *Democratic Socialism and the Cost of Defence* (London, Croom Helm, 1979).

27   *One Way Only*, op. cit., p. 8.

28   ibid., p. 8.

29   ibid., p. 9.

30   See the varying assessments of Atlanticists and left wingers in M. Kaldor, D. Smith and S. Vines (eds), *Democratic Socialism and the Cost of Defence*, op. cit., pp. 505–49, 67–92.

31   ibid., p. 523.

32   ibid., p. 525.

33   ibid., p. 523.

34   R. Neild, *How to Make Up Your Mind About the Bomb* (London, André Deutsch, 1981), p. 14.

35   Mary Kaldor, 'The non-nuclear alternative', *Catalyst*, vol. 1, no. 2 (Summer 1985), pp. 49–64, 58.

36   R. Neild, *How to Make Up Your Mind About the Bomb*, op. cit., p. 15.

37   Dan Smith, *The Defence of the Realm in the 1980s* (London, Croom Helm, 1980), p. 75.

38   Robin Cook and Dan Smith, *What future in NATO?* op. cit., p. 4.

39   Mary Kaldor, 'The non-nuclear alternative', op. cit., p. 58.

40   *Cards on the Table*, op. cit., p. 10.

41 ibid.
42 *One Way Only*, op. cit., p. 9.
43 ibid.
44 David Holloway, *The Soviet Union and the Arms Race* (London, Yale University Press, 2nd edn, 1984), p. 135.
45 ibid., p. 119.
46 ibid.
47 Mary Kaldor, 'Is there a Soviet threat?', in Michael Clarke and Majorie Mowlam (eds), *Debate on Disarmament*, (London, Routledge & Kegan Paul, 1982), p. 43.
48 M. Kaldor, D. Smith and S. Vines (eds), *Democratic Socialism and the Cost of Defence*, op. cit., p. 75.
49 A. Bullock, *Ernest Bevin*, op. cit., p. 106.
50 Philip M. Williams, *Hugh Gaitskell* (Oxford, Oxford University Press, 1982), pp. 206–8.
51 Eric Shaw, *Discipline and Discord in the Labour Party* (Manchester, Manchester University Press, 1988), pp. 172–7.
52 *Cards on the Table*, op. cit., p. 5.
53 ibid.
54 ibid., p. 11.
55 ibid., p. 12.
56 A. Bullock, *Ernest Bevin*, op. cit., p. 484.
57 R. Lowenthal, 'Co-existence with Soviet Communism', in T.E.M. McKitterick and Kenneth Younger (eds), *Fabian International Essays* (London, Hogarth Press, 1957), p. 23.
58 *One Way Only*, op. cit., p.10.
59 Mary Kaldor, 'Is there a Soviet military threat?' op. cit., p. 43.
60 See Michael Clark, *The Alternative Defence Debate: Non-Nuclear Defence Policies for Europe* (Brighton, ADIU, University of Sussex, 1985), pp. 17–18.
61 For a review of UK–US military cooperation consult Wm. Roger Louis and Hedley Bull (eds), *The Special Relationship: Anglo-American Relations since 1945* (Oxford, Clarendon Press, 1986), especially the chapters by Eberle and Gowing. See also John Simpson, *The Independent Nuclear State: The United States, Britain and the Military Atom* (London, Macmillan, 1984).

2 Labour's divided approach to defence, 1975–81

In the period from the mid-1970s to the early 1980s, the Labour Party changed fundamentally its approach to defence. In part, the change was generated by the shift in the leadership of the Party from the right to the left wing. That shift led in 1974–9 to a clear division on defence between the Labour government and the National Executive Committee of the Party. Following Labour's defeat in the General Election of 1979, the Party's defence debate became much more intense and bitter in tone.

Labour's changes on defence related especially to three issues, namely nuclear weapons, NATO and Britain's defence role. From the mid-1970s, Labour's policy on nuclear arms evolved from a muted opposition to reliance on such weapons to a passionate rejection of any role for them in Britain's defence. Second, while there was little debate about NATO in the Party during the mid-1970s, by the early 1980s Labour was vehemently opposed to both the strategy and the decision-making process of the alliance. Thus the dangers of nuclear war between East and West came to be seen as a greater threat to Western Europe than the Soviet Union. Third, in 1975 the Labour National Executive Committee established a Defence Study Group to examine the implications of reducing Britain's defence expenditure and role. The findings of the Study Group gave impetus to the Party's demand for achieving substantial defence cuts as rapidly as possible.

Changes occurring within the Labour Party or in the wider domain of British politics do not fully explain why the place of defence on the UK political agenda altered sharply in the years from 1975 to 1981. At the start of that era, it was not a particularly prominent or contentious issue, but by the early 1980s, defence had become a central and intensely divisive topic within the Party and outside. It is appropriate therefore to outline the international events and developments which contributed substantially to Labour's altered perspective on defence.

In the early to mid-1970s, the United States and the Soviet Union combined to develop sets of rules and institutions embracing major aspects of their security relationships. Thus they established regimes to stabilise their rivalry in nuclear weapons and to manage the risks of nuclear confrontation. But the improved superpower relations of those years were not sustained from the mid-1970s. Many US politicians lost confidence in Soviet–American *détente* following the humiliating US defeat in Vietnam (1975) and the apparent Soviet advances in areas such as Southern Africa. In their view the

United States was losing out in the competition with the Soviet Union, which was becoming the leading superpower in military terms.

By the end of the 1970s, Soviet–American relations had shifted from a mix of rivalry and negotiations to a situation where dialogue had collapsed and political confrontation was deepening. One year later, at the end of 1980, superpower relations manifested more hostility, mistrust and confrontation than they had for most of two decades. Moreover, US President Carter was giving way to a successor, Ronald Reagan, who had opposed the SALT process and who was determined to 'rebuild' US military strength.

Two events in particular exacerbated international fears regarding East–West conflict at the end of the 1970s. First, the Soviet invasion of Afghanistan in late December 1979 raised the gravest doubts in the United States and elsewhere concerning the predictability of Moscow's behaviour, given that it had ignored a central rule in relations between the superpowers. Second, earlier in the same month, NATO announced its decision to deploy ground-launched cruise missiles and Pershing-2 missiles. These missiles were designed to strengthen the security ties between the United States and Europe, links which were thought to be at risk with the introduction of Soviet SS20 missiles. NATO's decision, and the debate in 1977–8 about neutron bombs, stimulated widespread public concern about its nuclear strategy and the role of cruise missiles. It led to the emergence of a strong peace movement in Britain and other West European countries, which expressed great doubt regarding the US commitment to its allies. Taken together, the Soviet introduction of SS20 missiles and NATO's pledge to deploy cruise and Pershing missiles, along with the conditions which produced those decisions, generated severely strained relations between East and West by 1980.

The shift in Labour's approach to leadership, constitution and defence

In the years from the early 1970s until the end of 1981, three major changes occurred in the Labour Party. They affected its leadership, structure and policies. The changes refer to the shift in the leadership of the Party from Atlanticist centre right to left wing politicians, the redefinition of the constitutional relations between the various sections of the Party in the years 1979–81, and the Party's development of a new defence policy from the mid-1970s.

These developments were a product of strong feelings among Labour Party members and trade unionists that the Labour governments of 1964–70 and 1974–9 had failed in their policies for economic growth and industrial relations. Moreover it was believed that those administrations' foreign policy on certain issues (e.g. Vietnam in the 1960s, nuclear weapons in the 1970s) was profoundly repugnant to sentiment within the Party. At the same time, in the 1975 referendum on whether Britain should remain a member of the EEC, the majority in the Labour Cabinet advised in favour of no change. This recommendation placed Labour's leaders sharply at odds with the other decision-making bodies in the Party, and it demonstrated their alienation from the anxieties and attitudes of many Labour members and supporters.

Here the shifts or changes are reviewed, first by exploring the glaring contradictions between the operational defence policy of the 1974–79 Labour government and the declared defence policy of the Labour Party. Second, the major constitutional changes are analysed, and, third, the shift of power from centre-right to the left of the Party is considered.

The Labour Party led by Harold Wilson returned to government following the General Election of February 1974. At that time British voters were concerned especially about industrial relations, incomes policy and inflation domestically, and the assured supply and price of Middle East oil internationally. Five years later, the Callaghan-led government lost the support of Parliament and subsequently that of the electorate, due substantially to its perceived failure to manage industrial relations (e.g. particularly in relation to low-paid, public-sector employees) and economic–social issues in a satisfactory manner. During this period of Labour rule, when internationally the cooperative dimension of East–West relations seemed to be in the ascendant, defence policy was seldom near the very top of the political agenda. Yet the operational defence policy of the government was more inconsistent with that of the Party than was the case for any administration since 1945.

Here the approach of the Labour Party (as distinct from the Labour government) to defence is identified as the policy expounded in the Manifestos for the two General Elections of 1974, resolutions supported by the Annual Conference of the Party and the policy proposed by the National Executive and its subcommittee (namely the Study Group on Defence Expenditure, the Arms Trade and Alternative Employment). The defence policy of the Wilson–Callaghan administration was indicated by its decisions.

Although Labour's shift from the acceptance of NATO's defence policy to a non-nuclear approach was not completed until 1980–1, many signs of that trend were evident well before that date. From 1947, Labour in government worked to develop and sustain a separate British atomic-nuclear capability. But this can obscure the fact that since the cancellation of the Blue Streak missile in 1960, the Party did not explicitly support the acquisition or development of a new 'independent' nuclear capability. Such a lack of enthusiasm for a British nuclear force was entirely consistent with loyalty to NATO orthodoxy.

According to the Manifestos issued for the two General Elections of 1974 (in February and October) and in line with resolutions passed by Party Conference in both 1972 and 1973, Labour advocated the removal of the US Polaris base from the United Kingdom. While the Manifesto for the October election 'renounced any intention of moving towards a new generation of strategic nuclear weapons' both 1974 Manifestos favoured the progressive reduction of Britain's defence spending to the level of the main European members of NATO.

At the 1974 Labour Conference, for the third consecutive year considerable opposition was expressed to any strategy involving reliance upon nuclear arms. Resolutions articulating this sentiment attracted substantial, if minority support at Conference in 1976, 1977 and 1978. From the mid-1970s, the left wing and predominantly anti-nuclear (weapon) wing of the Party had gained a dominant position on the National Executive Committee. Reflecting this change, a Defence Study Group of the National Executive composed of left-wing members produced a report, *Sense About Defence*,[1] advocating a large reduction in UK defence spending. It also concurred with the 1974 Manifesto promise that no replacement should be obtained for the Polaris nuclear force.

The Labour government of the 1970s, far from seeking the removal of US nuclear weapons from the UK, in 1976 agreed to the stationing of many additional nuclear-armed US F111 aircraft in Britain. In the following year, the administration accepted the NATO decision to increase (from 1979) defence spending as part of the programme to strengthen the alliance's military capabilities. This promise was contrary to the 1974 Manifesto pledge, although the Labour government had succeeded in reducing the level of military spending (as a percentage of GNP) during its term of office. For this it was severely castigated by opposition leader, Margaret Thatcher. In 1978, the Labour government agreed with the report of NATO's High Level Nuclear Planning Group, indicating support for the modernisation of the alliance's long-range theatre nuclear weapons. Soon after coming to office in 1974, the Labour administration took a decision sharply contrary to the spirit of its election pledge when it agreed to enhance the penetration capability of the UK's Polaris nuclear force.[2]

Moreover there was little definite indication that the Callaghan government intended to 'renounce any intention' of acquiring a successor for the Polaris nuclear force. Rather, it arranged studies by the Ministry of Defence and the Foreign Office regarding a choice of successor for Polaris. Added to that, the Manifesto for the 1979 General Election, which was dictated by Prime Minister Callaghan, pledged the Party to a full discussion of the issue. A full discussion of the issue was much more favourable for a potential decision to replace Polaris than was the clear negative pledge contained in the Manifesto of October 1974. Moreover within the British Ministry of Defence, debate was concerned with the best system to succeed Polaris, not whether there should be a replacement nuclear force. In addition, Mr Callaghan discussed the option of a successor for Polaris with US President Carter in February 1979. But he warned the President that the full British Cabinet had not, as yet, considered the question, although a Cabinet committee had discussed the issue. Commenting on what might have happened if he were re-elected in 1979, Mr Callaghan observed that 'no Prime Minister can abdicate his overriding responsibility to safeguard national security, and once his mind is made up on the best course for the country, fight for his decision, and if he cannot get support then he should stand down.'[3]

The significant contradictions between the defence policy of the Labour Party and the Labour government in the 1970s can be explained in large measure by two factors. These were the political outlook of those involved and the quite disparate pressures experienced by Labour politicians in government and in opposition. With few if any exceptions, the Labour Ministers who had top-level responsibility for defence and foreign affairs from 1974 to 1979 (i.e. Prime Ministers Wilson and Callaghan; Secretary of

State for Foreign and Commonwealth Affairs: Callaghan, Crosland, Owen and their junior ministers) came from the centre and centre-right of the Party. Concurrently, those who enjoyed most influence in the Party National Executive Committee and thus on policy-making (e.g. Tony Benn, Ian Mikardo) were on Labour's left wing.

When in opposition, in the early 1970s, the Atlanticist Labour leadership felt intense pressure to convey an image of Party unity. This inhibited them from expressing hostility to the increasingly left-wing views of the majority of Labour activists, especially as many of those leaders openly or privately favoured UK membership of the EEC (which the Labour Party opposed).

On reaching office, the need to avoid very public and damaging arguments within the Party reinforced bureaucratic pressures on the Atlanticist leadership not to disclose important decisions, such as that to enhance the Polaris delivery system with Chevaline. Other exigencies, which pushed Labour ministers towards disregarding the (left-wing) pledges on defence issues in the Party's Election Manifestos can also be identified. These politicians believed that Britain was then, and should remain a reliable and key member of the NATO alliance. Therefore Labour ministers at the Foreign and Commonwealth Office and the Ministry of Defence were in a weak position to resist the alliance consensus of the mid-1970s that the member states needed to increase their defence effort. Added to which, many of those ministers probably agreed with NATO's decision and thus did not want to resist the consensus view, whatever the National Executive Committee proclaimed. Moreover from the middle of 1976, the Callaghan administration lost its overall Labour majority in the House of Commons. In consequence, Mr Callaghan made a pact with the leaders of the Liberal Members of Parliament, whereby the Liberals supported the government on a package of agreed measures until late 1978. Prime Minister Callaghan and his ministers had a clear understanding that their tenure of office could come to an abrupt end if they were tempted or persuaded to implement controversial measures touching on Britain's role in NATO or related defence issues.

With Labour's defeat in the General Election of May 1979, the contradictions between the defence policies of the government and the Party came to an end, but they were succeeded by deep and extremely bitter conflicts on defence within the Party. These conflicts and the promotion of defence to near the top of the British political agenda were substantially a result of a conjunction of developments within and beyond the United Kingdom in the period 1979–81. During that time, a series of international military, political and diplomatic events suggested to many Labour observers a real possibility of the outbreak of catastrophic war between the superpowers. These events confirmed the collapse of East–West *détente* at the end of the 1970s, the Soviet invasion of Afghanistan, and Soviet pressures on Poland. They included as well the actual or planned deployment of more sophisticated and apparently more threatening non-strategic nuclear systems by both blocs, and the advent of President Reagan in the United States. The new President was known to be profoundly sceptical of the superpower arms-control process as practised in the 1970s, and was committed to increasing the US military effort.

In Britain, the replacement of the Callaghan administration by the first

Thatcher Conservative government (1979–83) (which like the Reagan administration was pledged to a sharp increase in military spending) gave defence
issues much greater prominence than at any time in the preceding decade and
a half. Within fifteen months of its election, the Conservative government
accepted the deployment of 160 ground-launched cruise missiles on British
territory (consequent upon its support for the NATO decision of December
1979). It made public also the Chevaline project to enhance the Polaris
nuclear force, and decided to purchase Trident as the eventual replacement
for Polaris. In the same period the government published a civil defence
pamphlet (*Protect and Survive*), which claimed to advise households about
ways to mitigate the dangers if Britain suffered nuclear attack. These decisions and announcements played a primary part in stimulating keen concern about and interest in nuclear weapons. This was indicated in public
opinion polls suggesting widespread unease about the prospects of nuclear
conflict and a smaller but sizeable minority expressing opposition to Britain's
policy on nuclear arms. The latter opposition was signified also in a more
direct form by the rapid growth of the Campaign for Nuclear Disarmament
(CND) from a few thousand local (as distinct from national) members in 1979
to about a quarter of a million in late 1981. CND was foremost in organising
both large demonstrations throughout major British cities (some simultaneously with demonstrations in other European centres) and campaigns
and rallies across the United Kingdom.

In the same period, prominent professional and religious organisations
published serious reports on nuclear weapons, more than 150 local (government) authorities declared their areas 'nuclear free zones', and other bodies
concerned with nuclear arms were established, such as the World
Disarmament Campaign and European Nuclear Disarmament. A significant
political development of the peace movement was the emergence of groups
like Scientists Against Nuclear Arms and the Medical Campaign Against
Nuclear Weapons. But the sizeable minority support for unilateral nuclear
disarmament at the Liberal Party Assembly and the changing posture of the
trade unions were especially important. As the peace movement gained
momentum in 1980 and 1981, unions with long-established attitudes of
opposition to nuclear arms were joined by many others to form a majority at
the 1981 Trades Union Congress. At the 1981 Labour Party Conference (a
few weeks after the TUC), the trade unions affiliated to the Party voted by a
large but not quite two-thirds majority to reject a strategy relying on the use
or threat of nuclear weapons. Thus at the 1980 and 1981 Conferences, the
Labour Party rejected US cruise missiles in Britain and demanded the earliest
unconditional elimination of Britain's nuclear capabilities.

At the end of the 1970s it was the spread of deep anxiety about nuclear
weapons and nuclear war, within and outside the Labour Party, that transformed 'paper resolutions' into irresistible pressures on Labour leaders. The
anti-nuclear resolutions adopted by Labour Conferences in the early 1970s
had the appearance of pious aspirations which realistic politicians did not
have to take very seriously. From 1980, leading Labour politicians could not
disregard the strong determination of a large segment of active members in
the Party. Those members were determined that a future Labour govern-

ment should disengage from nuclear weapons, no matter what the cost of such action.

From mid-1979, as the Conservative government made plans to sustain a long-term nuclear dependent defence policy on the one hand, and as the peace movement's rejection of nuclear weapons generated wider support on the other, Labour's defence policy became a focus of intense contention. If the Party maintained continuity with the defence policy of previous Labour governments, it would, in the view of James Callaghan, Peter Shore and Roy Hattersley, be very beneficial for Labour. That course would require the Party to support NATO's nuclear policy, maintain US nuclear bases in the United Kingdom, and renounce Britain's nuclear capability, only on the basis of reciprocity and prudent negotiations. They contended that such a policy would avoid a sharp break in relations between Britain and NATO and prevent a haemorrhage of electoral support from Labour. Moreover, it would not involve senior Labour politicians reversing themselves on a vital issue of policy, which would damage their credibility and that of the Party with many potential Labour voters.

On the other side, in the early 1980s many Labour Party members believed that the peculiarly tense international conditions of the time were remarkably dangerous. In their view it was imperative that the Party should make every effort to assist in de-escalating the nuclear rivalry and acute tension between East and West. This perception and feeling in the trade unions and in the constituency Labour parties was of such scope and depth that the warnings and entreaties of Atlanticist leaders like James Callaghan and Peter Shore could not divert or halt it.

One circumstance in particular reduced considerably the influence and the standing of ex-Premier Callaghan and some other leaders. As E.P. Thompson, a prominent leader of the peace movement in the early 1980s, expressed it (in terms shared by many Labour activists), it was the Conservative Secretary of State for Defence, Mr Pym, who

> announced the near-completion of the 'Chevaline' programme to 'modernise' the warhead of our Polaris missiles—a programme costing £1,000 millions, which had been carried out in the deepest secrecy and without the knowledge of the full Cabinet, and in defiance of official Labour policy, on the authority of Mr Callaghan and two or three of his particular friends.[4]

The disclosure by Labour's political adversary, Mr Pym, confirmed some Labour Party members in the belief that their own leaders did not treat Election Manifesto pledges seriously. Moreover those politicians acted as if they were wedded to dependence on nuclear weapons in a way not fundamentally different from Conservative governments. Accordingly, the Party's spokespersons on defence in 1979 and 1980, namely William Rodgers, Brynmor John and other Atlanticist Labour leaders, were ill-placed to articulate Labour's increasingly anti-nuclear posture of opposition to US ground-launched cruise missiles and to Trident. Their task was rendered more difficult by Conservative taunts about Labour's decisions when in office and by the disbelief of left-wing Labour MPs and activists.

For many of the active members of the Labour Party, some organised in groups such as the Campaign for Labour Party Democracy and the Labour Coordinating Committee,[5] the disregard of Party policy displayed by the Wilson–Callaghan government of 1974–9 conveyed a stark message. In their view, these failures of relations within the Party, (together with the demotion of Tony Benn, the architect of Labour's radical programme, from the Department of Industry following the EEC Referendum in 1975) provided irrefutable arguments for making future Labour governments and oppositions accountable to Party opinion as expressed by Annual Conference and the National Executive Committee.

To secure this aim, from the mid-1970s they pressed for three major changes in the constitutional relations of the different sections of the Party. One of the proposals was that instead of being chosen just by Labour Members of Parliament, in future the leader and deputy-leader should be elected by an electoral college consisting of three sections, that is, affiliated organisations, MPs, and constituency Labour parties. A second reform contended that instead of there being major and very damaging (for the Party) conflicts when a constituency Labour party wanted to replace a sitting MP, each Labour MP should undergo a process of mandatory reselection. Thus they would be liable to be substituted by another candidate in the following General Election. The third change proposed was that at General Elections the Party Manifesto should be drawn up by the National Executive Committee alone, rather than at a joint meeting of the National Executive Committee and the Shadow Cabinet. In effect that gave the leader of the Party the final decision on the content of the Manifesto.

The left-wing advocates of constitutional change possessed a number of organisational and psychological advantages *vis-à-vis* the supporters of the *status quo*. The key persons planning for change displayed a very strong commitment to their task and they manifested much astuteness on tactics. By contrast, the right-wing and centre-right trade-union leaders who opposed the reforms were unable to unite around one common position. Second, the argument for widening the franchise was an attractive proposition for the increasingly assertive membership of the Labour Party. Therefore politicians opposing the change risked being viewed as conservative and élitist in outlook. Third, in the aftermath of the heavy electoral defeat in the 1979 General Election, many active members of the Party felt deep disappointment about the record of the Callaghan–Wilson government. In such circumstances, those suggesting ways of keeping Labour leaders closely attuned to the wishes of the rest of Party could expect a sympathetic hearing.

Accordingly, it was no surprise that two of the three constitutional changes received majority support. The third proposal for exclusive control of the General Election Manifesto by the National Executive Committee was defeated by a very narrow margin. Consequently, the mandatory reselection of Labour MPs was implemented and the electoral college for the election of Labour's leader and deputy-leader was instituted. The college allocated 40 per cent of the total vote to the section for affiliated organisations (mainly trade unions), 30 per cent to Labour MPs, and 30 per cent to constituency Labour parties.

When for the first time the college was brought into operation regarding the election of Labour's deputy-leader in 1981, it was evident that it was not an unblemished and consistent exercise in democracy. While some trade unions and constituency parties balloted their full membership and voted in accordance with those ballot results, others decided their choice by reference to their governing body only, or a similar organ. A number of trade unions lacked a reliable up-to-date register of all their members throughout the country. Nor did certain constituencies possess an accurate and full list of Party members. Some trade unions were also short of financial and other resources to conduct a proper ballot and therefore opposed demands which would require Labour Party affiliated organisations to consult their members directly in elections for the leader and deputy-leader of the Party. Moreover many of the left-wing supporters of the constitutional changes feared intervention by the national newspapers in Labour's elections. As a majority of those newspapers were quite hostile to the political outlook of Labour's left wing they were expected to make every effort to interfere in elections involving millions of trade unionists. They would do so by ensuring that left-wing candidates were depicted in the most unfavourable manner.

Both advocates and opponents of the constitutional changes believed that if the leadership and the MPs were directly dependent upon the votes of the active members of the Party (who were generally on Labour's left wing), the result would be to shift the policies of the Party in a left-wing direction. Thus centre-right MPs for constituencies where the Party members and the general management committee were left-wingers would alter their political behaviour; at the least they would not want to alienate those who possessed the power to end their tenure in Parliament by selecting another candidate. An MP who consistently supported policies and leadership candidates sharply opposed to those of their constituency party might well be inviting their own replacement. In the contest between Tony Benn and Denis Healey for the Labour deputy-leadership in 1981, where for the first time the way an MP voted was published, some MPs experienced strong pressures from their constituency party to support a candidate other than their own choice.

Although Denis Healey, a very prominent Labour Atlanticist, narrowly won the deputy-leadership (50.426 per cent of the electoral college to Benn's 49.574 per cent),[6] this victory did not mean the centre-right had retained its dominant position in the Party. On the contrary, it experienced a sharp decline to a minority presence in the Party by the 1980s. This can be illustrated by a sketch of the contests for the Party leadership from 1963 onwards, together with a review of the salient issues and constitutional changes of 1979–80.

Following Hugh Gaitskell's death in January 1963, Harold Wilson succeeded to the leadership. Although the beneficiary of support from left-wing MPs (due to his left-wing rhetoric and challenge to Gaitskell in 1960), his record in office and his choice of senior ministers made it evident he was not a left-winger. In fact, it could well be argued that none of the three leadership candidates in 1963 was from the left wing of the Party (i.e. Wilson, George Brown and James Callaghan). Almost a decade later in 1972, the candidate from the Party's left wing, namely Michael Foot, was heavily defeated (by Ted Short) in the contest for deputy-leader. But just four years later, Foot was a strong runner-up to James Callaghan in the leadership contest, obtaining well over 40 per cent of the MPs' votes. Four years on in 1980, Michael Foot narrowly won the Party leadership, defeating Denis Healey by ten votes.

It should be recognised that in 1980 Foot's total of votes included a sizeable number from MPs not on the left of the Party, some seeing Foot as a reconciling figure to hold the Party together in time of acute conflict. Yet the growth in his support from 1972 mirrored the growing strength of the left within the Parliamentary Labour Party. In turn, this increased strength reflected the left-ward shift of constituency Labour parties and trade-union leaderships in the late 1960s and in the 1970s. In many parts of the United Kingdom, 'Young graduates, fresh from reading politics or social science at university or polytechnic, joined their local Labour party', and due to their political expertise, 'they ousted old working-class activists from their positions as branch and ward officers.'[7] In the same period the leading positions in many trade unions were filled by persons who had received higher education and adhered to a left-wing outlook. These changes in two key bodies of the Labour Party led to two major changes in the 1970s. First, as ageing and more conservative-minded Labour MPs retired at the four General Elections of the 1970s (i.e. 1970, 1974, 1974, 1979) or died, they were often succeeded by politicians on the left wing of the Party. In large measure the success of Labour left-wingers was attributable to the fact that constituency Labour parties tended to be antagonistic to Britain's membership of the European Community and intensely critical of many aspects of the performance of the Labour administration. Both these factors put centre-right Atlanticist candidates at a severe disadvantage.

Second, the advent of more left-wing and articulate constituency Labour parties produced a series of highly publicised conflicts with sitting MPs, such as Dick Taverne at Lincoln (1972) and Reg Prentice in Newham North East (London, 1975). This same demand, that MPs and Labour leaders should be answerable to their constituency parties, reached its zenith in the debate about constitutional changes in 1979–80.

The transfer of the leadership of the Labour Party from the centre-right Atlanticists to the left wing occurred at different times in the various sections of the Party, but in every instance the shift was in the same direction. Thus the shift occurred on the National Executive Committee in 1973–4, in the Parliamentary leadership in 1980, but it did not express itself in the Shadow Cabinet until 1987. Given that the body entitled to elect the leadership of the Party was expanded from Members of Parliament to include constituency Labour parties and affiliated organisations such as trade unions, the prospects after 1980 for a centre-right Atlanticist politician to become Labour leader seemed quite bleak. This daunting outlook made Atlanticist MPs feel very anxious about the future policies and leadership of the Party.

It was in this atmosphere that prominent Labour Atlanticist politicians Roy Jenkins, David Owen, Shirley Williams and William Rodgers left the Labour Party to establish the Social Democratic Party in 1981. They decided that they could not remain in a Labour Party which, by then, advocated UK unilateral nuclear disarmament, sought Britain's withdrawal from the EEC, and where the leadership and MPs had been made accountable to mainly left-wing activists in the constituencies and in the trade unions. This exodus by politicians who had been members of the Labour Party for decades was heralded in organisational terms by the setting up of the Campaign for Social Democracy (by Dick Taverne in 1973), the Social Democratic Alliance (1975), and by the formation of the Council for Social Democracy as the embryo for the Social Democratic Party in 1981.

The seeds of the breakaway from the Labour Party on the issues of unilateral nuclear disarmament and Britain's membership of the EEC, were identifiable one or even two decades before the events of 1981. In 1960, when the Annual Conference's vote for unilateral nuclear disarmament threatened to split the Party, the newly established Campaign for Democratic Socialism played a key part in returning the Party to orthodox multilateralism. The Campaign's principal organiser was William Rodgers (and its supporters or members included Shirley Williams and Dick Taverne). Besides its successful efforts to defeat the nuclear unilateralists, it arranged the selection of its friends and adherents as Parliamentary candidates. Although the Campaign was wound up in 1963 the bonds created through participation in its activities 'remained very strong for many years'.[8]

British membership of the European Community divided the Labour Party to a limited extent in the 1960s, and quite deeply in the 1970s. In 1971 under the leadership of Roy Jenkins, almost seventy Labour MPs rejected the instruction of the Parliamentary Labour Party (i.e. the Party Whip) and voted with the Conservative government for the principle of Britain joining the EEC. Again in 1975, during the national referendum on Britain remaining in the European Community, Roy Jenkins, Shirley Williams and other Labour Atlanticist MPs, together with the majority of the Labour Cabinet, campaigned alongside Conservative and Liberal politicians. But most active members of the Labour Party opposed Britain's remaining in the Community.

For various reasons, questions arising from Labour's adherence to a non-nuclear defence policy were especially prominent within and outside the Party in 1981. Because it was a main factor in the establishment of the Social Democratic Party, the new Party strongly attacked the policy of unilateral nuclear disarmament when seeking support from former Labour voters and supporters, as did the Conservative Party.

Within the Labour Party, the contest for the deputy-leadership focused attention on defence issues. One of the three candidates, Tony Benn, supported a whole-hearted version of nuclear unilateralism and opposition to NATO's nuclear strategy. The other main contender, Denis Healey, was closely associated with the Atlanticist pro-NATO defence policy, not least because he was Secretary of State for Defence in the Labour government of 1964–70 and the Party's leading defence expert for many years. Accordingly Mr Healey had the extremely testing task of seeking support from a Party which advocated unilateral nuclear disarmament and which demanded the ending of any US nuclear presence in Britain, while not abjuring the commitments he had undertaken when in office. The third candidate, John Silkin, accepted nuclear unilateralism but he was much less vehement and less precise in his approach than Tony Benn. By opposing both the deployment of ground-launched cruise missiles in Britain and a replacement for Polaris (as well as offering cogent criticism of the security approach of the Reagan administration), Denis Healey moved a considerable distance in order to paper over the divisions between the Party's previous policy and its new approach to defence.

For Party leader Michael Foot, the handling of defence issues in 1981 was a particularly difficult matter. At the national level, the Conservative Party and the newly formed Social Democratic Party were accusing the Labour Party of betraying long-held commitments. They argued that Labour's new policy would leave Britain without a proper defence and would sunder Britain's relations with her allies. As the Social Democratic Party included many former Labour defence and foreign affairs specialists (David Owen, William Rodgers, James Wellbeloved, John Roper, John Cartwright, Lord Kennet), attacks from them were especially damaging for Labour.

Inside the Labour Party, many members of the Shadow Cabinet held the deepest reservations about unilateral nuclear disarmament and the non-nuclear defence policy. So also did ex-Prime Minister James Callaghan and former Labour politicians who served at the Ministry of Defence such as Roy Mason and John Gilbert. In most instances, these reservations were of such a nature as to prevent Mr Foot appointing some of his most effective and experienced colleagues to be the Party's senior spokespersons on defence. At the same time, the Party leader was aware that having lost some of the most respected Labour politicians like Shirley Williams and David Owen to the Social Democrats it was imperative to avoid impelling other Labour Atlanticists towards leaving the Party. Accordingly, it might be imprudent to appoint an unreserved advocate of a non-nuclear defence policy like Robin Cook to speak for Labour on defence. Michael Foot's decision was to replace William Rodgers (who was a founder member of the Social Democratic Party) with Atlanticist Brynmor John (in 1981), and to substitute the moderate left-winger and nuclear unilateralist John Silkin for Mr John towards the end of the year.

The delicacy of Foot's choice of defence spokesperson in 1981 reflected the problem of how to reconcile the majority of his Shadow Cabinet (and many Labour voters) to his leadership and to the uncongenial policies of a different wing of the Party. During Labour's period in office in the 1960s and 1970s, the Atlanticist centre right led the Party and dominated ministries handling defence matters. The acquiescence of the Labour left wing in a subordinate position was greatly facilitated by the relaxed nature of East–West relations and by the lack of public concern about nuclear weapons until the late 1970s.

By 1980–1, when the left gained the leadership of the Party, it was much more difficult for the now junior wing of Labour, the Atlanticists, to accept the role previously occupied by the left. In the 1980s the issues of defence and nuclear weapons were at the very centre of debate and concern within and between the British political parties. To a great extent those Labour MPs who then possessed expertise and experience of defence issues came from the Atlanticist section of the Party. That fact encouraged the Atlanticists to regard themselves as still the best qualified to speak on military security matters. Moreover the departure of prominent Labour Atlanticists to the SDP attracted greater scrutiny to the attitudes of those Atlanticists who remained with the Labour Party. Figures such as Denis Healey, Roy Hattersley and Peter Shore faced three possible options if they continued in party politics at the national level.

They might consider following former colleagues and joining the Social Democrats whose defence policy could be expected to be to their liking. A second course would be to maintain their loyalty to the Labour Party but to relinquish senior positions in the Party and retire to the back-benches. From there, they could express support for their long-held beliefs and policies. Such a route, would involve renouncing their opportunity to influence the presentation of Party policy which they enjoyed as members of the Shadow Cabinet. Moreover a decision by senior Labour politicians to retire to the back-benches could well attract the unwelcome attention of rival political parties and the media.

From early 1981, virtually all the Atlanticist members of the Shadow Cabinet took the course of minimising their public discussion of defence issues. Thus they witnessed, but could do little about the Party's adherence to a defence policy many of them considered electorally suicidal and probably incapable of implementation. By far the most demanding role for a leading Labour Atlanticist was publicly to explain and defend the non-nuclear defence policy. Such a role was filled in 1981 by Denis Healey. As the senior Labour spokesperson on foreign affairs and the Party's most respected defence expert, he was involved quite intensely in presenting a policy which at some points constituted a major shift from the postures he supported when in government. Because he was by far the most prominent Labour Atlanticist involved in presenting both the 'old' nuclear posture and the new non-nuclear stance (and due to his combative personal style), he became a target for sustained questioning by critics anxious to elucidate contradictions between his past and current postures on defence issues.

Labour's changing perception of the threats to Britain

In the mid-1970s, few if any of the leading elements of the Labour Party (i.e. the leader together with his senior colleagues, the National Executive Committee and the Annual Conference) believed that a deliberate Soviet attack on Western Europe and Britain was a likely event. Neither did the Party assume that a war in Europe involving the superpowers was a significant possibility. In so far as Labour's leaders compared the two threats, it was the risk of a Soviet attack that was the primary concern of the Labour government, although by 1975 the Party's National Executive Committee did not share that view.[9]

With regard to the danger of war in Europe, it was thought that the measures agreed in the early and mid-1970s to reduce the chances of nuclear confrontation between the superpowers (i.e. 'Hot-line' communication systems, US–Soviet agreements to notify each other in advance of certain missile launches and to consult when there was a risk of nuclear war) had diminished such threats to a great extent. Likewise, the early 1970s agreements on the status of Berlin were seen as enhancing stable relations in Europe.

By 1981, six years on from the mid-1970s, Labour fears about both threats, that is of a Soviet attack and of a war in Europe, had increased sharply, but by then Labour perceived the principal threat to be that of nuclear war between the blocs in Europe. This reversal of the order of importance of the military threats to Britain and Western Europe was of immense importance: because it was this change in Labour's basic assumption that led to the Party's rejection of NATO'S nuclear strategy and its adoption of a non-nuclear defence policy.

The heightening in Labour expectations of a nuclear war was due almost entirely to international developments, which also affected Britain in a direct fashion. But the elevation of the fear of nuclear war to the top of the list of perceived threats was attributable mainly to the shift in the leadership of the Party. From the late 1970s until 1981, various events and processes generated a strong expectation among the British public, and particularly within the Labour Party and the peace movement, that the outbreak of a nuclear war was becoming quite probable.[10] The events in question include the shift from the East–West *détente* of the mid-1970s to intense hostility at the start of the 1980s and the accession of a US President seemingly reckless in his approach towards nuclear weapons in Europe. They included also an inflexible Soviet leadership, which was willing to resort to force (as in Afghanistan and possibly against Poland) and which was quite insensitive to the impact of its actions (as in the case of the deployment of the SS-20 missile) upon Western countries.

Of even greater significance for the growth of Labour fears regarding nuclear war was the judgement that policies of nuclear deterrence were giving way to strategies which envisaged the waging of a nuclear war. In this regard, many in the Labour Party assumed that any nuclear weapons which were not designed solely and unambiguously for purposes of retaliation (in terms of location, accuracy, speed of delivery), were primed for waging nuclear war. These assumptions found corroboration in US strategic programmes, which stressed the need for Washington to possess a capability to counter Soviet nuclear war-fighting forces and in this way to maintain US deterrent options. More directly, it was thought that plans to deploy ground-launched cruise missiles in Britain (and in continental Europe) and Pershing-2 missiles in West Germany indicated a shift away from nuclear deterrence.

Although Labour Atlanticists and left-wingers alike shared the view that nuclear war had become more likely, nevertheless the Atlanticist view still assumed that the risk of nuclear war was somewhat less than that posed by the Soviet Union. By contrast, Labour's left wing, which had secured the leadership of the Parliamentary Party in 1980, adhered to the reverse perception. Thus in subsequent years Labour placed the focus primarily on the danger of nuclear conflict (arising from an international crisis, miscalculation or even accident) involving the people of Britain and the rest of Europe.

Labour's objections to nuclear weapons

Before Labour's objections to NATO's nuclear strategy in the period 1975–81 are elucidated, it is in order to clarify the Party's opposition to any role for, or reliance upon nuclear weapons. According to the anti-nuclear (weapon) perspective, which came to dominate the Party from 1979–80 (and which was shared by analysts within and outside the Labour Party and in the peace movement), there were compelling moral, political and military reasons why a civilised government or party should reject nuclear arms absolutely.

This perspective assumed that, like chemical and biological weapons, nuclear arms are in a separate category. Because of their characteristics, they cannot be viewed as normal or legitimate means for states to use in war, nor even to possess. One reason for this view is that it is assumed that virtually any large-scale use of nuclear weapons in populated areas would cause millions of casualties. It is believed also that it would result in the destruction of the means to sustain life, and would leave a deposit of poisonous radiation which would prevent the restoration of human habitation for many decades. Therefore in contrast with conventional weapons (which enable a victorious state in war to impose its will upon a rival and thereby secure political and economic benefit), the use of nuclear arms is likely to destroy human life and material values and might even eliminate the adversary. Moreover, in contrast with conventional war, the use of nuclear weapons does not usually permit the exercise of leadership, skill and commitment on the battlefield.

According to the criteria of the just war, the use of weapons, whether they be nuclear or conventional, should discriminate between combatants and non-combatants and should be proportionate to the objective sought. These criteria demand also that a state's resort to force against other states should only occur, if then, after all other non-violent means have been tried and failed. Although a sharply limited and carefully targeted attack on isolated military assets by nuclear weapons might satisfy the test of discrimination, it was considered quite improbable that a large-scale nuclear attack on populated areas could avoid the destruction of immense numbers of innocent people.

Anti-nuclear analysts and other observers believed that it would be extremely difficult, and more likely impossible, to halt and contain a limited use of nuclear weapons by the superpowers. It followed therefore that the use of such arms would very probably violate the moral norms of large sections of the people in the most fundamental way. Similarly, these analysts found it quite difficult to envisage circumstances where the use of nuclear arms would be justified, in the sense that the benefits gained therefrom would exceed the overwhelming costs associated with their use. Thus whether the anti-nuclear analysts subscribed to a morality of intentions or of consequences,[11] their assessment was to reject, without qualification, most probable uses of nuclear arms.

In the view of many Labour and other anti-nuclear analysts, it was not only the use of nuclear weapons which could not be accepted by civilized societies like Britain. It was also the very possession of such weapons which had to be renounced unambiguously. While many grounds were advanced for this rejection, two arguments were especially interesting. One proposition received comparatively brief treatment in the literature on nuclear-weapon issues. It asserted that a society or country which is serious about its adherence to justice and human rights cannot consistently defend its values by being willing to resort to 'the indiscriminate killing of civilians, regardless of age, sex or occupation', because such action 'constitutes mass murder that for no end whatever could anyone excusably take part, or acquiesce, or risk taking part or acquiescing, in such an act.'[12]

According to this perspective, the damage inflicted upon the moral principles and values of a civilised society by the very possession of nuclear arms was indeed extremely high. This was so because the domestic bases of that society were gravely corrupted and weakened by the means and signals it employed to ward off supposed external dangers. This damage was supposed to be inflicted upon the moral values of society by the conditional willingness to use deeply repugnant nuclear weapons, and by the complex arrangements required to give effect to a strategy of nuclear deterrence. Accordingly, those armed forces personnel who operated the aircraft, missiles and submarines charged with delivering nuclear weapons upon their targets were perceived to be implicated in potentially genocidal acts. It was also argued by some anti-nuclear analysts that the electors of Britain who supported a policy of nuclear deterrence 'become a party to the process or preparing for nuclear war'.[13] This might be the case even if many of their number were not fully aware of their complicity in such a repellent process.

In the view of Labour anti-nuclear critics, the profound moral difficulties associated with a nuclear strategy could be mitigated if those responsible could be assured that those weapons would never be used. But it was thought unrealistic to expect any system involving fallible human beings to produce such a result. In addition to the grave moral objections to nuclear arms, Labour observers contended that these weapons had a negative impact upon Britain's democracy. Specifically, it was contended that Parliament and voters were prevented from making an informed and timely judgement on the types of nuclear weapon which the United Kingdom acquired. Moreover it was suggested that the British House of Commons was often only told of NATO decisions affecting member states, long after the event.[14]

One notable example of an important government decision not being communicated unambiguously to Parliament until years after the determination refers to Britain's decision in 1947 to manufacture atomic weapons. Another concerns the choice by the Wilson government made public years later to enhance the Polaris nuclear delivery system with Chevaline. With regard to the future, anti-nuclear critics expressed the fear that in an international crisis between the nuclear powers, neither Parliament nor people would have an opportunity to influence directly decisions (taken by the UK government) affecting their very existence.

In the late 1970s and early 1980s, Labour and other anti-nuclear analysts articulated a set of criticisms regarding the perceived political and military defects of strategies of retaliatory nuclear deterrence.[15] Such basic shortcomings were seen to be of three kinds. These concerned their profoundly negative political and military consequences, the extremely limited utility (political and military) of nuclear arms, and the impediments which these strategies were believed to place in the way of the normalisation of relations between rival states and alliances. According to anti-nuclear and some other analysts, supporters of nuclear deterrence accepted certain propositions which led them to make a dangerous and a mistaken interpretation of how peace between the superpowers could be sustained into the indefinite future. Pro-nuclear advocates seemed to believe that the fear of nuclear devastation played a predominant part in maintaining peace in Europe since the late 1940s, and they expected that this would continue to be the case indefinitely. Anti-nuclear observers argued that this was a grave distortion.

While some accepted that such weapons had caused superpower leaders to behave in a more restrained fashion than would otherwise be the case, they identified other weighty factors which promoted stability in Europe. One was the view of many Labour observers that nuclear deterrence 'worked' because there was nothing to deter in the sense that it was quite improbable that the Soviet Union had intended to attack Western Europe. Another consideration was that the memory of the deep human catastrophe experienced by Europeans in the Second World War made them extremely determined to avoid a repetition thereof. Third, and probably of most significance, the relatively stable economic and political conditions obtaining in Europe clearly facilitated the maintenance of peace. Even among pro-nuclear analysts, very few asserted that the spread of nuclear weapons to unstable regions like the Middle East or South Asia would ensure peace in those areas.

Anti-nuclear observers agreed with pro-nuclear analysts that strategies of nuclear deterrence engender deep fear between the nuclear powers. But they judged that these strategies fed a profound hostility and a consequent, almost unending and perilous armed competition. One reason why nuclear weapons were thought to induce a special fear and to be highly provocative was that each superpower was acutely aware of the fact that its rival has targeted immense destructive power upon the most treasured assets of its society. In support of their assumption that nuclear deterrence feeds intense military rivalry between the superpowers, Labour observers pointed to the immense technological, engineering and economic resources allocated by the United States and the Soviet Union to enhance their nuclear capability in decades past. As a direct result of this huge investment, each superpower possessed not one but three immensely destructive branches (based on aircraft, submarines and land missiles) in its nuclear armoury. In combination, the United States and the Soviet Union possessed more than 50,000 nuclear warheads.

Given the catastrophic and inhuman consequences of a major use of nuclear arms, Labour analysts indicated that governments supposedly willing to act in this way were compelled to attribute great potential or actual evil intent to the adversary. To be willing to use such means against anyone less malevolent would be especially difficult to explain, still less justify. In this way, the rival power tended to be portrayed in terms which exacerbated the fears felt by the population which thereby supported the continuing military competition.

At the end of the 1970s, Labour analysts proferred a battery of arguments as to why the superpower nuclear rivalry was intensifying and why they judged that the breakdown of nuclear war was becoming increasingly likely. They pointed to the advent of immensely rapid and accurate nuclear weapons with multiple nuclear warheads on each missile, along with the perceived lowering of the psychological barrier against the use of nuclear arms. Accordingly, the temptation for a nuclear power in time of crisis to strike first its adversary's nuclear forces seemed to have grown much stronger. The perceived reduced inhibition against the use of nuclear arms was thought to be indicated by the intense discussion of the problems of how to conduct nuclear war in US political, strategic and academic circles. The US adoption of declaratory strategies aiming to sustain US advantage in the event of nuclear conflict also suggested a lowering of the taboo against nuclear war. Unguarded comments by President Reagan and members of his administration in the first year of his term exacerbated these perceptions in the Labour Party as did the very antagonistic state of East–West relations at that time.

Besides the apparent relentless and perilous nuclear rivalry of and deeply distrustful relations between the superpowers, Labour analysts noted other factors pointing (in their view) towards the eventual outbreak of nuclear war. Many shared the assumption of one prominent anti-nuclear figure that deterrence sometimes 'has worked for a while and sometimes it has not, but always in the end it has broken down.'[16] Whether this verdict was flawed because it seemed to accept that what happened in the pre-nuclear era was unlikely to change fundamentally in the present nuclear age is open to argument. But others suggest that even if the past is not a reliable guide, it remains the case that as the superpowers survived a number of confrontations (e.g. over Berlin, Cuba and the Arab–Israeli War of 1973) the cumulative risk of nuclear war became very high.[17]

Many Labour analysts accepted that nuclear war was unlikely to occur as a result of a surprise attack. Rather, there was general agreement that it was most likely to erupt in crisis conditions when governments experienced overwhelming fear and almost unbearable tension. Under such pressures, it would be quite possible for normally sober and responsible decision-makers to miscalculate about, or misinterpret the actions of its rivals. Similarly, in a crisis a government might fail to maintain full control over its own armed forces or the behaviour of its allies. Students of superpower confrontations such as the Cuban Missile Crisis do not deny that grave error or miscalculation can happen in such circumstances. Around 1980, British anti-nuclear observers thought that the spread of nuclear weapons to unstable regimes could result in a nuclear conflict which might entangle the superpowers on opposing sides. A US-Soviet nuclear war was believed to be more likely to emerge in such conditions than in a direct superpower clash in Europe.

With regard to the military and diplomatic utility of nuclear weapons, anti-nuclear commentators attributed a relatively limited value thereto in contrast with the assessment of some pro-nuclear analysts. In the view of the anti-nuclear observers, there was little if any positive military role for nuclear weapons if nuclear deterrence collapsed into war. In a war with another nuclear power, most potential uses of nuclear arms could only magnify the catastrophic consequences of the conflict. This consequence seemed especially probable if a relatively densely populated island like Britain found itself at war with a state possessing immense nuclear capability, such as the Soviet Union. Yet many Labour observers accepted, albeit reluctantly, that as long as 'British nuclear forces remained invulnerable to a Soviet first strike, they might deter the Soviet Union from attempting nuclear blackmail, or from launching an all-out nuclear attack on Britain which would mean that it would have nothing to lose by retaliating.'[18]

Labour's anti-nuclear analysts also contended that whatever the awesome destructive power of nuclear arms, there were few definite examples where a nuclear power successfully used the threat of the use of its capability to compel an adversary to do its will, and it was noted that it did not occur in the Vietnam War. Even in the case of the Korean War, it was not entirely clear that the US threat to use nuclear arms caused the cessation of the conflict.

According to anti-nuclear observers, the expected political costs of using nuclear weapons against a non-nuclear country almost always exceeded the military benefit accruing therefrom. That is to say that the damage inflicted by such behaviour upon the nuclear power's international image and especially upon its relations with friendly states and allies (and the deep divisions it would generate domestically) would be overwhelming.

According to Labour and like-minded analysts, the strategy of nuclear deterrence sustained a near impenetrable barrier in the way of establishing normal relationships between East and West. They argued that a threat-dominated relationship resting upon fear and worst-case interpretation of the adversary's intentions takes on a momentum which becomes almost impossible to reverse. This fierce impetus was a product of the coming together of three powerful forces. One concerned ideological rivalry of two great states for dominance in the international system. A second related to the unending search for more technologically sophisticated weaponry of all kinds, including nuclear arms. The third referred to the keen interest which all those who benefit from arms competition have in maintaining a relationship with the adversary which will not reduce their access to power, wealth or position.

Thus a policy of deterrence 'tends to encourage exaggerated rhetoric, to favour intransigence (as a demonstration of resolve), to discourage serious negotiation and the search for compromise, and to value a bellicose posture.'[19] In this way the 'dogmatists' of retaliatory nuclear deterrence offered a direction which did not act politically to mitigate the problems in superpower relations and thereby move away from the greatest danger, that of nuclear war. Instead, their advice enhanced greatly the probability of such an event, because they exaggerated the risk of aggressive behaviour by the adversary, while belittling the very grave danger of a nuclear conflict.

Support for the negative interpretation of the impact of nuclear deterrence was found by Labour analysts in the failure of the periods of East–West *détente* to endure for more than a few years between 1945 and 1980. Further evidence was adduced in the meagre success of superpower arms-control negotiations in halting, still less reversing the relentless qualitative enhancement of all branches of the superpower nuclear armouries. Anti-nuclear observers acknowledged that even if East–West relations were relatively free from deep fear and feeling of hostility, such international negotiations would have to manage severe and intractable problems. But they insisted that nuclear deterrence poisoned the atmosphere necessary for achieving far reaching measures of disarmament. Moreover, given that the superpowers associated the maintenance of peace with their possession of nuclear weapons, they would be very reluctant to consider dispensing entirely with these awesome capabilities.

Labour's objections to NATO's nuclear strategy

Before the main themes in Labour criticism of NATO strategy are discussed, it is necessary to consider briefly the context which influenced that negative assessment. In the decade after NATO adopted its flexible response strategy (in 1967), it attracted relatively little interest in Labour Party and other left-wing circles. Only in 1977–8, when the issue of NATO's production and deployment of enhanced radiation (neutron) weapons entered the public domain, did the long-dormant British peace movement begin to revive. In other words, so long as the NATO alliance was seen to combine political *détente* (as set out in the Harmel Report on the Future Tasks of the Alliance, 1967) with a strategy of military security which did not involve the introduction of new theatre nuclear weapons, the anti-nuclear instincts of many in the Labour Party remained quiescent.

However, from the late 1970s it was perceived that the development of dialogue and cooperation with the East was no longer on NATO's agenda. Instead it seemed determined to deploy dangerous new nuclear arms and to adopt worrying ideas on how to retain escalation dominance in a nuclear exchange. With the advent of President Reagan (1981), large segments of the Labour Party and peace movement thought NATO was led by someone quite insensitive to the dangers of nuclear war, opposed to serious arms control and keen to build up Western military capability. Many of Labour's objections to any policy of nuclear deterrence applied to NATO's strategy. But from the mid- to late 1970s, the Party's starting point was quite different from official NATO assumptions.[20] According to Labour and like-minded analysts, NATO exaggerated greatly Warsaw Pact advantages in many quantitative military indices (e.g. tanks, military personnel) while ignoring the Western alliance's superiority in other capabilities (e.g. naval forces, quality of military personnel). The Party judged also that NATO attributed potential malevolent intentions to the Soviet bloc without offering any credible evidence. It followed from this approach that the Party could identify no convincing rationale for NATO's heavy reliance upon nuclear weapons, weapons which it had come to reject vigorously in the late 1970s and early 1980s.

At that time, Labour argued that NATO's strategy was flawed fundamentally in three essential requirements. These concerned the credibility of the strategy, its propensity to promote or reduce stability in time of crisis, and its capacity to provide effective defence for Western Europe. Labour thought that NATO's strategy of a purported early recourse to nuclear arms was out of touch with reality. It lacked credibility because if NATO did resort to such a course of action it would be extremely likely to visit overwhelming costs upon Germany and probably other parts of Europe as well. This was so because NATO assumed that the Warsaw Pact deployed conventional and nuclear forces at least equal to those held by the Western alliance. Thus it would make little sense for NATO to escalate from conventional to nuclear arms even if no account was taken of Soviet military doctrine which asserted that it would not place limits upon its own nuclear response to a NATO first use of nuclear weapons. Rather, it seemed quite possible that any use of nuclear weapons by NATO would lead to a large-scale nuclear exchange. Therefore the threat or implied commitment to 'defend' the Federal Republic of Germany by measures which could lead to the destruction of its population, cities, land and industry was seen to carry little weight. That threat was thought to possess much greater credibility a decade before when the flexible response strategy was initiated because at that time NATO enjoyed an advantage over the Warsaw Pact in both strategic and battlefield nuclear weapons.[21] By the late 1970s, however, the strategy was judged by many within and without the Labour Party to be deceptively dangerous. In periods of *détente* it would seem quite effective, but in times of acute East–West tension it might induce the Soviet Union to risk a nuclear war knowing that NATO governments would be either extremely reluctant, or perhaps absolutely opposed to initiating the use of nuclear arms.

Labour anti-nuclear observers contended also that there was no satisfactory escape from this dilemma for NATO unless the alliance moved away from reliance upon nuclear weapons (whatever advantage nuclear arms possessed as symbols of shared dangers and unity within the alliance). If the alliance adopted 'smaller', more discriminating nuclear arms (which in some respects were almost comparable with conventional munitions), it increased the likelihood that any East–West armed conflict in Europe would slide into a catastrophic nuclear war. But if NATO reversed the trends of decades and deployed more destructive nuclear arms in Europe, the governments of the NATO member-states would endeavour to avoid using them, in almost every conceivable circumstance. Thus such arms might not deter the adversary from exerting strong pressure on the alliance, but they would have a potent 'self-deterring' impact on NATO.

According to Labour, the nature and location of NATO's weapons increased greatly the risk of nuclear catastrophe in Central Europe. The Party judged that the integration of nuclear and conventional arms in (the training and tactics of) NATO forces in Germany, along with the presence of thousands of short-range nuclear weapons, would mean that armed conflict between the blocs would become nuclear in a short time. Labour assumed that in the event of war breaking out in Central Europe, NATO's military commanders would, if they were facing defeat, be under almost irresistible pressure to release tactical nuclear weapons. Such pressures might be increased further if and when NATO came to deploy immensely rapid and accurate nuclear systems such as the Pershing-2 missile (which would be capable of reaching the USSR in a short time). By the same token, in crisis conditions Warsaw Pact forces would have the most compelling incentive to attack NATO's nuclear weapons first, in order to minimise the destruction such weapons would inflict on the Pact's military and other assets. In this way, NATO's strategy was thought to be one which threatened to turn East–West crises into catastrophic nuclear war.

Labour's objections to NATO strategy amounted to a sharp rejection of the alliance's approach to military security. In Labour's view the alliance was obsessed with nuclear deterrence rather than defence and it possessed awesome, indeed excessive capability to destroy enemy forces and values. The Party accepted that such a strategy and the forces necessary to implement it could give limited protection to states for a period. But in the longer term, the negative consequences of retaliatory nuclear deterrence meant it was not a reliable or acceptable system of security and defence. On the contrary, the likely eventual breakdown of nuclear deterrence could well destroy much of civilisation. Even in the short to medium term, it seemed that nuclear deterrence added further momentum to competition in nuclear weapons, which in turn diminished the security of the nuclear powers. Moreover, it seemed that NATO's flexible response strategy, in so far as it was understood by the public in Britain and other NATO countries, enjoyed only limited support. Often it appeared that public discussions of the strategy tended to frighten rather than reassure those whom the strategy was supposed to secure and protect.

Labour's objections to NATO's relationships and decision-making

In the decades following its foundation in 1949, NATO's relationships and decision-making attracted the strictures of left-wing observers within and outside the Labour Party, especially in periods of acute East–West tensions. As superpower *détente* ebbed away in the late 1970s, such criticism grew enormously in vehemence and in scope.

The basic point encapsulated by most of the censure was a feeling (shared by many in the Labour Party and in the peace movement) that decisions about war in Europe were the prerogative of a leader in another continent, namely the President of the United States. According to one prominent Labour figure, who used language reminiscent of President de Gaulle (in the mid-1960s), Britain's capacity to decide to make war or peace, a core element of national sovereignty, 'had long been ceded in law through a secret agreement with the USA: and in practice, by the very fact that no limitation on the use of US nuclear weapons based in Britain would be enforceable.'[22] This was to assert that neither government nor Parliament nor people in the United Kingdom could exert an effective influence on the most important issue concerning the fate of the country. It emphasised the uncomfortable fact that neither the United Kingdom nor any other European members of NATO could expect, realistically, to enjoy an equal voice with the United States on the control and the use of US nuclear weapons allocated to NATO. Thus membership of NATO, and the closely related UK–US military ties, involved Britain in handing over the ultimate decision about its future to another government. However, the nuclear capability and geographical location of the United States placed it in a very different category of vulnerability from the United Kingdom.

For many left-wing and anti-nuclear analysts, the presence in Britain of US nuclear weapons and facilities made it probable that in wartime those bases would bring down on the densely populated United Kingdom the most devastating nuclear attack. It was also thought that the presence of non-nuclear US military bases in Britain could diminish UK sovereignty and imperil the population in time of crisis and war.

Labour and other left-wing observers' concern about NATO's arrangements were not confined to what might occur in wartime. It embraced as well alliance relationships under normal conditions, which they judged led up to and produced high risks of war. Their anxieties focused upon three principal sets of relationships: United States hegemony or domination of key NATO institutions; the perceived excessively close ties of Britain's military and political élites with their counterparts in NATO and the United States; and the lack of means to make those élites accountable to the UK Parliament and people.

US domination of NATO was seen to be expressed in a variety of facts and arrangements. The United States supplied NATO's security guarantee, provided the alliance's nuclear weapons along with over 300,000 military personnel and conventional weapons, and gave leadership on matters of strategy and policy. Its dominant position was indicated by the filling of most important NATO military posts with US officers and by the United States near-monopoly of expertise and experience in the management of nuclear arms. The foundation for the dominant US role in the alliance was the assessment of the member states that the US contribution was indispensable for the coherence and the very survival of NATO. In the light of this judgement, European governments including the UK administration accepted that, 'The price for US military support in Europe is US dominance in NATO and pressure on European Governments to accept US policies.'[23]

Left-wing and other analysts objected to the virtual monopoly of the United States in deciding NATO's military strategy,[24] which for the most part they rejected. Also they considered it deeply inappropriate on grounds of status, political acceptability and the security needs of those states that the relatively wealthy and confident European countries continued to acquiesce in a subordinate role within the alliance. Such a role was understandable when the United States was both a military superpower and the powerhouse of the international economy.

Some of these analysts judged that UK Atlanticist politicians, senior officials in the military bureaucracy and intelligence services, along with military scientists, had subordinated Britain's 'real' security interests to the US-dominated alliance. These analysts believed those élites acted thus not only due to their ideological and political outlook but also due to institutional pressures not to question existing policies and arrangements.[25] Because these 'NATO-minded' officials held extremely influential positions in government, and often enjoyed strong professional relationships with their colleagues in the United States and in NATO, they were seen to constitute both a bulwark of the alliance and a formidable obstacle to radical change in Britain's security policy.[26]

A prominent and persistent strand in Labour and peace-movement comment on NATO (and UK) decision-making on nuclear weapons referred to a near-impenetrable barrier of secrecy surrounding that process and the lack of essential information and of effective means of making government accountable.[27] While the primary focus of this comment concerned the behaviour of the British government, or more accurately that of the secret subcommittees of the British Cabinets in 1947 and 1974, it was not confined to them. A senior Labour politician who had ministerial responsibility for nuclear energy observed that with respect to the firing of US nuclear weapons based in the UK, 'No Cabinet in which I have served has ever been told the true position and I can only suppose that the key US/UK arrangements are in effect only known to the president and the prime minister.'[28] Especially at the start of the 1980s (when superpower relations were in a state of frozen hostility), many left-wing analysts indicated anxiety regarding the nature of the agreement between London and Washington on US nuclear weapons in Britain.

With respect to UK consideration of relevant NATO decisions, it seemed to left-wing Labour analysts and others of like view that British governments failed to consult the House of Commons at a point when the House could influence the process. Thus following the defeat of the Callaghan government in 1979, those analysts expressed a sense of frustration on learning that the Labour government had participated in the NATO process which led to the decision of December 1979 (to deploy INF in Europe). It appeared to many British observers that they would learn much more about NATO consultations and decisions on sensitive issues from US Congressional and other sources than from UK ministers and officials. Thus while those ministers spoke in the name of the United Kingdom, they seemed determined to prevent Parliament and people from gaining access to essential information.[29]

Labour's objections to Britain's defence priorities

The Labour Party agenda on defence priorities from the mid-1970s was articulated and clarified by the Report of the National Executive Committee Defence Study Group on Defence Expenditure, the Arms Trade and Alternative Employment (i.e. *Sense About Defence*).[30] Many of its recommendations and much of its analysis became the official Party policy on defence after the left wing gained the Parliamentary leadership in 1980. The starting point for the Report's analysis was that UK defence spending was sharply out of line with the country's capacity. One benchmark used to support that view was that, according to NATO definitions, in the mid-1970s the United Kingdom allocated a proportion of national income for defence up to 50 per cent higher than France or the Federal Republic of Germany. This assessment could be challenged strongly on various grounds, particularly on the basis that as about half of West German and French military forces were conscripts (unlike the United Kingdom) those country's military budgets did not reflect the real economic costs of their defence effort.[31]

Nevertheless from the mid-1970s, the perception that the United Kingdom bore an excessive defence burden, both in relative and absolute terms, was widely accepted in the Labour Party. Some Party analysts suggested that the inappropriate UK effort 'would be less of a problem if the United Kingdom were economically strong and other NATO members weak. But exactly the converse is true.'[32] In their view, the heavy military burden (which could well be viewed as a result of the United Kingdom's low growth rates over many years) damaged the economic performance of the country in various ways.[33] Specifically it was thought that the highly disproportionate part of government research and development funds devoted to military purposes (e.g. electronics and electronic-engineering) diverted scarce resources from essential investment and reduced the export capacity of the country by imposing heavy demands on the engineering sector. Moreover, overseas military spending increased the strain upon Britain's delicate balance of payments. Thus the overall level of UK military spending was judged excessive in relation to three criteria. The first concerned the comparable European military effort, the second the perceived detriment inflicted by the military burden upon the UK economy, and the third the unmerited priority given to defence compared to other vital sectors (including investment in manufacturing, education, housing and health).

In the view of many Labour Party analysts, Britain's military effort in the 1970s was not a result of a prudent and balanced assessment of the country's defence requirements. Rather, major roles were sustained by the United Kingdom due to a mistaken belief that there was a 'correlation between military power and importance and standing in the world.'[34] The British political and military establishment was believed to be desperate to retain a strong influence with the United States and within NATO by way of its excessive military effort.

Labour observers' conviction about the excessive level of UK military expenditure was not translated into a fully worked-out alternative policy. Instead they proffered a cost approach to defence somewhat similar to that pursued by the 1964–70 Labour government. They suggested cuts in anti-submarine cruisers, reductions in the British Army on the Rhine, the cancellation of the multi-role Tornado aircraft, and the early retirement of the Polaris nuclear force.[35] All of this was designed to reduce UK defence spending to an appropriate 'balanced' level.

By the early 1980s, the Party which by then was in opposition clarified its view of what changes it sought in UK defence roles.[36] Labour was forced to articulate its own posture by the decisions of the Conservative government, and by the insistent charge of that administration that when in government Labour had neglected the country's defences. In its early years in office, the Thatcher administration decided to replace the Polaris nuclear force with the Trident system. It demonstrated the special priority it gave to defence by making one of the largest sustained increases in the defence budget for decades, while reducing spending on housing, education and overseas aid. Labour's response was to make a commitment to cancel the Trident nuclear force, to phase out most of Britain's 'out-of-area' capabilities, and to move away from costly so-called 'gold-plated' systems. Given the very substantial costs of the proposed Trident force and the explosion of anti-nuclear sentiment in the early 1980s, the proposal to end Britain's strategic nuclear role was highly attractive for many elements in the then divided Labour Party. Similarly, many of the 'out-of-area' capabilities seemed unnecessary at a time when Britain no longer enjoyed a world role.

Notes and references

1 *Sense about Defence: The Report of the Labour Party Defence Study Group* (London, Quartet Books Ltd., 1977).
2 According to Tony Benn, the enhancement of Polaris was discussed in Cabinet on 20 November 1974. See *The Benn Diaries, 1973–1976* (London, Century Hutchinson, 1989). Acerbic letters from Tony Benn and Michael Foot on the issue appeared in the *Guardian* newspaper, 14 and 15 February 1989.
3 James Callaghan, *Time and Chance* (London, Collins, 1987), p. 558. The lack of trust between Labour leaders in government and the Party was indicated in the suggestion that Prime Minister Callaghan personally authorised studies for a successor to Polaris 'so that Secretary of State for Defence, Fred Mulley, who was a member of Labour's National Executive, could say he had authorised no such thing', Hugh Miall, *Nuclear Weapons: Who's in Charge* (Basingstoke, Macmillan Press, 1987), p. 61.
4 E.P. Thompson and Dan Smith (eds), *Protest and Survive* (Harmondsworth, Penguin Books, 1980), p. 19.
5 These groups are discussed in David Kogan and Maurice Kogan, *The Battle for the Labour Party* (London, Fontana Paperbacks, 1982).
6 If the Transport and General Workers' Union vote had been cast as its ordinary members had indicated, Mr Healey would have won by a large margin.
7 Ian Bradley, *Breaking the Mould: The Birth and Prospects of the Social Democratic Party* (Oxford, Martin Robertson, 1981), pp. 48–51.
8 ibid., p. 47.
9 For an exposition of the differing views of the Labour Government and the National Executive Committee see M. Kaldor, D. Smith and S. Vines (eds), *Democratic Socialism and the Cost of Defence* (London, Croom Helm, 1979), pp. 505–48, 51–92.
10 See Gregory Flynn and Hans Rattinger (eds), *The Public and Atlantic Defense* (London, Croom Helm, 1985), Chapter 2.
11 This is briefly examined in Jeff McMahan, *British Nuclear Weapons: For and Against* (London, Junction Books, 1981), pp. 119–25.
12 Michael Dummett, 'Nuclear Warfare', in Nigel Blake and Kay Pole (eds), *Objections to Nuclear Defence* (London, Routledge & Kegan Paul, 1984), pp. 28–40, 36.
13 Alternative Defence Commission, *Without the Bomb: Non-Nuclear Defence Policies for Britain* (London, Paladin Books, 1985), p. 6.
14 See Scilla McLean (ed.), *How Nuclear Weapon Decisions are Made* (Basingstoke, Macmillan Press, 1986), and *Who Decides? Accountability and Nuclear Weapons Decision-Making in Britain* (Oxford, Oxford Research Group, 1986).
15 These defects are analysed in *Defence Without the Bomb*, op. cit., and by Michael MccGwire, 'The insidious dogma of deterrence', *Bulletin of the Atomic Scientists*, vol. 42, no. 10 (December 1986).
16 Edward Thompson, 'Deterrence and addiction', in C.F. Barnaby and G.P.

Thomas (eds), *The Nuclear Arms Race: Control or Catastrophe* (London, Frances Pinter, 1982), p. 52.

17 For an interesting consideration of this issue, see Karl W. Deutsch, *The Analysis of International Relations* (New Jersey, Prentice Hall, 2nd edn, 1978), pp. 154–61.

18 Report of the Alternative Defence Commission, *Defence Without the Bomb* (London, Taylor & Francis, 1983), p. 29.

19 M. MccGwire, 'The dilemmas and delusions of deterrence', in Gwyn Prins (ed.), *The Choice: Nuclear Weapons Versus Security* (London, Chatto & Windus, The Hogarth Press, 1989), pp. 75–97, 96.

20 Labour's objections to NATO strategy are expounded in *Defence and Security for Britain* (London, The Labour Party, 1984). For further and fuller discussion of these issues by analysts close to the Labour approach, see *Defence Without the Bomb*, op. cit., *Sense About Defence*, op. cit., G. Prins (ed.), *Defended to Death* (Harmondsworth, Penguin Books, 1983), and Paul Rogers *et al.*, *As Lambs to the Slaughter: The Facts About Nuclear War* (London, Arrow Books, 1981).

21 See Jane E. Stromseth, *The Origins of Flexible Response: NATO's Debate over strategy in the 1960s* (Basingstoke, Macmillan Press, 1988).

22 Tony Benn, *Arguments for Democracy*, edited by Chris Mullin (Harmondsworth, Penguin Books, 1982), p. 13.

23 The Report of the Alternative Defence Commission, *Defence Without the Bomb*, op. cit., p. 86.

24 Consult, for example, Dan Smith, *The Defence of the Realm in the 1980s* (London, Croom Helm, 1980), Robert Neild, *How to Make up Your Mind About the Bomb* (London, André Deutsch, 1981), and Edward Thompson, 'Deterrence and Addiction', op. cit., note 16 above.

25 Edward Thompson, 'Deterrence and addiction', op. cit.

26 The potential opposition of sections of the armed forces to the implementation of a non-nuclear defence policy in Britain is noted in P. Dunleavy and C.T. Husbands, 'One last chance: the case for a nuclear referendum', *New Scientist*, no. 19 (November 1984), pp. 7–12, and in Patrick Dunleavy 'A non-nuclear, non-NATO Britain: is there an electoral pathway?' in G. Burt (ed.), *Alternative Defence Policy* (London, Croom Helm, 1988).

27 See Gwyn Prins (ed.), *Defended to Death*, op. cit., Robert Neild, *How To Make Up Your Mind About The Bomb*, op. cit., Tony Benn, *Arguments for Democracy*, op. cit., Hugh Miall, *Nuclear Weapons: Who's in Charge*, op. cit., and Scilla McLean, *Who Decides? Accountability and Nuclear Weapon Decision-Making in Britain*, op. cit.

28 Tony Benn, *Arguments for Democracy*, op. cit., p. 13.

29 See Hugh Miall, *Nuclear Weapons: Who's in Charge*, op. cit., and Scilla McLean, *Who Decides? Accountability and Nuclear Weapon Decision-Making in Britain*, op. cit., and E.P. Thompson, 'Protest and survive', op. cit.

30 *Sense About Defence*, op. cit.

31 This is discussed by Paul Cockle, 'Observations on the proposal to align UK defence expenditure with the average percentage spent on defence by the FRG, Italy and France', in M. Kaldor, D. Smith and S. Vines (eds), *Democratic Socialism and the Cost of Defence: The Report and Papers of the Labour Party Defence Study Group*, op. cit., pp .130–6.

32 *Sense About Defence*, op. cit., p. 13. In the 1980s, the fullest official Party publication on the economic costs of defence spending was issued in the 1986 *National Executive Committee Statement to the Eighty-fifth Annual Conference, Defence Conversion Costs*. See also Malcolm Chalmers, *Paying for Defence: Military Spending and British Decline* (London, Pluto Press, 1985), and Malcolm Chalmers,

The Cost of Britain's Defence, Peace Studies Paper Number 10 (London, Housmans, 1983).

33 See *Sense About Defence*, op. cit., and Malcolm Chalmers, *The Cost of Britain's Defence*, op. cit.

34 *Sense About Defence*, op. cit., p. 72.

35 ibid., Chapter 2.

36 See *Defence and Security for Britain*, op. cit.

3 Labour's defence policy and NATO, 1982–87: concepts, issues and priorities

This chapter will examine three sets of issues, for the period from 1982 until the General Election of 1987. First, it explains the circumstances leading to Labour's adoption of the then relatively new concepts of common security and defensive deterrence. That in turn requires an analysis of the implications for Britain and NATO should such ideas be adopted.

Second, the chapter examines Labour's objective of matching Britain's defence role with its capability. For many years, members of the Party had argued that British governments had espoused unrealistic notions about the country's international status and influence. In consequence, it was suggested that the United Kingdom had undertaken an unsustainable defence burden.

Third, there is an analysis of Labour's efforts to devise a defence policy which would reconcile many conflicting demands. From 1982 until 1986, the anti-nuclear movement had a decisive impact upon Labour's policy. But for reasons which will be elucidated, other pressures gained in weight and influence from the latter part of 1986.

Common security and East–West relations

In the early 1980s, when fears of nuclear war in the United Kingdom and elsewhere were most acute, the central focus of debate on security within the Labour and other political parties was upon nuclear weapon systems and whether they reduced or exacerbated the risks of nuclear war. Therefore, only gradually did Labour come to articulate and expound its approach to the political dimension of security which gave context to, and was more fundamental than any array of weapons.

The immense impetus behind the anti-nuclear dimension of Labour's non-nuclear defence policy emerged with the growth of the peace movement at the end of the 1970s and the early 1980s. But the common security component in Labour's defence posture was not fully reflected until the Party's defence statement of 1984, *Defence and Security for Britain*. Labour's adoption of the common security approach was facilitated by the studies of two separate commissions, the one international, the other British, which met in the first years of the 1980s. The international commission was composed of prominent political figures and was led by Sweden's Prime Minister, Olof

Palme. The members of the British Alternative Defence Commission included some whose thinking on defence was very close to that of the Labour Party. The publication of the *Report of the (Palme) Independent Commission on Disarmament and Security Issues, Common Security: A Programme for Disarmament* (1982) and *The Report of the Alternative Defence Commission, Defence Without the Bomb* (1983) disseminated similar ideas in the period when Labour was in the process of composing the 1984 defence statement. Those ideas concerned non-provocative defence, the interdependence of states' security, and reassurance of the adversary.

For Labour, the common security concept was of profound importance in giving at least a degree of coherence to its defence policy. (It should, of course, be recognised that the defence policies of all the major British political parties exhibited some inconsistencies and questionable assumptions.) That is to say that it provided Labour with a response to the question, asked insistently by political opponents and by some sympathisers and supporters, as to how Britain and NATO could be defended without nuclear weapons. It could now reply that appropriate non-provocative deployment of weapons, combined with reassuring diplomatic strategies, would gradually make that concern irrelevant. As the Party's 1986 defence statement *Defence Conversion and Costs*, noted, the non-nuclear, non-provocative posture 'will provide reassurance, enhance crisis stability and reduce the likelihood of war'.[1]

In *Defence and Security for Britain* (the 1984 Statement to Annual Conference by the National Executive Committee), a demand for the restoration of *détente* is asserted. At the same time, the documents published in December 1986, *Modern Britain in a Modern World*, stated the aim of Labour policy to be 'New *Détente*' in East–West relations.[2] In Labour's view the 'old' *détente* of the 1970s 'lacked momentum and soon became an exercise in political systems management.' The Party's concept of the 'new' *détente* aimed for a changed East–West relationship. This would be underpinned by strengthened economic ties and fostered by a whole variety of mutually beneficial interactions between the governments and peoples in the two parts of Europe. In contrast with the 'old' *détente*, which was seen as mainly to do with relations between governments, the 'new' *détente* embraced '*détente* from below'. That would involve multifaceted contacts of diverse kinds between people in all walks of life (e.g. businessmen, students, performers, sportspersons).

In the mid-1980s, according to Labour the successful promotion of *détente* could alter East–West relations in at least four significant ways. First, the development of more relaxed inter-bloc relations would strengthen the Soviet political leadership by reducing the risk of war and by 'raising living standards and promoting political stability.'[3] Various groups in the Soviet Union 'stand to make special gains from *détente*',[4] such as industries, which would benefit from Western technology, the ministries of foreign trade and foreign affairs, and export industries. In this way those of a 'dovish' disposition would gain in influence relative to Soviet 'hawks'. Second, in consequence of the strengthened position of those favouring *détente* within the East and the West, the impetus for improved relations between the blocs was expected to gain momentum. Third, cooperation between East and West in sharing and in solving, or at least attempting to solve, problems like nuclear safety, health and transport (integrating international passenger and freight networks) 'can bring benefits to Britain and the rest of Europe.'[5] Fourth, even if some instances of cooperation, such as East–West exchanges of artists and performers, sportspersons, students and teachers, might seem small steps, 'they have enormous potential for building confidence between nations.'[6]

According to *Defence and Security for Britain*, the pursuit of '*détente*, trade and communications with Eastern Europe at all levels will greatly reduce military tensions and therefore aid true deterrence of war.'[7] Among the principal means of communication mentioned in the 1984 Statement and discussed at greater length in the 1986 publicity documents (*Modern Britain in a Modern World*) were proposed new mechanisms for joint East–West crisis management and contact groups drawn from different parts of Europe (i.e. East, West and neutral states). These were supposed to assist in giving early warning of problems, or in acting as back-up channels and providing notification about military manœuvres between the two alliances.

Turning directly to the military dimension of common security, Labour's 1980s defence policy statements explicitly accept the principles enunciated in *Common Security: A Programme for Disarmament: The Report of the Independent Commission on Disarmament and Security Issues under the Chairmanship of Olof Palme*.[8] According to the Palme Commission, countries should adhere to the following principles in their security policies:[9] all nations have a legitimate right to security, military force is not a legitimate instrument for resolving disputes between nations; restraint is necessary in expressions of national policy; security cannot be attained through military superiority; reductions and qualitative limitations of armaments are necessary for common security, linkages between arms negotiations and political events should be avoided.

The Palme Commission Report observed that profound differences of interest, ideology and outlook should not be expected to disappear. This was the case concerning relations between East and West, North and South, or neighbouring states engaged in long-standing rivalries. Rather, 'the task is only to ensure that these conflicts do not come to be expressed in acts of war, or in preparation for war',[10] because in this nuclear era war could result in the destruction of all values.

Defence and Security for Britain acknowledged that the determined pursuit of mutually beneficial interactions in the sphere of trade, environment, sport and culture can do much to reduce misunderstandings and to build inter-bloc confidence. It contended also that measures of arms control and disarmament have a great potential to diminish mutual fear as have changes in the doctrine, deployment and character of weapons systems. Specifically, Labour accepted that weapons which were perceived as especially threatening by one's rival, far from enhancing Britain's and NATO's security, had the opposite effect. As the section on the objectives of defence policy commented, 'In a nuclear age no one is secure unless we are all secure.' It went on to say that British and NATO policy must make sure not to engage 'in an aggressive search for superiority and a relentless arms build up with which to threaten [the Soviet

Union].'[11] To insist that the security of Britain is dependent upon the security of its military and ideological adversary might seem like an example of harmless rhetoric. But if UK military planners had to take into account how the deployment of British weapons would be viewed in Moscow, and perhaps to alter their plans if the Soviet Union manifested a deep anxiety about that deployment, that would constitute a very far-reaching change.

The short- and medium-term aim of Labour's defence policy was to prevent war in Europe and to avoid any diminution in the independence of Britain and its allies. The longer-term aim was stated to be 'the establishment of a new security system in Europe and the mutual and concurrent phasing out of NATO and the Warsaw Pact.'[12] This aim, which Labour had formally supported since the 1950s, had not received serious analysis by the Party.[13] It may be unrealistic to expect a major political party concerned necessarily with mainly short-term events and developments to have worked out solutions to processes of many decades ahead. In this regard the transformation of relationships between the countries of the European Community, whereby force or the threat of war no longer played any part in managing conflicts, had only a limited relevance. This was the case because after the Second World War the states of Western Europe adopted compatible political ideologies and outlooks, and they had come to perceive that they must renounce force in their future relationships. In the early to mid-1980s after decades of intense hostility, few analysts in Britain (or elsewhere) expected that the Soviet Union and West Europeans would come to adopt similar political ideologies and attitudes in the foreseeable future. Thus the task of East and West managing their differences of interest, ideology and outlook without resort to force seemed a formidable one. Labour's statement, *Defence and Security for Britain*, commented that 'defence policy cannot be isolated from foreign policy but must be determined by it.'[14] But there was little evidence in the mid-1980s, that the Party harboured definite notions on what foreign policy it needed to give clear long-term direction and context to its defence policy.[15]

Defensive deterrence

In the section dealing with the objectives of the policy, *Defence and Security for Britain* declared that defence policy 'must be consistent with and part of foreign policy.' Likewise, throughout the document the need for the United Kingdom to follow a well-integrated political and military policy is reiterated. Given Labour's vehement rejection in the late 1970s and early 1980s of NATO's strategy the signposts for Labour's new security policy, especially on which directions not to take, were clearly set out.

Accordingly, the new policy could have no role for nuclear weapons (except as a short-term compromise with existing realities) and must focus on reassuring rather than frightening the adversary. In addition, it had to respond to British public opinion which believed that the United Kingdom required an effective defence capability. It also had to reflect Party opinion, which considered that successive British governments had failed to match UK military spending to the country's economic capacity. At the same time, the policy needed to ensure adequate defence for the United Kingdom. Thus Labour defence policy, as proclaimed in the Manifestos for the General Elections of 1983 and 1987, was depicted as non-nuclear and defensive in character. That policy was elaborated in *Defence and Security for Britain* (1984), *Defence Conversion and Costs* (1986), and in *Modern Britain in a Modern World* (1986).

To assist in elucidating Labour's defence policy, it may be advantageous to divide it into three categories. These were the measures with which the Party gave a strong commitment to implement when next in government, measures which it hoped to persuade its partners in NATO to carry out, and actions which necessitated the agreement and support of countries both within and outside NATO.[16] Labour gave a strong commitment to remove nuclear weapons from the United Kingdom and to press for the adoption of a defensive deterrent strategy by NATO. Otherwise the Party was rather tentative about the reforms it advocated in NATO tactics and deployments, while Labour's policy aims in the third category were largely matters of aspiration.

Denuclearising the United Kingdom

In *The New Hope for Britain*, the Party's Manifesto for the General Election of 1983, Labour proposed

> that Britain's Polaris be included in the nuclear disarmament negotiations in which Britain must take part. We will, after consultation, carry through in the lifetime of the next parliament our non-nuclear defence policy.

The ambiguity of this commitment, in the sense that it was not clear what would happen to the Polaris force if the negotiations proved inconclusive, was removed from *Defence and Security for Britain* (1984) and from the Manifesto for the 1987 General Election. In both documents Labour promised to decommission the Polaris system, and in the 1987 Election campaign Neil Kinnock made a commitment to begin that process immediately upon taking office as Prime Minister. Throughout the period 1982–7, Labour declared an unqualified opposition to the acquisition by Britain of a successor system for the Polaris force. This was in contrast with the hesitations which surrounded Labour's view of the circumstances when it would be right to give up Polaris.

The Party's promise to cancel the Trident purchase from the United States was founded primarily upon its general rejection of a separate nuclear force for Britain. It was, however, based also upon the specific character-istics of that system and it related to the implications of Britain possessing Trident. In terms of resources, it was thought that the cost of Trident (£9.4 billion in 1984 according to *Defence and Security for Britain*) 'seriously damages Britain's real conventional defence.'[17] Even more important in Labour perceptions, Trident 'will tie us into US technology and missiles for the next 40 years and, like Polaris, it will not in any sense be truly independent.'[18]

Unlike the Conservative government, Labour dismissed the proposition that Britain might need its own nuclear capability in the last resort as 'dangerous, expensive nonsense'. The Party's condemnation of Trident was particularly strong on the basis that it would escalate enormously the nuclear arms race by increasing fourteenfold the number of targets the United Kingdom could attack. This development was regarded by the Party as precisely the opposite of what Britain should be doing. It was also thought to violate the spirit of the nuclear Non-Proliferation Treaty, which Labour viewed as a major bulwark of international security.

Virtually any major variation in Britain's nuclear capability would have an impact upon its relations with its NATO partners. It was evident, however, that the main elements of Labour's non-nuclear policy, that is the decommissioning of Polaris, the cancellation of Trident, and the withdrawal of tactical nuclear weapons from UK-based aircraft or submarines, were fully within the prerogative of the UK government. Most other parts of Labour's non-nuclear defence policy could have a far-reaching impact upon Britain's NATO partners and required the support of those allies if they were to be implemented.

In the General Elections of 1983 and 1987, Labour advocated the removal of US-owned nuclear weapons from bases in Britain. That would mean the removal of nuclear-armed submarines from Holy Loch in Scotland, the withdrawal of nuclear bombs from US F111 aircraft based at Heyford and Lakenheath, and the ejection of any other US nuclear weapons stored in the United Kingdom. In 1983, the Party sought the removal of US nuclear bases as well as nuclear weapons, aims which were repeated in *Defence and Security for Britain* (1984). Labour's 1986 publicity documents, *Modern Britain in a Modern World*, restated the objective of removing US nuclear arms from the United Kingdom, and it promised also that a Labour government would 'negotiate a treaty to govern the maintenance of US military bases in the UK to ensure that British sovereign national rights are fully applied.'[19] In 1987, the Party's Manifesto reiterated the commitment to dispense with US nuclear weapons but it was silent about nuclear bases. Party leaders had made it clear that US F111 aircraft could remain in Britain provided they were converted to an exclusively conventional role.

Leading up to the General Election of June 1983, Labour assigned great significance to preventing 'the deployment here or elsewhere in Western Europe of Cruise or Pershing missiles.'[20] By the 1987 Election, the Party strongly supported the US–Soviet talks which heralded the elimination of intermediate range nuclear weapons under the terms of the prospective INF Treaty.

Shifting to a defensive posture

In its 1984 statement on defence, Labour observed that an effective non-nuclear defence policy 'should make sure that any attempt at invasion or conquest is so costly to the aggressor that the latter will not think aggression worth while', but 'the nature and deployment of such defence forces should not themselves provoke hostility and tension.'[21] Elaborating on this, it declared Britain required a

> true defensive deterrence which is capable of successful resistance; which exacts a high and unacceptable cost from any aggressor's forces: which as far as possible does not escalate the conflict and which is consistent with a wider policy of promoting security and disarmament.[22]

Thus the approach had two central purposes. One aim was to facilitate the construction of multifaceted confidence building ties between the rival states and alliances. The other objective was to ensure that Britain and NATO possessed adequate military capabilities to prevent an aggressor succeeding. It was also implied that NATO's political and military signals to Moscow should dissuade the Soviet Union from harbouring ideas that it could grab Western territory without much risk or cost.

Labour's analysis made the assumption that if Britain and NATO put aside offensive weapons (such as long-range aircraft) and eschewed military deployments and exercises of an offensive character, this posture would be perceived in that way by other governments. Some UK military analysts questioned whether a defensive orientation could be distinguished from an offensive approach. But an adviser to the working group which produced *Defence and Security for Britain* commented that such a strategy could be recognised by the overall setting and by the fact that 'the build-up, training, logistics and doctrine of the armed forces are such that they are seen in their totality to be unsuitable for offence but just sufficient for a credible defence without nuclear weapons.'[23]

Labour's adherence to a defensive deterrent strategy did not explicitly provide for the retention of a substantial counter-attack military capability. Such a capacity could be used either to disrupt enemy aircraft and forces before they reached NATO territory or to dislodge those forces if they occupied NATO areas. Orthodox military analysts contended that a defensive strategy which eschews substantial counter-attacking capability and which commits itself not to using force against the territory of the adversary denies itself the means for an effective defence. Labour's approach to a defensive strategy might have a place for limited counter-attacking and extensive surveillance capabilities to warn against surprise attack. Similarly it might allow NATO forces to take the initiative if it seemed probable that an attack by enemy forces was imminent. But it excluded any role for nuclear weapons, which many in the Party rejected absolutely.

The Party's defence statements were uninhibited in their condemnation of NATO's 'deep-strike' strategies such as Follow-on-Forces Attack (FOFA). FOFA was thought to be incompatible with a defensive deterrent strategy and to be provocative and unstable in crisis situations, while leaving NATO forces quite vulnerable if it failed in its initial aim.[24] Similarly, *Defence and Security for Britain* rejected US Air–Land Battle doctrine because it involved the potential use of nuclear and chemical weapons and because it would be viewed as offensive by the Soviet Union and the countries of Eastern Europe.

Proposed changes in NATO and UK deployments and capabilities

In the context of NATO, Labour's defence policy sought the removal of nuclear and chemical arms from the arsenal of the alliance and the bringing about of significant changes in its force dispositions and weapon systems. According to *Defence and Security for Britain*:

> The most important and necessary reform of all must be the removal of nuclear weapons from NATO's forces on the Central Front. This will itself release resources for conventional defence. It is a precondition for moving towards an effective, non-suicidal defence for NATO.[25]

In this way Labour sought the establishment of a nuclear weapon-free zone in Central Europe as suggested by the Palme Commission and as recommended by the Alternative Defence Commission. This would involve the removal of all battlefield nuclear weapons from the British Army on the Rhine and Royal Air Force units in West Germany. Such a displacement of nuclear weapons from the Central Front would also be a major step towards the realisation of a highly valued Labour objective: NATO's adoption of a policy of No First Use of nuclear weapons.

Labour's defence policy statements of 1984 and 1986 and Neil Kinnock's speech at Harvard University in December 1986[26] insisted that Britain and NATO would enhance their existing military capabilities by converting dual-capable (i.e. able to carry nuclear and conventional arms) aircraft, missiles and guns to a solely conventional role. This, it was argued, would occur for three main reasons. First, since many dual-capable systems were reserved for their nuclear role, they were not available to perform their full range of capability. As Neil Kinnock commented regarding the US F111 aircraft (stationed in the United Kingdom), it fulfils only one task (i.e. theatre nuclear strike role) when it could carry out six roles. Second, as most of the supposed nuclear roles did not in Labour perspectives make military sense, those tasks were a wasteful deployment of scarce military resources. Third, because dual-capable systems would be regarded as nuclear systems by the adversary, NATO would need to be very careful about the preparation and deployment of such weapons in time of crisis. The conversion of dual-capable weapons to a non-nuclear function would also release those forces assigned to transporting and protecting NATO's nuclear systems.

With regard to the level and disposition of NATO military forces, in 1984 Labour judged that there

> is now a rough conventional balance in Europe between NATO and the Warsaw Pact. Nato has a numerical superiority in some categories: the Warsaw Pact has superiority in others . . . [but] there is some strength in the argument that NATO should improve its defensive conventional capability on the Central Front.[27]

Labour's defence statements of 1984 and 1986 accepted, with qualification, the view that the Soviet bloc did not possess sufficient military strength to guarantee victory should it attack NATO. But the 1986 statement was deeply critical of the assessments made by the United Kingdom and NATO of the

East–West military balance. In particular it rejected the 'current over-dependence on US intelligence analyses',[28] the 'interpretations of Soviet military capabilities generated by current "worst case" analyses.'[29] It promised that a future Labour government would 'publish a more realistic assessment of the balance of forces, nuclear and non-nuclear, between the two blocs.'[30]

Along with the demand for changes in NATO's arsenal and posture, Labour wanted the alliance to adopt greater in-depth defence to enable NATO 'forces to capitalise properly on the intrinsic tactical advantage that defensive forces hold over offensive ones.'[31] To make better use of NATO forces, Labour sought action in three fields: reserves, electronic barriers, and equipment.[32] Thus in the context of a redesigned Central Front, the Party's defence statements demanded the reorganisation of equipment and the expansion of NATO and UK reserve forces. The strengthened UK reserve forces could be used either for the defence of Britain or for the rapid reinforcement of the British Army on the Rhine.

Probably the most radical of Labour's proposals concerned major shifts in the make-up of NATO's weapons inventory, along with consequent changes in the alliance's command and force structure. Labour advocated a sharply reduced role for 'large and very expensive weapons platforms' such as costly and sophisticated, long-range aircraft, warships and main battle-tanks. That proposal assumed that such platforms were becoming increasingly vulnerable in war conditions. The Party contended that it would be better to rely on 'smaller and simpler vehicles and aircraft which would be more manœuvrable, easier to conceal and which could be produced in larger quantity because of their lower costs.'[33] Such a drastic shift in NATO's military systems would mean a diminished role, or in the longer term no function at all, for the highly centralised command structure the alliance had up till then required to control highly complex and sophisticated weapons platforms.

According to *Defence and Security for Britain*, NATO should take advantage of what was termed the revolution in 'precision-guided munitions' which because of the 'enormous increase in the precision and power of weapons has in certain areas greatly strengthened the hand of the non-nuclear defender in any war against the aggressor.'[34] Specifically, it commented that the advent of precision-guided munitions should diminish in great measure NATO's anxiety regarding the Warsaw Pact lead in tank numbers.

Labour's defence statements implied, but did not make explicit, the judgement that the adoption of precision-guided munitions and of cheaper, smaller, more manœuvrable platforms indicated a shift to small, fairly autonomous and highly mobile combat units. It was suggested that such units, whether countering enemy tanks, aircraft or artillery, could use sensors, electronics and data and signal processing to slow down or halt an aggressor. In that task, *Defence and Security for Britain* argued that the deployment of electronic barriers and obstacles close to the East–West border could have a big impact. In times of crisis, it 'could greatly enhance the prospects for successful defence and decrease the relative effectiveness of a given offensive force by as much as 40 per cent.'[35] Extrapolating the Party's analysis, it may be assumed that highly trained professional forces would operate on land and in the air just behind the electronic barrier, to inflict heavy costs upon the attacking force. At the same time, less experienced reserve personnel would be placed further back in Germany with 'simple anti-tank and anti-aircraft missiles'.[36]

Turning to other areas of NATO's defence arrangements, Labour's statements identified major weaknesses in the alliance's naval role in the Eastern Atlantic, as it did in Britain's defence of the home base. For example, *Defence and Security for Britain* commented that NATO had a serious weakness in its capacity for rapid transport by sea of military equipment from the United States to Western Europe. Regarding the North East Atlantic, Labour argued that NATO, and specifically the Royal Navy, should end its anti-submarine warfare operations against Soviet ballistic missile-armed submarines. This was essential because such operations utilised nuclear depth bombs and was perceived to be offensive and provocative. The Party was determined to remove nuclear weapons from all branches of Britain's armed forces and to renounce offensive military action. Labour proposed to shift the UK submarine fleet to diesel-electric-powered vessels. It had in mind to assign them to protecting Britain's long coast (Britain having the twelfth-longest coast in the world), ports, fisheries and oil rigs. The Party suggested the United Kingdom should give a much higher priority to defending the country against invasion and guaranteeing the maintenance of trade and communications between Britain and other states, especially those of Western Europe. Labour's 1984 defence statement demanded a major role for the Merchant Navy and a strong shipbuilding base. This would contribute to an integrated maritime policy which together with the Royal Navy would, it was claimed, sustain Britain's security in time of war and its prosperity in peacetime. The opposition of the Party to multipurpose, 'gold-plated' and extremely expensive weapons platforms meant a shift towards greater dependence on large numbers of simpler vessels possessing shore patrol and surface attack capabilities.[37]

Defence and Security for Britain was quite definite in its judgement that 'The key to a successful defence of the United Kingdom is air power', noting that for an invasion force to succeed 'air superiority is essential.'[38] Just as Labour advocated greater priority for naval forces to defend Britain at sea, so it proposed greater investment 'in radar, communications and effective IFF (electronic equipment which makes it possible to identify aircraft as friend or foe).' It advocated a redirection 'of resources in the RAF towards air-defence, coastal and naval aviation'. Such a shift of resources would require the transfer of a substantial proportion of Air Force squadrons such as 'the longer range bomber version of Tornado' to a 'covering role in the North East Atlantic and a battlefield interdiction role in Central Europe'.[39] According to Labour's 1986 publication, *Modern Britain in a Modern World: The Power to Defend Our Country*, 'all the evidence is that . . . would give NATO the means to contain and defeat an attack by conventional means.'[40] These changes referred to increases in NATO reserves, the establishment of a barrier near the inner German border and a shift in the weapons inventory from multipurpose and costly systems to defensive precision guided munitions.

Changing Britain's defence role and capability

Labour's 1984 defence statement observed that 'Britain's current defence policy bears little relationship to a realistic assessment of our roles and responsibilities.' The 1986 defence document *Defence Conversion and Costs* reiterated that assessment, noting that it formed the basis upon which the 'next Labour government will approach its responsibilities for the defence and security of Britain.'[41]

According to Labour, a realistic appraisal of Britain's status and position would clearly recognise that the country had become a medium-sized West European power possessing limited economic and other capabilities. Therefore it could no longer sustain the five major defence roles that it had maintained in the decades since the late 1940s. Instead it should concentrate its defence efforts on 'the non-nuclear defence of the United Kingdom and our allies in Europe.'[42] This meant maintaining three roles: the commitment of UK forces to the defence of the European mainland; a major contribution to the defence of the North Eastern Atlantic; and the defence of the United Kingdom itself. It indicated ending the strategic nuclear role and making substantial reductions in the fifth task of retaining a capacity for global military intervention.

By cancelling the Trident nuclear system, decommissioning the Polaris nuclear force, and closing the facilities for the production and development of nuclear arms, Labour expected to achieve substantial savings. These were estimated at 10 per cent of the defence budget by the third year of a Labour administration.[43] Outside the NATO area, the UK military role involved the protection of territories such as the Falkland Islands, Brunei, Belize and Hong Kong, and the maintenance of military exercises and deployments in the Caribbean, the Gulf and the Indian Ocean. With regard to that role, Labour promised to hold 'an immediate review aimed at reducing and then ending'[44] Britain's commitment. However, the Party explicitly accepted that Britain would retain a capability of contributing to international peacekeeping and disaster relief.

In the three years from the publication of *Defence and Security for Britain* in 1984 to the issue of Labour's Manifesto for the General Election of June 1987, the Party modified its posture on how to allocate the resources released by the winding up of major defence responsibilities. In 1984, the Party's defence document declared its aim to be one of moving Britain's defence budget towards the average of its main European partners. It clearly rejected any suggestion of achieving that objective in 'the lifetime of a single parliament' because that would require severe reductions in UK conventional capability. At the same time, the Party favoured the transfer of resources formerly used for defence purposes to non-military ends.

In 1986, *Defence Conversion and Costs* proffered a highly qualified view on how a Labour administration would decide the appropriate overall level of UK military spending. It listed the factors which should be taken into account by a Labour government as follows: the trend of Soviet military strength which, if strongly upwards or downwards, would encourage a like response from the United Kingdom and NATO; the nature of the cuts made by the Conservative administration to the defence budget so that reductions in areas like the pay of forces personnel would need to be restored; and the general strength of the economy inherited by a Labour government. However, the 1986 statement differed from the Party's 1984 posture in one important question concerning defence savings. It accepted that a significant proportion of the savings gained from cancelling nuclear weapons should be used 'to restore the short-term economies in conventional defences which the Conservatives will need to introduce to pay for Trident.'[45]

In December 1986, the Party's campaign paper, *Modern Britain in a Modern World: The Power to Defend Our Country*, shifted the focus of Labour's declared defence concerns on to two topics. One was the so-called distorted nuclear-biased character of the defence policy of the then Conservative government; the other discussed how the next Labour administration would 'rejuvenate' and 'restore' Britain's conventional military strength. Far from attention being directed at how a Labour government would reduce UK military spending, *The Power to Defend our Country* asserted that 'We, however, accept the view that NATO's conventional capability will need to be enhanced. Britain will contribute towards that enhancement by committing the sums saved on Trident towards additional conventional strength.'[46]

In like fashion, Labour's Manifesto for the General Election of June 1987 commented that

> Labour has a proud record of acting in defence of Britain . . . We will maintain a 50-frigate and destroyer navy. We will play a full part in the development of the European Fighter Aircraft. We will invest in the best up-to-date equipment for the British Army of the Rhine.[47]

Thus the non-nuclear dimension of Labour's defence policy was sustained throughout the period 1982–7. But the public presentation of the policy shifted from a negative tone towards British defence spending in 1982–6 to a quite positive commentary on the need to strengthen UK conventional capability in 1986–7.

Labour's evolving defence policy and developments in the Party and in British politics, 1982–87

Addressing the 1983 Labour Conference, Neil Kinnock, the newly elected leader of the Party, warned the delegates: 'Just remember how you felt on that dreadful morning of June 10th, just remember how you felt then and think to yourselves, June 9th 1983, never ever again.'[48] Mr Kinnock's injunction reflected accurately the feelings and hopes of the Party.[49] It was agreed generally within the Party that Labour's worst election result for half a century or more was not difficult to explain. In that election, Labour obtained 209 seats in a House of Commons of 650 seats and gained only 27.6 per cent of the popular vote, that figure being just 2 per cent ahead of the Liberal–SDP Alliance vote. In brief, the defeat owed much to the public perception that Labour was deeply divided and lacked effective leadership.

Moreover it was thought to espouse unpalatable policies, and to be infiltrated by extreme elements.[50]

Such perceptions were in substantial part a product of Labour's extremely public contention regarding defence in the years 1980–3. That was highlighted in 1981 with the departure of senior politicians to form the Social Democratic Party, as defence was one of the main reasons why they left the Labour Party. Similarly, the 1981 contest for the deputy-leadership of the Party, between Denis Healey, Tony Benn and John Silkin, called attention to Labour divisions on defence and other issues. When Prime Minister Margaret Thatcher announced the General Election for 9 June 1983, the Labour National Executive study group on defence (established in 1981) had not completed its deliberations.[51] Largely to maintain a semblance of Party unity, Labour's Election Manifesto expressed an ambiguous compromise on Britain's Polaris nuclear force. Thus the Party's defence stance straddled the positions of the multilateral Atlanticist and the anti-nuclear unilateralists.

As E.P. Thompson, the leading anti-nuclear campaigner noted, 'an expert axeman splitting a log looks first for the hairline cracks in the wood and strikes there.' In this way, the Conservative 'axeman' had studied Labour's defence policy and had identified the 'crack' before the election. When the election commenced, 'They struck again and again; "one-sided disarmers", leaving Britain "defenceless" . . . "unilateralism" '[52] and so on. But the 'golden opportunity' for Labour's opponents occurred in a few days (22–5 May 1983) during the campaign.[53] First, Michael Foot, the leader of the Party, was seen to disagree openly with deputy-leader Denis Healey on what would happen to Britain's Polaris nuclear force if international negotiations were unsuccessful. Mr Foot indicated that Polaris would be decommissioned whatever the result of the negotiations, while Healey proffered a contrary view. Second, James Callaghan, the former Labour Prime Minister, publicly rejected the unilateral dimension of Labour's policy on nuclear weapons.[54]

Labour's highly publicised confusion and disarray on the very important issue of defence had a number of significant political consequences. It provided the most apt conditions for Labour's political rivals to dictate the election agenda on defence issues. As a result of that dominance, it rendered powerless Labour's effort to promote its favoured defence issues on topics such as the cancellation of the Trident nuclear force. The articulation of Labour's non-nuclear defence policy was in addition seriously impaired by the fact that some Party spokespersons appeared short of confidence in the policy, nor had they fully mastered the analysis underlying it.[55]

As a result of Labour's incoherence and divisions on defence, it became, for the first time in decades, a central issue in the election. This in turn diminished Labour's electoral appeal by highlighting its most unpopular policy. The Labour divisions on defence probably assisted the Conservative Party, too, by diverting attention from some of the latter's less popular policies. But Labour suffered its most damaging electoral setback by giving the impression, and by permitting its opponents to reinforce that impression, of being not only anti-nuclear but also anti-defence. Labour's two-pronged approach, of advocating the elimination of all nuclear weapons from the United Kingdom while simultaneously reducing Britain's defence spending, made it much easier for its rivals to depict the Party as being hostile to any defence for the country. In May 1983, national surveys indicated that a majority of the electorate opposed the reduction of military spending and 'thought that Britain would not be properly defended under a Labour Government.'[56] Such perceptions were fatal to Labour's claim to form the government of the United Kingdom.

Labour's politicians accounted for that injurious and widespread image of the Party's defence policy in diverse ways. According to Denis Healey:

> The reason we were defeated, in so far as defence played a role, is that people believed we were in favour of unilaterally disarming ourselves. It wasn't the confusion, it was the unilateralism that was the damaging thing. And all the opinion polls have shown that . . . I remember vividly the very first election meeting I went to. It was at Allerton Bywater Colliery just outside Leeds . . . I was torn to shreds in the miners' canteen by miners saying to me 'We're never going to vote for a party which is in favour of unilaterally disarming Britain'.[57]

Jo Richardson, a left-wing member of the Party's National Executive Committee, had a similar experience of canvassing to that of Denis Healey. She argued that Labour had failed to explain its defence policy to the electorate. Most of the constituents canvassed by Jo Richardson, who were Labour voters,

> were very nervous. And they had swallowed completely the very heavy Tory line, very much reinforced by the media, that our policy was going to leave Britain defenceless. I may have lost some votes that way . . . but there clearly would be areas where the myth of Britain being defenceless would put people off.[58]

In the aftermath of the General Election, the judgement of Roy Hattersley, the Party's deputy-leader, was that the evidence of the surveys and of Labour's own canvassing was damningly clear: 'unilateral nuclear disarmament, getting rid of our nuclear weapons when other countries did not get rid of theirs, was the most unpopular policy on which the Labour Party has ever fought a general election.'[59] Opposition to Labour's defence policy was deepened, in Hattersley's view, by the contradictions evident therein: 'We said that NATO remained our protection. But we refused to accept our NATO obligations. We promised effective conventional defence. Yet we insisted that a Labour government would cut the defence budget.'[60]

At the 1983 Labour Party Conference, held some months after the disastrous General Election, a resolution seeking 'a credible, comprehensive and effective non-nuclear defence policy' received a large majority. This clear acknowledgement, that Labour lacked such a policy, did not specify exactly what that policy would comprise. In effect, what the resolution sought was a non-nuclear defence policy which incorporated the lessons learned from the débâcle of the 1983 General Election campaign. It suggested a policy which expressed the widest possible unity of, and consensus within, the Party, which had maximum appeal to the electorate, and which offered the minimum of 'targets' to Labour's political opponents.

A majority of Labour's Shadow Cabinet favoured a multilateral, pro-NATO, nuclear approach, while the dominant voice at Labour's Conference was unilateralist and anti-nuclear. The British electorate supported a multilateral, pro-NATO policy, with a clear preference for UK possession of nuclear arms, but it tended to oppose the presence of US nuclear arms in Britain. Thus no likely policy could expect to attract the unreserved assent of the various sections of the Party and the electorate.

The process of considering and producing a new defence policy could not prudently ignore the fact that since the mid-1970s a deep split had emerged within the leadership of the Labour Party. On the one hand, Annual Conference and the National Executive Committee, with a left-wing anti-nuclear majority, had the prerogative of making Party policy. On the other hand, the Cabinet, when in office, or Shadow Cabinet, when in opposition, with a centre-right majority, had the responsibility for implementing and articulating policy in Parliament and other fora.

If the new defence and security policy was to engender broad-based support within the Party, it had to express certain irresistible demands. Especially prominent among these claims were the requirements that Britain's defence be non-nuclear, that the UK maintain full membership of NATO, and that the country reduce overall defence expenditure. The instruction issued by the 1983 Annual Conference for a non-nuclear policy reflected the clear dominance of the peace movement in the Party. Any suggestion that Labour should sustain a nuclear-dependent policy, which senior Party figures like Peter Shore advocated, could not succeed. In any case, Labour had just elected an anti-nuclear leader (i.e. Neil Kinnock), and the anti-nuclear perspective was strongly shared by most Party organs, with the exception of the Shadow Cabinet.

Similarly, advice proffered in the mid-1980s by prominent Labour politicians like Tony Benn, that Britain should withdraw from NATO, would, if accepted, have torn asunder the extremely delicate unity of the Party. It would in all likelihood have led to the exodus of many senior politicians from leading positions in the Shadow Cabinet and some from the Party itself.[61] Moreover, most leading members of the Party believed that such a policy would be electorally suicidal at a time when the new Social Democratic Party was performing relatively well in public opinion polls and by-elections, and disaffected Labour Atlanticists had a potential credible refuge. They might well flee to that refuge if Labour were to deny one of their core values, namely protecting Britain, in partnership with West Europeans and North Americans, within the NATO alliance. Moreover, in the years 1983–4, it seemed prudent for Labour not to make optimistic assumptions about potential Soviet behaviour in Europe. Therefore avoidable proposals which seemed likely to disrupt the Western alliance had little to recommend them. Instead, the best solution for the United Kingdom was to gain maximum influence within NATO. In this way, a Labour-ruled Britain could at the very least pursue both a reduced alliance reliance on nuclear weapons and improved East–West relations.

However, the two core commitments in Labour's defence policy, namely the non-nuclear and the NATO undertakings, conflicted with each other. The depth of that tension depended on the priority assigned to them and the time allowed for implementing the policy. On the face of it, the Party's keenly expressed determination to move the United Kingdom to an exclusively non-nuclear defence posture was incompatible with Britain's full and active membership of NATO. For decades the alliance had assigned a central role to nuclear arms. In specific terms, the possibility of an acute collision between Labour's NATO and its non-nuclear obligations seemed quite considerable on two issues: the future of US nuclear bases in Britain, and the nuclear weapons assigned to the British Army on the Rhine.

According to *Defence and Security for Britain*, a Labour government, 'will take appropriate action to ensure that the US Government removes its nuclear weapons and nuclear delivery systems from British territory and British territorial waters.'[62] In addition, it promised to consult NATO allies about the role of the British Army on the Rhine. But if the alliance failed to remove battlefield nuclear weapons, the 'British Government should take independent action to remove all battlefield nuclear weapons from British Army and Royal Air Force units in Germany.'[63]

Thus the 1984 Labour defence statement reflected the Atlanticist perspective in asserting an unqualified support for UK membership of NATO. Simultaneously, it adhered to the anti-nuclear position on key aspects of the consequences of Britain's participation in the alliance. In this way, the contradiction in the Party's position on NATO, manifest in the 1983 General Election, was not resolved by the new defence policy issued in 1984. Paradoxically, Roy Hattersley (deputy-leader of the Party from October 1983), who had called attention to the damage inflicted by Labour's inconsistency on defence in the General Election of 1983, 'moved, and Neil Kinnock the leader seconded, the adoption'[64] of *Defence and Security for Britain* at the National Executive Committee in the Summer of 1984.

Hattersley's and other Labour Atlanticists' apparent acceptance of, or acquiescence in the robustly anti-nuclear thrust of the 1984 defence policy did not mean they had renounced their own approach to those issues. Rather, as interviews with senior Labour spokespersons confirmed, they were keenly aware of, and took comfort from the comment in the introduction to *Defence and Security for Britain*. That comment noted: 'We do not suggest that our defence policy—any more than policy in any other field—will remain immutably unchanged between now and the next General Election.'[65] Labour leaders indicated that if domestic and/or international circumstances altered in a way which enhanced the persuasiveness of their analyses, they might secure substantial modifications in the content and presentation of the Party's defence policy.

In the two and a half years from Labour's adoption of *Defence and Security for Britain* until the General Election of June 1987, such changes did occur. Atlanticists like Denis Healey, the Party's spokesperson on foreign affairs (and its most authoritative expert on defence issues), and Roy Hattersley, together with a majority of the Shadow Cabinet, succeeded in changing drastically the presentation of the Party's defence policy. At the same time, they secured identifiable modifications in the content of the policy.

The success of Labour Shadow Cabinet Atlanticists in shifting the Party's defence policy during the year preceding the General Election of June 1987, was attributable to three factors. First, the Labour leadership was profoundly anxious about the fact that the British electorate continued to regard Labour as 'weak' on defence. That perception inflicted enormous damage on the Party in the 1983 General Election. Second, the United States exerted considerable pressure on Labour to secure a less radical defence policy. Third, largely due to the influence of those two factors, the advice proffered by Atlanticists like Denis Healey gained momentum.[66]

In late 1986, 'intensive private polling and group research'[67] by Labour's embryonic shadow communications agency[68] revealed that Labour's public standing on defence had improved little from the disastrous perception of the earlier years of the 1980s. These findings provided a basis for an internal strategy paper of the National Executive Committee. The paper suggested ways in which Labour might seek to remedy its 'weak' defence image.[69] Specifically, the paper contended that Labour would 'become the Party that puts the defence of Britain first; that believes in strong, usable effective defence; that believes in spending more on the Royal Navy, the Airforce and the Army; that is a staunch and committed member of NATO.' The Conservatives were, according to the paper, to be depicted as the party that 'saps our defences in order to pay for Trident and Cruise; that has run down our essential armed forces in order to buy and maintain unusable nuclear weapons.'[70]

Modern Britain in a Modern World, Labour's campaign publication of December 1986, reflected not only the analysis and the approach of the National Executive Committee strategy paper. It adopted, as well, the 'language, style and themes' of the paper.[71] The publication had two main aims. First, it sought to reassure the British electorate that Labour could be trusted to defend the country. Second, it aimed, at the very least, to minimise the impact of Labour's negative image on defence. Thus *Modern Britain in a Modern World* emphasised how the Conservative government had 'eroded' Britain's defences. This erosion, it suggested, was indicated by the spreading of inadequate resources on conventional manpower, weapons and equipment. The resources were claimed to be inadequate, largely because of an outdated effort to sustain an unusable nuclear capability.

By contrast, Labour highlighted its promise to strengthen UK conventional defences, while the Party's deep attachment to nuclear disarmament was presented in a low key.

The case for renouncing nuclear weapons was presented in pragmatic strategic terms rather than as a moral imperative. That is to say, Labour expressed its argument as an issue of resources whereby it contended Britain had to choose 'between either proper levels of spending on our navy, air force and army or spending on nuclear weapons'.[72]

On two other issues, *Modern Britain in a Modern World: The Power to Defend our Country* exhibited notable shifts. The concept of defensive deterrence or defensive defence (which places much weight on the political methods of preventing war) occupied a prominent place in both *Defence and Security for Britain* (1984) and *Defence Conversion and Costs* (1986). Although reforms in military strategy associated with defensive deterrence, like precision guided munitions and the use of barriers, are discussed in *The Power to Defend our Country*, the publication contains little explicit analysis of the concept. In part, this probably reflected the view of Labour's leadership, that above all else it must persuade British voters that, unlike 1983, Labour was 'terribly strong on conventional armament,'[73] and that it was anxious to enhance Britain and NATO's conventional military capability. In psychological terms, Labour's leadership probably judged that if it was to succeed in its primary objective (of restoring its image as a Party which could be trusted on defence), it could not afford to highlight measures designed to reassure the adversary and to build mutual confidence.

If Labour had stressed its belief in defensive deterrence, it might also have exposed itself to Conservative Party charges that it no longer viewed the Soviet Union as a serious military threat. That could well have retarded the Party's effort to reassure the British electorate about its approach to defence. It should also be understood that in the years 1985 and 1986 Labour's leadership felt it imprudent to challenge, openly, the conventional wisdom that the Soviet Union remained a potentially formidable military threat to the West. Labour's weak public image on defence made it unacceptably risky for the Party to call into question the long-established British perception of the Soviet Union. With specific reference to defensive deterrence, few Labour leaders, except Denis Healey, showed particular interest in the concept. That was in contrast to some of the academic specialists who advised the Joint Working Party, which produced *Defence and Security for Britain.*[74]

Another significant change in Labour's defence policy expressed in *Modern Britain in a Modern World: The Power to Defend our Country* concerned the objective of reducing UK defence expenditure. The Party's defence statements of 1984 and 1986 maintained that objective. But they acknowledged that a reduction to the average defence expenditure of European countries could not be attained for some years without causing unacceptable damage to Britain's defences. That expression of Party policy indicated that some of the savings deriving from the cancellation of Trident, and the decommissioning of Polaris, would probably be available for non-military purposes.

The Power to Defend our Country, however, promised that 'the sums saved on Trident' would be committed to enhancing Britain's 'conventional strength'.[75] That promise was considered essential by Labour to give credibility to the Party's claim that it would, in government, remedy Britain's over-stretched conventional forces. But it did not fit well with Labour's long-standing aim of diminishing defence spending. Moreover, the commitment was made without the authority of the Party's policy-making body, namely the Annual Conference, and it reversed the policy decided a few months earlier. Accordingly, it attracted challenge and strongly-expressed doubts by many within and outside the Party.

Much paradox surrounded Labour's publicity campaign, *Modern Britain in a Modern World*, of December 1986.[76] The anti-nuclear element in the Party, which was vocal in demanding a publicity effort on defence in 1985 and 1986, did not get the presentation or policy it had sought. On the contrary, the Atlanticists and those nervous of any Labour initiative on defence, dominated the campaign.

Labour leaders and senior figures at Labour headquarters were reluctant to arrange a campaign for a variety of reasons. Prominent among those reasons was their worry 'that doing anything at all to campaign on defence policy might open up a repetition of the damaging splits experienced in 1983.'[77] Such fears were not without foundation. Some of the most senior members of Labour's Shadow Cabinet were profoundly uneasy about the possible consequences if a Labour administration implemented the non-nuclear policy, especially that involving US nuclear weapons in Britain. Public discussion on such matters might lead to Party divisions like those exposed in 1983. Far from advancing Labour's defence policy, such splits would set back the whole Party.

But by the end of 1986, the balance of factors which had impeded a campaign previously turned in a favourable direction. These included the Chernobyl nuclear accident of April 1986 and the bombing of Libya by US aircraft based in Britain. Both events seemed to offer support and encouragement to Labour's non-nuclear policy, including its concern about US nuclear bases.[78] In addition, much of Labour Atlanticists' opposition to a defence publicity campaign was diminished when they were reassured about its character. That is to say, they were content to support it when it became clear the campaign would be presented in terms they supported and was aimed principally at raising public confidence in Labour's approach to defence.

The changes in Labour defence policy contained in *Modern Britain in a Modern World* were not the only significant developments of the policy in the period leading up to the General Election of 1987. In 1984, Labour Atlanticists had acquiesced in the compromise defence policy of *Defence and Security for Britain*. But they were acutely aware that the aim of removing US nuclear weapons from the United Kingdom could jeopardise satisfactory Anglo-American relations.

Since the early 1980s, the objective of removing US nuclear arms from the United Kingdom had been a central concern of the Labour Party. Labour Atlanticists and other members of the Labour leadership recognised that one way of easing their uncomfortable position was to inject more flexibility into the mode of implementing the policy. They sought also to reassure the United States about vital non-nuclear elements of that country's military presence in Britain and about Labour's willingness to avoid the disruption of NATO strategy. These issues are examined further in Chapter 4.

Four years after Labour's disastrous failure in the General Election of 1983, a disaster partly attributable to Labour's confusion and division on defence, the Party faced another General Election, where defence was a prominent issue. The Labour leadership had hoped that the defence would decline in electoral importance on the UK political agenda. But the reverse happened after the highly publicised division among the Liberal–SDP Alliance in September 1986.

Labour contributed in its own way to the increased interest in defence by assigning it a prominent place at the 1986 Annual Conference and by its publicity campaign *Modern Britain in a Modern World* in December 1986. Neil Kinnock's visits to the United States in December 1986 and March 1987 had a similar impact. Labour's concentration on defence in the latter part of 1986 and early 1987 was designed to limit the political and electoral damage to the Party. Party leaders assumed that if Labour attempted to avoid and evade discussion of the non-nuclear defence policy, then rivals like the

Conservative Party would exploit the situation. They would probably wait for an opportunity during the General Election to depict Labour's policy in the most unfavourable light possible. Accordingly, Labour's best chance of publicising and explaining its approach to defence was to select a time well before the election campaign. The partisanship and the acute tensions and emotions generated during an election campaign were expected to reduce dispassionate debate to a minimum. In addition, by presenting the policy prior to the election, Labour hoped to blunt the impact of the attack they had every reason to expect from their main rivals during the General Election.

In the months preceding the General Election of June 1987, former Prime Minister James Callaghan expressed his rejection of key elements of the Party's defence policy. This in turn led to a public row with a member of Labour's Shadow Cabinet, John Prescott, in the House of Commons.[79] Similarly, former Foreign Secretary Michael Stewart attacked the Party's policy on defence. Together with other apparent signs of unease by senior Labour figures,[80] these events raised the profile of defence. They conveyed an image that the proclaimed unity of the Labour leadership on defence was extremely fragile. Labour's effort to present a united image was seriously undermined by the disparate attitudes of Neil Kinnock and Denis Healey regarding the US nuclear umbrella. While Mr Healey recognised Britain's need for US nuclear support to deter potential Soviet pressure, Mr Kinnock indicated many reservations about the efficacy, reliability and morality of any US nuclear shield or umbrella.[81]

In the lead up to the General Election of June 1987, the Conservative Party identified three key weaknesses in Labour's search for electoral support: 'defence, the "loony left", and economic competence.'[82] Labour's leadership, keenly aware of Conservative perceptions, endeavoured to pursue its own agenda of topics to highlight during the campaign. The National Health Service, unemployment and divisions between classes, communities, and rich and poor in the United Kingdom, were prominent in Labour's campaign. Its effort to minimise discussion of defence, at the daily press meetings with the national and international media produced accusations that Labour was running away from the issue. It culminated in Neil Kinnock devoting an entire session to defence.

In the 1987 General Election, the 'golden opportunity' for Labour's opponents emerged in Mr Kinnock's response to a television interview query (by David Frost). His answer to the question, 'If you haven't got nuclear weapons, the choice in that situation would be to subject your forces to an unfair battle?' referred to 'using all the resources you have to make any occupation totally untenable.'[83] Thus Conservatives portrayed Labour's defence policy of getting rid of nuclear weapons as being the equivalent of dismantling the country's entire defence, and relying ultimately on guerrilla warfare. Mrs Thatcher commented: 'The leader of the Labour party even talks about occupation. Occupation? Occupation of Britain? After winning two world wars without a single enemy soldier on British soil? We Conservatives will never take risks with Britain's security.'[84] Arising from Kinnock's mention of occupation in the television interview, the single most effective attack on Labour's defence policy during the campaign was the

Conservative Party poster depicting a soldier with his hands in the air, labelled 'Labour's Policy on Arms'.

During the 1987 campaign, the Conservative Party and the Liberal–SDP Alliance supported and supplemented their condemnation of what they represented as Neil Kinnock's 'defence policy' by means of various arguments. Specifically, they contended that a Labour government which was serious about implementing its defence policy would undermine the foundations of the NATO alliance. In making that attack they were able to call in support the public anxieties articulated by Supreme Allied Commander in Europe General Rogers and US Secretary of Defense Caspar Weinberger.

Cumulatively, the sustained attack on Labour's defence policy by political opponents left the Party looking highly defensive and beleaguered on the issue.[85] As in the 1983 General Election, Labour was unable to focus public debate upon its own preferred defence agenda. Thus topics like the affordability of Trident and the need to reduce the level of nuclear weapons received comparatively little public discussion. Instead, Labour had the difficult task of explaining why a policy designed to shift from nuclear to conventional defence was the best course for Britain and for NATO. Concurrently, its Conservative rival could plausibly claim that such a change would reduce the psychological barriers to war and coercion. In addition, it would require an even larger defence budget and would bring no identifiable gain for the country's security. In this way Labour's sustained effort, in the period 1984–6, to present itself as a Party committed to strong, effective defence (which it highlighted in its publicity campaign *Modern Britain in a Modern World* in late 1986) failed to shift public perceptions. Labour was widely regarded, still, as being weak and unreliable on defence.

According to some surveys, about a quarter of the voters whose support Labour sought in 1987 said that the Party's policy on nuclear weapons was 'the main reason why they were deterred from supporting labour.'[86] It seems likely that a segment of voters used their dislike of Labour's defence policy as a surrogate or a synonym for their unease about other aspects of the Party's policy, behaviour and image. A number of observers, including some Labour supporters, judged that a defence policy which cried 'out against all natural experience', in claiming 'that if you throw away your most devastating weapon then you will be much safer', cost the Party about 3 per cent of the votes in the General Election of 1987.[87] Scarcely any serious observer could deny that, in 1987 as in 1983, Labour had not produced a successful policy. Such a policy would be acceptable to and reassuring for three quite disparate groups. These were the active members of the Party, the British electorate, and the United Kingdom's allies, especially the United States.

Within the Party, there was broad agreement that it faced huge difficulties in gaining public support for the policy. One obstacle was the British press. For the most part, the tabloid newspapers treated the non-nuclear policy in a very hostile and distorted fashion. Another more important difficulty was that Labour challenged long-established notions on a topic where 'most people are not willing to listen to rational or logical arguments [and] see nuclear weapons as a kind of national status symbol.'[88] There was less consensus in the Party on the degree to which it might have secured greater support for the defence policy. According to some anti-nuclear politicians on the left of the Party, the evident nervousness of the leadership about the policy encouraged Labour's rivals to attack it even more fiercely, and it meant that a potential avenue for advancing the policy was unexplored.[89] These critics had in mind the refusal of the Party leadership to promote its own defence agenda in 1985 and for most of 1986 and the postponement of the publicity campaign until six months before the General Election. Moreover it was thought futile and unwise for the Party to present itself in the 1987 General Election as 'stronger' on defence than the Conservatives. That effort challenged the well-established image of the Party as one which gave priority to issues such as the National Health Service, housing and education. Thus it had little prospect of succeeding.

According to Labour Atlanticists, the real difficulty for the Party was not the absence of public campaigning on defence by a hesitant leadership. It arose from the fact that, in colloquial terms, Labour was asking the 'British people to believe six impossible things before breakfast.'[90] In their view, the Party should maintain its non-nuclear objective, but it should approach that aim in a careful, incremental manner. That meant that it should take due account of the British preference for multilateral over unilateral measures and should be sensitive to the anxieties of Britain's allies. In the Atlanticists' judgement, it was very unwise for Labour to alienate potential voters with an unacceptable policy on defence. The only result of so doing was to prevent the implementation of any Labour policy, including defence.[91]

Notes and references

1 *Defence Conversion and Costs*, Statement by the National Executive Committee to the Eighty-fifth Annual Conference of the Labour Party, 1986, pp. 35–42 of *Statements to Conference* (London, Labour Party, 1986), p. 35.

2 For a valuable discussion and account of how the 1984 Report was put together, see Mike Gapes (the senior Labour research officer on international affairs), 'The evolution of Labour's defence and security policy', in Gordon Burt (ed.), *Alternative Defence Policy* (London, Croom Helm, 1988), pp. 82–105. The fullest exposition of the Party's perspective on *détente* is found in *Modern Britain in a Modern World: Europe: New Détente* (1986).

3 *Defence and Security for Britain*, Statement to Annual Conference 1984 by the National Executive Committee (London, Labour Party, 1984), p. 20.

4 ibid.

5 *Modern Britain in a Modern World*, 'New Détente for Europe' (London, Labour Party, 1986).

6 ibid.

7 *Defence and Security for Britain*, op. cit., p. 20.

8 See *Defence and Security for Britain*, op. cit, *Defence Conversion and Costs*, op. cit., and *Modern Britain in a Modern World*, *A Power for Good* (1986).

9 *Common Security: A Programme for Disarmament: The Report of the Independent Commission on Disarmament and Security Issues under the Chairmanship of Olof Palme* (London, Pan Books, 1982), pp. 8–11.

10 ibid, p. 8.

11 *Defence and Security for Britain*, op. cit, p. 6.
12 ibid, p. 3.
13 The Alternative Defence Commission explored possible new patterns of relations in Europe in the early 1980s. See *Defence without the Bomb* (London, Taylor & Francis, 1983), and *The Politics of Alternative Defence: A Policy for a Non-Nuclear Britain* (London, Paladin, Grafton Books, 1987).
14 *Defence and Security for Britain*, op. cit., p. 14.
15 For a well-informed and interesting academic analysis of possible long-term policy aims for a non-nuclear British government, see Ken Booth and John Baylis, *Britain, NATO and Nuclear Weapons: Alternative Defence versus Alliance Reform* (London, Macmillan, 1989), especially Chapter 3.
16 A similar categorisation was proffered by Denzil Davies, MP, Labour's main spokesperson on defence in O. Ramsbotham, *Choices: Nuclear and Non-Nuclear Defence* (London, Brassey's Defence Publishers, 1987), pp. 201–18, 212–13.
17 *Defence and Security for Britain*, op. cit., p. 27.
18 ibid.
19 *Modern Britain in a Modern World*, 'Changing NATO Strategy' (London, Labour Party, 1986).
20 *The New Hope for Britain*, op. cit., p. 36.
21 *Defence and Security for Britain*, op. cit., p. 22.
22 ibid.
23 Frank Barnaby and Egbert Boeker, *Defence without Offence: Non-Nuclear Defence for Europe* (Bradford, Bradford University School of Peace Studies, 1982), p. 26.
24 See *Defence and Security for Britain*, op. cit., p. 14. In interviews with Labour defence specialists, there was little evidence that the Party had a clear definition of its defensive deterrent strategy. Thus while the Party leadership faced the passionate and intense interest of members on all matters touching on nuclear weapons, it enjoyed much more room for manœuvre on issues like the nature and the sequence of the policy for defensive deterrence.
25 ibid., p. 29. See also Denis Healey, 'A Labour Britain: NATO and the bomb', *Foreign Affairs*, vol. 65, no. 4 (1987), pp. 716–29.
26 *Components of Security: Defence, Democracy and Development*, speech by Neil Kinnock at the Kennedy School of Government, Harvard University, 2 December 1986.
27 *Defence and Security for Britain*, op. cit., pp. 10–12.
28 *Defence Conversion and Costs*, op. cit., p. 38.
29 ibid., p. 38.
30 ibid.
31 *Modern Britain in a Modern World: The Power to Defend Our Country* (London, Labour Party, 1986), p. 8.
32 ibid.
33 *Defence and Security for Britain*, op. cit., p. 30.
34 ibid., p. 13.
35 ibid., p. 29.
36 *Defence without the Bomb*, op. cit, p. 170. For further relevant discussion, see G. Prins (ed.), *Defended to Death: A Study of the Nuclear Arms Race* (Harmondsworth, Penguin Books, 1983), pp. 267–87.
37 For an analysis of these issues by an adviser to the working party which wrote *Defence and Security for Britain*; see Gwyn Prins (ed.), *Defended to Death*, op. cit., pp. 267–87.
38 *Defence and Security for Britain*, op. cit. pp. 31–2. There is a strong similarity in the wording of the last paragraph of p. 31 and the first paragraph of p. 32 of

Defence and Security for Britain, and the last paragraphs of p. 270 and the first paragraph of p. 271 of G. Prins (ed.), *Defended to Death*, op. cit.

39 *Modern Britain in a Modern World: The Power to Defend Our Country*, op. cit., p. 8.
40 ibid.
41 *Defence Conversion and Costs*, op. cit., p. 36.
42 ibid.
43 ibid.
44 ibid.
45 ibid, p. 37.
46 *Modern Britain in a Modern World: The Power to Defend Our Country*, op. cit., p. 7.
47 *Britain Will Win, Labour Manifesto, June 1987* (London, Labour Party, 1987), p. 15.
48 D. Butler and D. Kavanagh, *The British General Election of 1987* (London, Macmillan Press, 1988), p. 51.
49 The profound impact or imprint made by the disastrous General Election of 1983 was noted by virtually all the Labour figures I interviewed.
50 D. Butler and D. Kavanagh, *The British General Election of 1983* (London, Macmillan Press, 1983), pp. 140–3.
51 See Mike Gapes, 'The evolution of Labour's defence and security policy', op. cit, p. 82.
52 E.P. Thompson, 'The might will return', *New Statesman*, 24 June 1983, pp. 8–10, 9.
53 See D. Butler and D. Kavanagh, *The British General Election of 1983*, op. cit., especially pp. 93–7 and Chapter 4.
54 For a full expression of Mr Callaghan's view of unilateralism and British defence policy, see 'Why Britain must not go it alone', *The Guardian*, 19 November 1982. Neil Kinnock commented that Callaghan's speech stalled 'the Labour campaign for a week in terms of public perception'. See interview with Kinnock, *Tribune*, 5 July 1983, p. 6.
55 See E.P. Thompson, 'The might will return', op. cit., pp. 9–10.
56 D. Butler and D. Kavanagh, *The British General Election of 1983*, op. cit, p. 282. The majority opposed to reduced defence spending was in the Harris Poll. See *Observer*, 22 May 1983.
57 'Interview with Denis Healey', *Marxism Today* (April 1986), pp. 24–9.
58 Jo Richardson, 'What is the Labour Party doing about defence?' *Sanity* (October, 1985), pp. 14–19, 15.
59 Interview with Roy Hattersley, *Tribune*, 19 July 1983, p. 6.
60 Roy Hattersley's manifesto in the campaign for the leadership of the Party published in the *Guardian*, 18 July 1983, p. 2.
61 This was confirmed in my interviews with senior Labour figures in late 1986.
62 *Defence and Security for Britain*, op. cit., p. 21.
63 ibid.
64 Mike Gapes, 'The evolution of Labour's defence and security policy', in G. Burt (ed.), *Alternative Defence Policy*, op. cit., p. 84.
65 *Defence and Security for Britain*, op. cit., p. 3.
66 See 'Labour and defence, 1983–1987', paper by Dr Eric Shaw, Social Science Department, Manchester Polytechnic (1989), pp. 9–11.
67 Mike Gapes, 'The evolution of Labour's defence and security policy', op. cit., p. 92.
68 According to C. Hughes and P. Wintour, *Labour Rebuilt: The New Model Party* (London, Fourth Estate, 1990), the shadow communications agency 'worked more like a siphon than a vessel. It was not an organisation, so much as an

affiliation of mostly anonymous Labour sympathisers to a core group, which in turn was steered by Gould and Mattinson. Those two worked wholly to Mandelson, which in turn derived his sole authority from Kinnock', p. 58. Here Gould refers to Philip Gould, an advertising expert who together with Deborah Mattinson formed Gould Mattinson Associates. Mandelson was Labour's Head of Campaigning and Communications. Most of the affiliates mentioned above came from advertising and marketing. The key task of the shadow communications agency was to advise the Labour Party on its image and policies and how best to make the greatest impact in order to gain electoral success.

69 The internal strategy paper 'Defence Strategy', October 1986, is discussed by Dr Eric Shaw in his paper 'Labour and defence, 1983–1987', op. cit., p. 18.

70 ibid.

71 ibid.

72 *Modern Britain in a Modern World: The Power to Defend our Country*, op. cit., p. 3.

73 *Guardian*, leader, 11 December 1986.

74 In my interviews and meetings with Labour politicians, advisers and specialists, I found little evidence of much curiosity about defensive deterrence, but advisers like Mary Kaldor indicated a keen interest in the notion.

75 *The Power to Defend our Country*, op. cit., p. 7.

76 At Party headquarters it was, according to one account, 'a standing joke that the campaign was effectively closed the day it was launched', see C. Hughes and P.Wintour, *Labour Rebuilt*, op. cit., 69, p. 17. A very different perspective was offered by Mike Gapes (Labour Senior International Research Officer) who considered the campaign was a sophisticated, professional and effective effort. See Mike Gapes, 'The evolution of Labour's defence and security policy', op. cit., p. 101.

77 Mike Gapes, ibid. According to C. Hughes and P. Wintour, *Labour Rebuilt*, op. cit., Labour's Director of Campaigns and Communications, 'was convinced that the less the party said about defence the better', p. 16.

78 Mike Gapes, 'The evolution of Labour's defence and security policy', op. cit., p. 101.

79 In March 1987, Mr Callaghan warned that the Soviet Union would give nothing in return for unilateral nuclear reductions by Britain. See *Hansard, House of Commons* (10 March, 1987), cols. 53–4. On that day (9 March) Mr Prescott accused the former Prime Minister of damaging (i.e. 'snookering') Labour's election prospects.

80 Lord Stewart warned in a House of Lords debate in December 1986 that it would be a 'suicidal policy' for Britain to seek to persuade NATO to give up its nuclear arms. See *Guardian*, 4 December 1986. An article highly critical of Labour's defence policy by Richard Heller, an adviser to the Shadow Cabinet a few months (10 March 1987) before the General Election, offered hints that senior figures in Labour's leadership felt anxious about the policy. During the Party's 1986 Annual Conference, one (Sunday) *Observer* analysis contended: 'Though no one dares speak out publicly, probably a majority of the Shadow Cabinet have reservations over the policy and a small minority regard it as electoral suicide.' See Adam Raphael and Robert Taylor, 'H-ban Kinnock's unexploded bomb', *Observer*, London, 5 October 1986, p. 4.

The leader column in *The New Statesman* of 5 December 1986 (written by editor John Lloyd but without the support of other members of the editorial staff) demanded that Labour should discard the unilateral element of its defence policy. My own interviews with Labour officials confirm the judgement proffered by the respected journalist Hugho Young that multilateralists like Roy Hattersley, John

Smith and Gerald Kaufman agreed to 'defend the policy they did not support. Or at least they will not attack it'. See *Guardian*, 4 November 1986.

81 In his 1987 *Foreign Affairs* article, Denis Healey observed: 'Belief in the need for the American nuclear umbrella remains as strong in Britain as on the Continent', in 'A Labour Britain: NATO and the bomb', op. cit., p. 728. In various television interviews in the second half of 1986, Neil Kinnock asserted that there were no circumstances in which he would want nuclear weapons used on Britain's behalf and he also indicated that the United States could not reasonably be expected to risk nuclear attack upon itself in order to 'defend' Europe. See (London) *Independent*, 14 November 1986.

82 D. Butler and D. Kavanagh, *The British General Election of 1987*, op. cit., p. 105.

83 ibid., p. 103.

84 ibid., p. 117.

85 Labour's General Election coordinator Bryan Gould commented: 'The major problem for us was that we were not clever enough in dealing with the defence issue. On this I think we took too long to get ourselves off the hook of an essentially defensive posture.' See Alan MacDougall, 'Fear and loathing on the campaign trail', *Chartist*, no. 116 (July/August 1987), p. 17.

86 Mike Gapes, 'The evolution of Labour defence and security policy', op. cit., p. 102.

87 The quote is from Hugh MacPherson, Parliamentary Column, *Tribune*, 26 June 1987. According to Simon Hoggart, 'Labour Leader Neil Kinnock will stick to his defence policy—even though the Party's own polls suggest it lost him about 3 per cent of the vote at the General Election.' Simon Hoggart, 'Kinnock: we're sticking to our guns on defence', *Observer*, 21 June 1987, p. 5. In Ivor Crewe's analysis of the 1987 General Election, defence was the second most important issue for voters. Among the 35 per cent who said defence was an important matter, the Conservatives led Labour by 64 per cent as the preferred Party. Thus 'Defence swung voters away from Labour and to a lesser extent from the Alliance to the Conservatives'. Ivor Crewe, 'Tories prosper from a paradox', *Guardian*, 16 June 1987, p. 4. In the election aftermath defence was identified as a vote-losing issue for Labour by Tom Sawyer, a key member of the Labour National Executive Committee. 'Divisions that Labour can heal', *Guardian*, 19 June 1987, and Roy Hattersley, 'Kinnock pleads for smooth policy', *Guardian*, 16 July 1987. That interpretation was reiterated by Robert Harris, 'Sitting on top of a time-bomb', *Observer*, 27 September 1987, p. 20. Whether coincidence or not, it can be noted that a remarkable shift of public opinion from Labour to Conservative occurred in December 1986 when Labour's publicity campaign on defence was launched. See report on the Gallup Poll in the *Daily Telegraph*, 20 December 1986.

88 Mike Gapes, 'The evolution of Labour's defence and security policy', op. cit., p. 104. See also Peter Kellner, 'Labour's future: decline or democratic revolution', *New Statesman*, 19 June 1987.

89 According to Joan Ruddock (who became a Member of Parliament in the 1987 General Election), who was a leading member of the Campaign for Nuclear Disarmament, Labour's defence policy contained two key weaknesses. First, it lacked a foreign policy context which replaced the Cold War relationship of distrust, hostility and military 'solutions'. Second, Labour rarely promoted it with 'real enthusiasm' and failed to conduct 'consistent, determined, high-profile campaigning, year-in year-out.' See J. Ruddock, 'Labour must link unilateralism with a new approach to foreign policy', *Tribune*, 17 July 1987, p. 7. Another Labour MP, Gavin Strang, contended that the absence of an appropriate foreign policy framework and of consistent campaigning by the Party damaged its chances

as did its emphasis on 'how to mount a more effective defence against a possible Russian attack'. See G. Strang, 'Unilateralism should not be abandoned', *Tribune*, 25 September 1987, p. 6.

90 Richard Heller, 'Labour's great vote deterrent', *Times*, 10 March 1987.

91 Writing in 1987, Peter Shore, MP, a prominent figure on the right of the Party, commented: 'The clear majority of our people stubbornly, and rightly, continue to believe that a Britain without nuclear weapons, while America, Russia, China and France retain them, would be far more vulnerable, would be far less secure and much less influential than she is today. They will not be shifted.' *Guardian*, 25 September 1987, p. 9. Bill Jordan, President of the Amalgamated Engineering Union, was quite vehement about Labour's defence policy. He wrote 'Forty per cent of Labour voters oppose our defence policy, 39 per cent want to keep the British deterrent. The floating voters, whose support we require, are even more adamant.' *Labour Party News*, September/October 1988, p. 16.

4 Labour's defence policy and NATO, 1982–87: implications for UK relations with the United States, Europe and the Soviet Union

In principle, a Labour government committed to implementing its non-nuclear defence policy would be free to decide how and when it eliminated UK nuclear arms. But that process, which might be remarkably difficult to achieve, would be a beginning only in attaining the Party's wider objectives. Labour deemed it essential to alter both NATO's strategy and its approach to defence and deterrence. That in turn would raise major issues for Britain's relations with leading members of the alliance such as the United States and the Federal Republic of Germany. Clearly the prospects for securing fundamental changes in NATO's strategy and attitude would be keenly influenced by the behaviour of the Soviet Union, including its response to initiatives by members of the Atlantic alliance. Therefore it is essential to examine in some detail the implications of Britain's adherence to a non-nuclear strategy for its relations with the United States, West European countries and the Soviet Union. In practice, that involves a review of Labour's interaction with US political leaders and with European socialist parties. This chapter also includes an examination of Labour's approach to the Soviet Union during the period 1982–7.

Labour's defence policy and the United States

In the years 1982–7, Labour's non-nuclear defence policy had many potential implications for Anglo-American relations. One starting point is to identify the disparate perspectives and attitudes of the Labour Party and of the United States, that is, to elucidate, briefly, how factors such as geography, history and ideology influenced the perspectives of political leaders in the Labour Party and in the United States.[1] Naturally, the geographical location of the two countries conditioned the way each viewed the possibility of war, especially nuclear conflict, with the Soviet Union.

In Britain, and in continental Europe, such an event threatened the very survival of society. It did not appear quite as menacing, or perhaps as real a prospect in the United States. Thus in October 1981, President Reagan's comment regarding a superpower nuclear exchange being limited to Europe evoked strong feelings in the British Labour Party. It reinforced UK perceptions that the United States viewed itself as quite distant from the European members of NATO.

Speaking in 1984, Labour's leader Neil Kinnock noted:

> It has been US policy to stampede Europe into accepting the new 'first strike' strategy. It is not a matter of blaming one or other of the super-powers for the arms race. It is a matter of denying them the right to launch the third world war from Europe.[2]

With regard to the impact of their history upon the perceptions and attitudes of Europeans, an American analyst wrote: 'Innumerable attempts to change national boundaries, to alter political realities by the use of force, have produced death and destruction.'[3] By contrast, Americans have both a history and a psychology which 'inclines us to reach beyond our grasp and to regard limits as new frontiers to be crossed, rather than as boundaries to be observed.'[4] Therefore Americans tend to take greater risks *vis-à-vis* the Soviet Union than West Europeans considered judicious. In an era when each alliance possessed enormous destructive capability, Labour politicians believed behaviour which involved a high risk of the catastrophe of nuclear war should be avoided at all costs.

In geographical terms and in some aspects of history, West Europeans were much closer to the Soviet Union than were Americans. They were inclined to have a less hostile perception of the Soviet Union than many, or most Americans. Thus there was a considerable ideological contrast between Britain and Western Europe on the one side, and the United States on the other. For many members of the British Labour Party, the Marxism of the Soviet regime, or more precisely its proclaimed adherence to Marxism, was not in itself a repellant factor. Rather, it was the terror and repression of Stalin's rule, albeit modified by his successors, which in Labour perspectives made the Soviet Union an enemy of democratic socialists.

Socialists of any variety were notable by their almost complete absence from the Congress and the administration of the United States. The approach of Marxists and communists to politics and society was viewed by most Americans as repugnant to their basic values and incompatible with their way of life. In the early 1980s, President Reagan described the Soviet Union as the 'evil empire'. At that time, Mr Kinnock did not see much to choose between Soviet and US foreign policy. For the most part, Mr Kinnock and Mr Healey were fiercely critical towards many aspects of Mr Reagan's policy (e.g. arms control, nuclear arms, Central America), but they were relatively restrained in their strictures of Soviet policy.

In some respects, the sharpest difference of perspective between Labour and US politicians derived from their disparate foci and assumptions. While Labour was concerned primarily with events in Europe, US leaders had a world-wide focus. Since the late 1940s, the US role as leader of the Western World meant that it was interested in, and often had a military presence in most areas of the globe. Accordingly, US administrations, and especially that led by President Reagan, viewed political events and developments in Central America, Southern Africa and elsewhere through the lens of East–West rivalry. By contrast, Labour politicians emphasised the regional and national dimension of such issues.

After Britain withdrew from East of Suez in the late 1960s and concentrated on Europe, Labour was of the view that henceforth the United Kingdom lacked the resources to sustain a major military role outside of NATO. Rather, as anti-nuclear sentiment came to dominate Labour Party attitudes in the early 1980s, the focus of many in the Party retreated even further from Europe to the United Kingdom. These rather inward-looking perspectives were manifest in Labour's opposition to British membership of the European Community, and particularly in its commitment to rid the United Kingdom of nuclear weapons, whatever course was taken by other nuclear weapon states.

Viewed from the United States, Labour's anxiety to remove nuclear arms from the United Kingdom unilaterally seemed to expose the most intense parochialism.[5] In Washington's view, it suggested also a gravely mistaken perception of how such unilateral action would affect Britain's military security.

In the period 1982–7, a significant element in the profound lack of empathy between Labour and US politicians derived from the absence of satisfactory contacts between them. In 1981, a large proportion of Labour Atlanticist Members of Parliament (former and current) who had specialised in foreign affairs and defence left the Party to join the newly established Social Democratic Party. Thus Labour lost figures like David Owen and Shirley Williams, who were well known to politicians and analysts in the United States. By the same token, the very departure of respected politicians from Labour, partly because of the Party's non-nuclear defence policy, reinforced US distaste for the new Labour policy. In addition to Labour's loss of leading Atlanticists to another Party, most of the remaining prominent Atlanticists known in the United States were out of tune with Labour's unilateral non-nuclear defence policy.

At the start of the 1980s, not only did Labour lose many of those who had represented it through contacts with US opinion-formers, analysts and politicians. Indeed, many of the new or existing defence and foreign affairs spokespersons were ill placed to establish or re-establish regular and effective relations with their US counterparts.

Given the strongly inward-looking mood of the Labour Party in 1981–4, it was not easy for its spokespersons to devote much effort to rebuilding relations with their opposite numbers in other NATO countries, and especially in the United States. The intense hostility of anti-nuclear Labour activists towards dialogue and consultation with US officials and politicians discouraged Party representatives from having frequent contacts with their US counterparts. Those pressures were enhanced by the strong feelings of Party activists that the Labour Atlanticist politicians who left the Party had been excessively close to US attitudes and preferences.

On top of the greatly diminished flow of contacts between US and Labour politicians in the years 1981–4, other sources of information and advice were not equipped adequately to promote US understanding of the assumptions underlying Labour's approach to defence. For example, an important source of information on British politics used by US analysts,[6] the London *Economist* newspaper, was generally hostile to Labour's defence policy.

British institutes enjoyed extensive contacts with US visitors, such as the Royal Institute of International Affairs (Chatham House) and the International Institute for Strategic Studies. Those bodies could facilitate dialogue and consultations between UK and US politicians, but they were not in the business of compensating for inadequate communication between them. Thus on the one hand, Labour's defence and foreign affairs spokespersons were, with a few notable exceptions like Denis Healey, inhibited about sustaining clear and effective communication with American politicians. The latter group, on the other hand, did not have satisfactory access either to Labour representatives or to analysts who were open-minded about Labour's approach to defence.

In the period 1982–4, when East–West relations were severely strained, the issues for UK–US relations arising from Labour's non-nuclear security policy were ones of substance, of symbolism and of procedure.

Turning first to substantive issues, Labour's rejection of nuclear weapons conflicted in the most vehement manner with US approaches to defence. In particular, Labour opposed American perspectives on how to maintain deterrence and peace in Europe. According to US strategic doctrine and policy, the presence of its nuclear weapons in Western Europe was the fundamental expression of the US commitment to defend Europe. There was little if any dissent among US political and military leaders that its forces could remain in Europe only if they had the protection of appropriate inventories of nuclear arms. It was assumed that such weapons would deter attack from its nuclear-armed adversary, namely the Soviet Union.

Given that three categories of US nuclear delivery system were based in the United Kingdom, the possible advent of a British government dedicated to eliminating such weapons would be a particularly significant matter for the United States. This refers to the presence in Britain, in the mid-1980s, of US nuclear submarines, F111 aircraft carrying nuclear weapons, and land-based cruise missiles. Along with those weapons, the United States used more than one hundred bases and facilities in the UK, many of which related to the operation of its nuclear forces.

The issue of whether the British Army on the Rhine would retain British and US-supplied nuclear arms was also a matter of great potential moment for NATO's commanders. If a UK government refused to have anything to do with nuclear weapons, NATO's long-established mode of operation and the US role in the alliance would be altered in a basic manner. It was suggested that such changes might be viewed as a virtual invitation to attack by Soviet forces, which would themselves be free from the threat of nuclear response by British forces.

First, if US nuclear arms were ejected from the United Kingdom, that action would necessitate either their relocation in another European NATO country or their return to the United States. In all probability, such developments would impose intense strains on the unity of the alliance. This could be expected because some of Britain's partners might conclude they were being asked to bear an excessive share of nuclear responsibility due to the United Kingdom's abdication from its accustomed role in NATO.

Second, if the United Kingdom was no longer willing to sustain nuclear weapons, whether of British or United States ownership, NATO's military plans (which rested on a complex mixture of conventional and nuclear weapons) would be affected to quite a significant extent. Third, it was evident that a denuclearised British Army and Air Force in Germany would not be compatible with NATO's strategy of flexible response. If Britain insisted that its forces located in a specific part of the Central Front (in Germany) refuse all nuclear munitions, it would nullify the military strategy of the NATO alliance.

A matter of even greater potential significance for UK–US relations was the issue of leadership in the NATO alliance. For most of four decades, the United States and the United Kingdom enjoyed a particularly strong and close relationship on key aspects of military security issues. Therefore Labour's demand to terminate some of the most important of these ties was received with disbelief in the United States. US leaders found the prospect of a UK request to wind up its nuclear links especially disturbing for two reasons. These were based on the fact that the demand came from the country and the Party which was prominent at the creation of the NATO alliance. Moreover, Britain had close affinities in language, ideas, institutions and international outlook with the United States. If implemented, the anti-nuclear policies advocated by the Labour Party would leave the United States as the only nuclear weapon state participating fully in NATO. It would deprive Washington of its junior partner and its most loyal lieutenant in the alliance.

The conversion of Britain, its loyal supporter in NATO, to a status of a semi-aligned non-nuclear member of the alliance would, in US perspectives, be a profoundly damaging event. It would mean that the United States would be deprived of a principal benefit of its role in NATO whereby it could 'influence the defence and foreign policies (and, to a lesser extent, economic and trade policy) of its allies.'[7] The United States also had reason to be anxious that, in the event of the United Kingdom adopting a non-nuclear defence policy and becoming unresponsive to US preferences and leadership, other European countries would act in a similar way. That is, that if the United Kingdom gave up nuclear weapons largely in order to diminish the risk of being attacked by an adversary, then fellow members of NATO might well feel compelled to reduce their exposure to potential attack by refusing also to possess or accept any nuclear weapons on their territory.

Should such an unravelling process initiated by a core NATO member gain momentum, the United States would be left isolated in sustaining the main risk of nuclear devastation if war broke out in Europe. It would accentuate the weakening of European–American relations already diminished partly as a result of shifts away from an Atlanticist orientation by new generations of US political leaders. More pointedly, it would raise in acute form the question, 'How can the American people be expected to put themselves at risk on behalf of Europeans when the Europeans refuse to accept these risks themselves?'[8]

Perhaps the single most significant symbolic issue in contention between the Labour Party and the US approach to nuclear issues in the 1980s concerned the matter of the US nuclear umbrella for the European members of NATO. In the second part of 1986, and to a lesser extent the first part of 1987, it received particular attention from politicians and the media in Britain. The great majority of US political leaders and analysts assumed that the best way to protect peace and security in Europe was to deter any temptation that Moscow might harbour about using force against NATO members. Deterrence could be expected to work if the alliance maintained an effective mix of conventional and nuclear capabilities, including the essential component of US nuclear forces in Europe.

By contrast, Labour's leader Neil Kinnock indicated that he did not expect the United States to risk the very survival of its own society if it could contain the conflict within Europe. He made it very clear that he did not want the United States to use nuclear arms on behalf of Western Europe in any circumstances.[9] For Mr Kinnock and some other Labour politicians, the credibility of the US nuclear guarantee to the European members of NATO was quite low, given that the use of such weapons could lead to an unqualified disaster for the United States.

In one sense the dispute about the US nuclear guarantee had to remain a matter of individual belief. Writing in early 1987, Denis Healey, Labour's chief spokesperson on foreign affairs, noted: 'Although the Labour Party believes that it is no longer wise or credible to rely on the threat of nuclear retaliation against a conventional attack . . . the overwhelming majority of Europeans regards the so-called American nuclear umbrella as essential for deterring a Soviet nuclear attack on Western Europe.'[10] Therefore in contrast with Neil Kinnock's unqualified rejection of nuclear arms, Mr Healey recognised the need for a Western nuclear capability to deter a potential Soviet nuclear attack. However, in late 1986,[11] Mr Kinnock acknowledged that, whatever a Labour-ruled Britain did, the United States could be expected to retain an impressive strategic nuclear force so long as the Soviet Union had a similar capability. In that way, the US nuclear guarantee to Western Europe could be expected to continue for some years.

In another sense, UK and US observers could not be certain that the Soviet Union had ever intended to act in the manner which NATO's nuclear weapons were supposed to deter. Therefore, according to some Labour politicians, there was no Soviet danger or threat which would give a meaningful role to the US nuclear umbrella. In the view of US politicians and analysts, the latter approach was, to say the least, profoundly imprudent. This was so because if the umbrella had in the past, or might have in the future, done anything to dissuade the Soviets from using or threatening to use force in Western Europe (and they contended a sensible analyst would not completely dismiss that), then it was an immense asset in the protection of Western security.

From mid-1986 until the General Election of June 1987, various US officials publicly expressed hostility towards and anxiety about Labour's non-nuclear defence policy. In the autumn of 1986, during the Annual Conference of the Labour Party, US Secretary of Defense Caspar Weinberger asserted that the implementation of key elements of Labour's policy would gravely weaken NATO and would increase the probability of war.[12] In particular Labour's plans to remove or eject US nuclear weapons from the United Kingdom would, according to Weinberger, undermine domestic US support for maintaining extensive US forces in Europe and for sustaining the US nuclear guarantee to Europe.

Secretary Weinberger contended that a British rejection of US nuclear arms and nuclear presence in the United Kingdom (which was an integral part of NATO's defence arrangements) would seriously weaken the alliance's strategy of flexible response. Such a rejection would also strengthen greatly isolationist impulses in the United States. As to Labour's plans for unilateral nuclear disarmament, Mr Weinberger warned that, far from promoting balanced and mutual arms reduction, they would destabilize East–West relations.

The hopes of Labour's leader Neil Kinnock, that US officials would not make public statements on Labour's policies, turned out to be ill founded. Labour regarded such statements as interference in Britain's domestic politics. Mr Kinnock's initial suggestion that Secretary Weinberger did not speak for the US administration proved to be incorrect and unfounded.[13] Instead, US Assistant Secretary for Defense Richard Perle spoke of Labour's defence policy in even harsher terms than Secretary Weinberger. In an interview on British television in the autumn of 1986, Mr Perle spoke of Labour's defence policy in very stark terms. He commented as follows:

> The programme of the British Labour Party under Neil Kinnock is so wildly irresponsible, so separate and apart from the NATO strategy, that I think a Labour government that stood by its present policies—and I rather doubt that they would—would, if it didn't destroy the alliance at least diminish its effective ability to do the task for which it was created.[14]

In more diplomatic language, NATO's Supreme Commander and the Commander in Chief of US forces in Europe, General Rogers, warned (in early December 1986) against Labour's policy. The General observed that the expulsion of US nuclear bases by a Labour administration might lead the US Congress to bring home its forces from Europe.[15] His comment led Mr Kinnock to retort: 'I would not expect him as a man who knows his responsibilities to seek to inhibit the conduct of events in any of the constituent democracies of NATO.'[16]

General Rogers' intervention coincided with Mr Kinnock's visit to the United States. That visit included a keynote speech at Harvard University, meetings with senior members of Congress and with the board of the *Washington Post* newspaper, and a talk by Mr Kinnock at the National Press Club.

From Neil Kinnock's standpoint, the visit was unsuccessful in gaining his main objectives. First, the Labour leader sought to reassure his US hosts (politicians, opinion-formers and analysts) that the Party remained strongly committed to NATO. Therefore he emphasised his support for sustaining

US (non-nuclear) military and intelligence bases and facilities, and he underlined Labour's proposals to enhance the conventional capabilities of Britain and NATO.[17] At the same time he sought to minimise the radical nature of Labour's proposals for changing NATO. He noted that the Party policy did not have 'the purpose of "chain reaction" amongst the European allies in NATO, nor will it have that consequence.'[18]

Second, Mr Kinnock hoped to influence his listeners in the United States, US visitors to London (like Vice-President Bush in late 1985, Senators Pell and Sarbanes, and Congressman Solarz in late 1986), and US Ambassador Price by presenting them with a better insight into and a grasp of Labour's approach to defence. He endeavoured to explain to them why the policy appealed to many British citizens even if they themselves rejected its assumptions. In this way, he hoped to assuage the fear that the election of a Labour government would lead directly to a deep crisis for NATO and for Britain's role in the alliance. Such notions were disseminated quite assiduously by Labour's domestic political rivals who gained much credibility from the allegations of US officials such as Defense Secretary Weinberger. Mr Kinnock was anxious to avoid a repeat of the Labour débâcle on defence which occurred in the 1983 General Election. This he hoped to do by discussing, and thus defusing, defence issues well before the General Election in 1987.

Mr Kinnock's discussions in the United States during late 1986 did not result in consensus with his American counterparts on key issues such as the value and the future of US nuclear weapons based in Britain. Instead, his meeting with Senator Warner was described as ' "a 30 minute good constructive exchange" in which they agreed to differ. Senator Warner said Labour plans would "unravel" NATO.'[19] In substantive terms, Mr Kinnock's talk with Senator Warner probably differed little from his discussions with other members of Congress. These included Senators Hart, Kennedy, Moynihan and Congressman Aspen. Those discussions indicated that a Labour administration would experience much difficulty in achieving a good working relationship with the United States and other NATO allies if it insisted upon implementing its non-nuclear policy.

The feeling that a Labour administration could face difficulties in its relations with fellow members of NATO was deepened when Mr Kinnock (and Denis Healey) made a further visit to the United States in late March 1987. His meeting with President Reagan was held in a blaze of hostile media attention.[20] It was stated by the White House spokesman to be a useful and constructive meeting. But the President was reported to have told Mr Kinnock that Labour's defence policy would seriously damage NATO unity and would undercut the US position in the Geneva (i.e. US–Soviet) disarmament talks.[21] During the UK General Election campaign a few months later, the President reinforced the message that voting Labour could lead to high risks for Britain and for NATO. He commented that Labour's policy of nuclear disarmament was a 'grievous error'.[22]

From the perspective of the United States, the prospect regarding Labour's defence policy in the years 1986–7 could be summed up as follows. The starting point of this interpretation is that US politicians did not agree with, or want to be seen to concur with Labour's approach to military security. Apart from the Reverend Jesse Jackson, few if any prominent US politicians assented to most of the Party's defence policy. Former Defense Secretary McNamara and other figures could agree with Labour's demands for the strengthening of NATO's conventional forces and the adoption of a 'No First Use' strategy by the alliance. More significantly, many mainstream members of the US Congress were able to 'digest the individual slices'[23] of Labour policy. Yet few US observers found the Labour promise to strengthen UK conventional capability credible and, unlike Labour, most wanted to give first priority to that reform and then to consider further diminishing NATO's nuclear reliance.

In sum, most US politicians considered Labour's approach to be unrealistic and potentially dangerous. In their view, Labour quite mistakenly regarded Britain's position in NATO as fairly comparable to that of Canada, Spain or Norway. The Party seemed to want the United Kingdom to abdicate from its centuries-old role as a major European power. They realised also that for a US politician to be seen to be close to the policies or personnel of the British Labour Party could make them deeply vulnerable to the attacks of their rivals in their re-election campaign.

A second pertinent question was whether it made any difference to the President and Congress of the United States that the leading opposition party in Britain had adopted a defence policy incompatible with NATO's strategy. In the 1980s, it was evident that US leaders did not welcome the fact that a sizeable section of British opinion adopted an anti-nuclear attitude. But in practical terms the issue manifested itself in two parts: would the Labour Party gain office in the forthcoming general election, and if it did, would it implement its declared policy for the removal of US nuclear weapons?

In the period leading up to the 1983 General Election, scarcely any objective analyst within or outside the United Kingdom expected Labour to win office. Therefore while in the Falklands conflict of 1982 the United States administration 'attached great importance to the survival of the Thatcher government',[24] it had little reason for anxiety regarding the 1983 General Election. Three years later, British public opinion polls gave Labour a modest advantage, which could be interpreted to mean that it might win office in 1987–8.

Some members of the US Congress considered that the most prudent response was to avoid overt intervention in British politics. Such action was unnecessary and it could be counter-productive.[25] They recognised that Labour had an electoral mountain to climb before it became the government of the United Kingdom. American observers recalled that, despite ideological differences, past Labour governments had worked effectively with US administrations. In their view it was unlikely that a Kinnock government would break completely with the habits of goodwill and mutual accommodation which had characterised the relations of the United States and previous Labour governments.

In 1986, other US officials judged that the time was opportune to warn against or otherwise impede the election of a UK government determined to implement a non-nuclear defence policy. This is to suggest that the interventions of President Reagan, Secretary Weinberger and General Rogers had a twofold objective. First, they aimed to diminish Labour's chances of winning the General Election, due by 1988 at the latest. Second, they sought to persuade the Labour leadership to pull back from the unilateral aspects of its policy and to eliminate specific policy aims and precise timetables from its declared commitments.

It is very probable that, cumulatively, the repeated warnings of senior US officials (September to December 1986) weakened further British voters' already fragile confidence in Labour's capacity to govern effectively. There is little doubt that the two visits by Mr Kinnock to the United States (at the end of 1986 and March 1987) inflicted considerable damage upon the prestige and standing of the Labour leader. That arose from the depictions of his American meetings (albeit by a largely unfriendly British media) as severe rebuffs. In sharp contrast, Prime Minister Thatcher's reception in that period, by both Washington and Moscow, was presented in the most favourable light.

Members of the US administration and Congress had considerable success in persuading Labour to be more flexible about the implementation of its defence policy, largely because they were operating in tandem with like domestic pressures and with the grain of international events. In a newspaper interview in February 1987, the United States Ambassador to Britain, Charles Price, observed: 'Mr. Kinnock had perhaps been influenced by Democratic politicians on his recent visit to the United States. You get the impression, in terms of the time it might take to negotiate the withdrawal of American bases.' In response to the interviewer's question suggesting that the timing of the removal of US nuclear weapons from the United Kingdom was being fudged, the Ambassador noted: 'That it's fudged to some extent, because suddenly it's moved from [*sic*] and they will be gone within one year to, well, discussions may have to go on somewhat longer.'[26]

It is clear that the Labour leadership shifted the emphasis of its stance on the twin issues of (i) whether a UK government would fully consult the United States about the removal of its nuclear arms, and (ii) whether the United Kingdom would insist on their removal in accordance with a strict timetable. Between 1985 and late 1986, Labour's language on these issues revealed a definite evolution.

In 1985, Labour's chief defence spokesman commented as follows on US nuclear arms based in the UK: 'It would take about a year to negotiate and remove them.' He went on to say: 'the Americans will have to accept that we have our rights and if they don't like what we do they will have to lump it.'[27] By the end of 1986, Mr Kinnock's view of discussions between a Labour government and the United States had changed. Now he accepted that 'In other cases, it will be longer, both for reasons of political discussion and the maintenance of the unity of NATO, and also because of the technical requirements of actual removal.'[28]

For some years, Labour's foreign affairs spokesperson Mr Healey had warned his colleagues that 'To expel American bases from Britain without consultation, in the first few days of a new Labour government, would create a serious danger that America would reduce her conventional contribution to

NATO.'[29] In the six months or so leading up to the 1987 General Election, Mr Healey indicated even greater flexibility than Mr Kinnock about US nuclear arms. He noted that discussions on the removal of such arms from the United Kingdom 'would have no time limit though we would expect to conclude them well within our first term.'[30] He also offered hints that the full implementation of the removal process could take a considerable number of years.[31]

Mr Healey's promise that a Labour government would acknowledge that 'NATO strategy must be indivisible', and would 'continue to cooperate in the existing strategy, until we succeed in changing it',[32] was of immense importance. It signalled that neither NATO nor the United States should expect any precipitate action like the sudden withdrawal of the nuclear weapons held by the British Army on the Rhine.[33] Unilateral action of that kind would greatly disturb NATO's command, not least because in the event of a Soviet attack it would severely disrupt an effective coordinated response by the alliance.

Labour's shift on UK-based US nuclear arms was accompanied by undertakings that US nuclear vessels (which at that time were banned by the New Zealand Labour government) would remain welcome under a Labour administration. But the most significant assurance given by Labour leaders was their pledge that, if elected, they would subscribe to NATO strategy until they succeeded in changing it. Given that in the mid- to late 1980s no major alliance member had a government which fully supported Labour's non-nuclear approach, the United States had at least put off the prospect of NATO's strategy being altered against its will.

Similarly, the Labour leadership modified its stance on the very contentious issue of cruise missiles, which were viewed by the peace movement as the most objectionable (as well as the most recent) UK-based US nuclear weapon. In September 1985, Mr Kinnock had promised that 'There will be no circumstances in which a Labour government from its first day will allow the movement or deployment of Cruise missiles.'[34] In the 1987 General Election campaign, the Party accepted that cruise could be retained in Britain, while the then ongoing US–Soviet INF negotiations had a chance of being successful.[35]

From one perspective, the Party's position in mid-1987 expressed Labour's view that a combination of unilateral and multilateral measures was the best way to pursue disarmament. From another view, the Party's shift on this issue was part of a wider pattern. In other words, Labour came to adopt an approach to the implementation of its policy on cruise missiles, which was much less unilateralist and less specific than previously. It was also infinitely less obnoxious to Washington.

With regard to other (other than cruise) UK-based nuclear arms, American politicians had gained significant commitments from their Labour counterparts. These modified positions might indeed turn into reality, Denis Healey's noted comment, that if Britain's allies wanted it, it was 'not inconceivable' that those arms would remain in the United Kingdom under a Labour government. That is to say that if a Labour government were elected, the United States would have the most compelling incentive to prolong for a maximum period discussions on its UK-based nuclear arms. Thus it would secure the fullest opportunity for domestic opponents of the non-nuclear policy (whether in Cabinet, Parliament, the armed forces or in the media), to mobilise their case for postponing, modifying or even halting the policy. At the same time, NATO's complex consultative arrangements might involve delays of some years if leading member-governments were determined to procrastinate.

Such deliberate attempts to postpone the implementation of a UK decision would have the advantage of allowing for the British government to reverse its policy, due either to shifts in domestic politics or changes in international circumstances. It might also give time for the election of a British adminis-tration adhering to a nuclear-reliant policy.

In any event, an analysis of the issue suggested that US politicians pos-sessed a strong and probably a winning bargaining position. That analysis read as follows. First, the Labour Party was committed to unqualified membership of, and participation in the NATO alliance. Because the unity and the electoral survival of the Party required it, Neil Kinnock and other senior Labour figures felt it essential to underline that 'No Labour govern-ment would allow itself to risk the disintegration of the alliance.'[36] Second, NATO without the United States would not be NATO, and the United States insisted that it would not allow its troops in Europe without nuclear 'cover'. Therefore Labour's real choice was involvement in a nuclear alliance or disengagement from NATO. It could be safely assumed that the strongest and most enduring pressures would have a decisive influence on a Labour government. Accordingly, it seemed highly probable that Mr Healey's ad-mission about US nuclear arms remaining in Britain was a candid recognition of the likely outcome of events.

Labour's defence policy and Europe

According to Labour in the early 1980s, the twin aims of a prudent defence policy were (i) to diminish the risk of confrontation and war between the two nuclear-armed alliances, and (ii) to maintain a conventional military capa-bility sufficient to dissuade an opportunistic Soviet attack upon Western Europe. Labour's 1984 statement, *Defence and Security for Britain*, noted the primacy of the political dimension of these objectives. But it acknowledged that the military obstacles to reforming East–West relations were quite formidable.[37]

Labour's proposals for improving relationships between the blocs came directly from its interpretation of what it assumed caused the then seemingly perilous superpower interaction. The Party judged that the source of the existing security dangers was located in three interrelated domains. These were relations within the two alliances (i.e. NATO and the Warsaw Pact), political ties between East and West, and the military strategy pursued by each alliance towards the other.

An important strand in Labour thinking about security which received little attention in the public presentation of Party policy contended that the existing pattern of hierarchical relations (especially evident in the Warsaw

Pact) within the two blocs was a formidable obstacle in the transformation of East–West relations. It was assumed that each superpower, with its own distinctive ideology, political institutions and socio-economic system, was competing for leadership of international society. In that 'race', the quality and magnitude of their military resources were a major element.

Further, the assumption was made that the pursuit of global leadership required the United States (and the Soviet Union in its sphere) to maintain political and military hegemony in Western Europe. As *détente* between the United States and the Soviet Union developed from the late 1960s, the hierarchical relations within the NATO alliance were weakened. Thus West European governments became more assertive and they adopted increasingly independent positions. The change of relationships within NATO were partly connected with the shift of relative economic power from the United States to Western Europe.

It was contended that the internal unity and cohesion of NATO (and the Warsaw Pact) depended largely upon a shared perception of deep conflict with, and antagonism towards its rival. Therefore the West European governments were depicted as willing to accept alliance discipline only when superpower relations deteriorated from the end of the 1970s. At that time, for example, governments agreed to deploy cruise and Pershing missiles in the face of strong domestic hostility.[38] The logic of Labour's approval to East–West relations was that if Britain wanted to reduce bloc confrontations and to diminish the risk of nuclear war, it must seek major changes in relations between the European members of NATO and the United States.

Background factors, 1982–87

Assessing the mix of opportunities and constraints facing the potential implementation of Labour's defence policy in the 1980s, the main issues can be placed in one of three categories. These were issues solely within the competence of the UK government, matters to be decided by NATO and issues to be effected by other international actors such as the superpowers and the United Nations. Even on issues formally within the prerogative of the British government, the support, hostility or neutrality of the major European members of NATO could exert a compelling influence. The attitude of those states could probably have a decisive impact if combined with a similar United States policy.

At the start of the 1980s, the dominant sentiment in Labour's approach to the outside world was rather insular. It was dogmatically unilateralist on nuclear weapon issues and hostile to British participation in the European Community. Therefore the international dimension or implication of Labour's foreign and defence policy tended to be subordinated to intense internal demands and pressures. As a consequence, those policies were ill matched to the conditions determining their potential implementation and were thus unlikely to attain their proclaimed objectives.

The reasons why the Labour Party came to emphasise the unilateral aspect of its defence policy, especially regarding the removal of all nuclear weapons from Britain, were not difficult to discern. Except for France, Britain was the only European country which possessed its own strategic nuclear force. Evidently, it would be easier to denuclearise the United Kingdom than to convert NATO to a non-nuclear strategy. On the face of it, advocates of unilateral nuclear disarmament by Britain had to secure a three-part programme. First, they had to persuade a major political party to adopt that aim; second, that party must be elected to government; third, that government must carry out its declared policy. The anti-nuclear movement succeeded in persuading Labour to oppose the acquisition or enhancement of nuclear weapons in 1964 and 1974 and the Party secured office in those years. But the Labour government failed to implement the non-nuclear policy.

For many anti-nuclear members of the Party, Britain's possession of nuclear weapons violated their own moral sense and the values of the Party in a fundamental way. Their disillusion with, and bitterness against the Labour government of 1974–9 was profound, as it was to an extent for those who opposed British nuclear weapons on pragmatic grounds, such as cost. The multilateral route to nuclear disarmament by Britain seemed to most anti-nuclear Labour activists to be a delusion. Nuclear arms control negotiations had few notable successes, and in any case they did not for the most part directly involve the United Kingdom. Moreover, the credibility of multilateral nuclear arms control was undermined for many in the Labour Party because of what they considered the fulsome, but bogus verbal support given by prominent UK politicians to that approach.

In the intense and often bitter internal Labour debates of 1979–82, much consideration was given to the best method for ensuring that the next Labour government kept its pledges on unilateral nuclear disarmament. It was realised widely that the failures of past Labour administrations were a tribute to the skill, experience and determination of Britain's political and military élite in retaining a valued symbol of Britain's former position as a great power.

Labour leaders recognised also that it would be immensely difficult to secure wide electoral support for a policy requiring Britain to put aside the most powerful weapon it possessed, and with it a capacity which gave the UK a very special status. But the advocates of the policy, who dominated the National Executive Committee and the Annual Conference, believed the Party had no choice but to overcome the daunting battery of impediments.

For the reasons listed above, the unilateralist facet of Labour's defence policy received more attention than it merited. Moreover, an impression was given that Labour was not very interested in multilateral arms reductions between East and West.

At the start of the 1980s, Labour's unilateralism, insularity and opposition to membership of the European Community set it apart from its fellow European socialist parties. But from 1982 onwards, a variety of pressures, processes and events eroded that isolationist mood. Such influences greatly enhanced the voice of those arguing for more outward-looking policies and attitudes.

The impact of the first Reagan administration (1981–4) was the single most important pressure signalling to socialists in Britain and other European countries the need to concert their approach. Socialist parties in Britain, West Germany, Denmark, the Netherlands, Norway and elsewhere were deeply opposed to President Reagan's confrontational style of managing superpower relations. They were also sharply at odds with his policies regarding nuclear arms control, adherence to the SALT ABM Treaty, the Strategic Defence Initiative, and Central America. European socialist parties, including the British Labour Party, realised the logic of their deep alienation from the leader of the NATO alliance. That realisation made them more aware of the need to reduce their security dependence on the United States by building cooperative arrangements with each other.

In the early 1980s, British Labour Party leaders learnt some valuable lessons from their French socialist colleagues about the different domain of economic management. The French Socialist government, elected in May 1981, made determined efforts to raise the living standards of the disadvantaged and to promote growth and employment, but it came up against insuperable obstacles.

Specifically, the Mitterand government found that in an open international economy, where the major countries were deflating, its strategy for growth collapsed by mid-1982. For the Labour Party, which favoured social and economic changes similar to those which failed in France, the lesson was clear. In brief, it was that 'To seek to implement policies without the fullest reference to what is happening beyond national borders is to invite disaster.'[39] There was good reason to think that judgement applied also to defence issues.

In the General Election of June 1983, one of the most serious obstacles to harmonious and significant cooperation between the Labour Party and its European counterparts was dealt a mortal blow. With the overwhelming electoral defeat of the Party, the Manifesto commitment that 'British withdrawal from the Community is the right policy for Britain—to be completed well within the lifetime of the parliament'[40] lost its credibility. That commitment had become unrealistic given that Britain would have been a member of the Community for about fifteen years by the time another Labour administration could hope to be elected. By then, Britain's trade and investment flows would be so integrated with the EEC that withdrawal would involve unsustainable economic costs and the severe disruption of political relations.

In late 1983 and in 1984, Labour's leadership handled the issue of withdrawal from the Community not by promoting an incisive and perhaps divisive debate. Initially it proceeded by accepting a fudged and contradictory expression of Party policy. Thus the 1983 Annual Conference reiterated the commitment to withdraw from the European Community. But it also adopted what was the *de facto* policy of accepting EC membership and 'regarding withdrawal as a last option',[41] not a definite commitment.

Except for opposition from Labour Members of the European Parliament, the shift in policy attracted little attention largely because interest within the Party had shifted from EC membership to nuclear weapons. Moreover, advocates of withdrawal could do little to implement their policy. That was unlikely to change given that the 'British people are frightened of the word "withdrawal" hinting as it does of a desperate journey into the unknown.'[42]

Labour's leaders faced the important elections for the European Parliament (due in June 1984) by emphasising the reform of EC institutions and policies, particularly the Common Agricultural Policy. They also used the occasion of the European elections to campaign on domestic UK issues like unemployment. Labour attached much significance to the elections for the European Parliament. They were the first opportunity it had had since the disastrous General Election to demonstrate that it was still the leading opposition party in Britain. Party strategists recognised that Labour had to fight the European elections on a positive programme. Their analysis was proved correct in that Labour's performance was an immense advance on the result of the 1983 General Election.

A number of senior Party figures had also come to appreciate (or had consistently done so) that, whatever the obstacles the Community might place in the way of achieving important social and economic aims of a Labour government, it 'will need all the allies it can get or at the very least it will need understanding friends.'[43] In their view, a Labour administration had little choice but to endeavour, with the support of like-minded governments, to alter the EC.

Following the 1984 elections, Labour members of the European Parliament had one of the largest national party representations in the Socialist Group. In this way, the European Parliament enabled some of Labour's most active members to promote Party policy in a significant transnational forum. This gain was made at a time when Labour could make little impact in the British Parliament.

In the mid-1980s, the decisions of two European governments underlined the durability of the constraints facing a British Labour government which pursued a unilateralist and/or non-nuclear defence policy. In 1981, the Panhellenic Socialist Movement (PASOK) led by Andreas Papandreou won the Greek General Election, the first victory by a socialist party in that country. It pledged itself to negotiate the removal of US military bases from the country and to leave NATO. Six years later, even after the Pasok government had won a second term (in 1985), those bases remained in Greece.

The United States possessed various means to deflect the Greek socialists from their declared policy. These included the vulnerability of the Greek economy and its dependence upon US aid. Moreover, Greece realised that the expulsion of US bases might well leave Athens very isolated in its disputes with Turkey, which remained allied to the United States. That instance suggested that the United States commanded an immense capacity to persuade an ally to alter its policy.

The other example refers to the Socialist government in Spain. Prime Minister Felipe Gonzales was elected on the basis of opposition to Spain's participation in NATO. Within a few years, he played a leading part in persuading the electorate to support NATO membership in the referendum of 1986. Together, the examples of Greece and Spain suggested that however alienated opposition socialist parties might be with NATO, when in government they would find the attraction of adjusting to the alliance irresistible.

During the Spanish referendum, NATO's Secretary-General Lord Carrington accepted that Madrid was entitled to select its own 'menu' and to reject other elements associated with NATO membership. At the time, British Labour politicians, like Denis Healey, contended that a Labour-ruled United Kingdom should be treated similarly. In their view, NATO should accept that Britain could be a loyal member of the alliance and simultaneously pursue a non-nuclear defence policy. But that argument seemed to appeal more to logic than to history.

Finally, the Chernobyl nuclear accident of April 1986 deepened immensely awareness of the international dimension of nuclear and security issues both in Britain and throughout Europe. It underlined the point that a nuclear war in Europe could well inflict countless human and economic costs upon Britain, whatever the status (i.e. nuclear or non-nuclear) or alignment of the country.

Thus it emphasised the fact that unilateral measures could form only one part of a coherent British defence strategy. Any party which was concerned to reduce the risks of the war should also devote the fullest attention to the wider international aspects of security.

Specific policy, 1982–87

Labour's approach to the European NATO countries may be divided into two periods, that is 1982–3 and 1984–7. In the first period, Labour was winding down a cycle of intense internal conflict on many issues, including defence. Therefore the Party had little inclination to take account of the attitudes and preferences of its sister socialist parties on the continent. At that time of transition, much of the Party leadership's time and energy was devoted to maintaining a public semblance of unity. It was immensely concerned also with preventing a further haemorrhage of voters and members to the newly established Social Democratic Party.

Labour's Manifesto for the 1983 General Election included commitments which had a potential to impinge quite sharply upon other European countries. Especially important were the pledges to withdraw from the European Community, reduce UK defence spending to the level of 'the other major European NATO countries',[44] and to remove US nuclear bases and weapons from the United Kingdom. Taken together, the promises to diminish Britain's defence efforts, to alter the United States military presence in a core NATO country, and to leave the EC were profoundly unpalatable for many continental socialist parties. Most of those parties accepted both the European Community and NATO. European socialists could support some parts of Labour's programme, such as the aim to shift NATO towards a non-nuclear strategy. But the total package signalled that Labour was not sensitive to the concerns of its colleagues in Europe.

Judged by the attitudes expressed at Labour's Annual Conference, the Party seemed to have turned its back on Europe. Anti-NATO sentiment dominated the views expressed, if not the votes cast, in defence debates, while hostility to UK membership of the EC was the norm when the Community was discussed. That is to say that Labour sought to leave the principal economic organisation in Europe, and the Party's defence policy threatened to sunder the main security organisation of Western Europe (i.e. NATO).

By the early 1980s, Labour had become insular and unilateralist, despite its declared support for 'the fullest international co-operation'.[45] Further, the public disarray of the Labour leadership on defence policy during the 1983 General Election campaign did not generate confidence that the Party was capable of effective cooperation with other European parties, still less with the United States.

The second period in Labour's approach to Europe commenced in the aftermath of the 1983 General Election. Then Labour chose a new leader, began a recovery from its internal strife, and became increasingly aware of the need to be outward-looking. Within the United Kingdom, that meant re-establishing relations of trust and responsiveness with the electorate. Internationally it included a concern to restore and strengthen ties with other socialist parties. Labour removed one of the most prominent obstacles to improved relations with those parties within a a short period when it adopted a policy of leaving the EC only as a last option. Second, the Party's new defence statement issued in mid-1984 included limited points of reassurance for some other European parties.

One instance of that concerned the handling of the issue of the British Army on the Rhine (BAOR). As the Party document notes, 'A total withdrawal of British forces in Germany could lead to substantial savings in the defence budget, but there would be considerable political and military implications.'[46] It went on to say that ending the role of BAOR would make it more difficult for NATO to adopt a 'No First Use' policy and might hasten the emergence of a Franco-German nuclear force. The document was silent about one vital consideration. If Labour had advocated the withdrawal of the British Army on the Rhine, it could well be interpreted by socialists and others in Germany as meaning the Party had renounced both nuclear weapons and the defence of Western Europe. In such circumstances, Labour could expect very little understanding and support from German socialists (SPD) in pursuing major security objectives.

With regard to Labour's policy for reducing defence spending, it seems probable that Europeans looked with favour on the shift in the Party's attitude. In contrast with the 1983 Labour Manifesto, the 1984 defence statement, *Defence and Security for Britain*, pledged that the projected saving 'could not be achieved in the lifetime of a single Parliament without major cuts in our conventional forces which we do not recommend.'[47] This was a more considered approach to the complex issue of military spending than the policy Labour had espoused in the early 1980s.

It should be noted that even limited cooperative arrangements between European socialist parties required more than broad agreement on what they rejected. The parties also needed a consensus on what set of alternative defence arrangements would meet their concerns and objectives. By the mid-1980s, the socialist parties of Britain, West Germany, Scandinavia and the Benelux countries had reached considerable agreement on their preferred approach to European security.

A key concept in that approach was the notion of common security which was popularised by *Common Security: A Programme for Disarmament: The Report of the Independent Commission on Disarmament and Security Issues under the Chairmanship of Olof Palme* (1982). The thrust of the Report had to do with the search for 'common security through multilateral agreement between the super powers and their allies',[48] including measures like confidence-building arrangements and non-aggression pacts. The common security approach did not concern itself with the relative merits of unilateral or multilateral nuclear disarmament. But it gave more comfort to advocates of an outward-looking multilateral analysis than to dogmatic unilateralists in the British Labour Party.

Socialists from North European countries, including the Labour Party, agreed also that there should be a 'larger and more independent European role in Western defence.'[49] The dissatisfaction of many Europeans with US leadership of the alliance in the late 1970s was increased immensely with the advent of President Reagan in 1981. These parties agreed that NATO should diminish sharply the place of nuclear weapons in its strategy and reject offensive strategies of 'deep strike'. Instead, the alliance should apply the logic of common security by adopting unambiguously defensive doctrines and weapon deployments.

The Scandilux forum of the socialist parties from Denmark, Norway, Belgium, the Netherlands, Luxembourg, West Germany, Britain and France was one significant grouping of mainly like-minded politicians. It was formed in 1980 in response to NATO's decision to deploy cruise and Pershing 2 missiles in Europe. The main functions of Scandilux were 'information sharing, policy discussion and policy-making'.[50] Except for the French socialists, the participants in Scandilux broadly supported the interrelated defence approach based on common security, a larger European role in NATO, and a defensive orientation for the alliance. The Labour Party was an observer at the meetings of the group and it was usually represented by the leader. It used the meetings 'to keep track on developments in other parties.'[51]

Labour participated also in other European groupings of socialist parties such as the NATO group of Socialist and Social Democratic Parties. There was considerable diversity on defence issues in that rather large forum. For example, Danish and Norwegian socialists espoused an anti-nuclear policy, while French and Italian socialists took a contrary view. Therefore the group could not produce a detailed programme on defence.

By contrast, Labour's Joint Commission with the German SPD was considered quite important by the Labour leadership. The Joint Commission on security produced a communiqué in November 1986. (Due to their disparate approaches towards the role of nuclear weapons, the Labour Party and the French socialists had little prospect of reaching substantial agreement on defence issues).

The principal reason that Labour leaders attached particular importance to their relations with their West German counterparts was quite evident. At the heart of Labour's concern to alter UK and NATO defence policy was the attitude of the actual or potential government of the Federal Republic of

Germany. The disposition of the Federal Republic on an issue such as Labour's policy for the removal of US nuclear weapons could have a major and perhaps a decisive impact.

If the West German government was vehemently opposed to such a policy (as it might be if the consequence of expelling US nuclear weapons was likely to be the breakup of NATO), it could do much to frustrate it. West Germany could counteract Labour's policy if it accepted the transfer of US nuclear weapons ejected from Britain. In Germany, those additional nuclear weapons would, in Denis Healey's view, 'appear very much more provocative to the Soviet Union than they are in Britain.'[52] According to Labour's defence spokesperson, Denzil Davies, the shift of US nuclear arms to the Netherlands and West Germany 'would be a very foolish and silly thing for the Americans to do. Our policy is part of an attempt to move NATO away from its present nuclear strategy.'[53]

Whether it would be provocative or foolish for the United States to transfer nuclear arms evicted from the United Kingdom to West Germany, such a move would free Britain from foreign nuclear weapons. But it would mean a failure to modify NATO strategy. Long before US nuclear weapons were moved out of Britain, the United States in league with West Germany might have persuaded London to delay, alter or even reverse its policy. That is to say that it would be immensely difficult, and probably impossible, for a Labour government to remove UK-based US nuclear arms in the face of the combined hostility of the United States, West Germany, France and other states. European governments might oppose a British non-nuclear policy because of their fears for the survival of the Atlantic alliance.

Labour leaders had a clear understanding that the policy of West Germany and other European NATO members could virtually determine whether Britain would be able to implement its policy, which was formally within its own domain. In 1984, *Defence and Security for Britain* argued that shifting NATO in a non-nuclear direction depended upon achieving political changes in West Germany, Belgium and the Netherlands. In combination with the governments of Norway and Denmark (which did not accept nuclear weapons on their territory), and with the support of Greece, these pressures 'could have a profound impact on the internal politics of the Alliance and therefore on the USA itself.'[54] The 1984 statement placed considerable stress on the tensions and conflicts between Europeans and the United States and it argued for 'a stronger assertion of European interests within NATO'.[55]

Two years later, in mid-1986, the Labour statement on defence and security, *Defence Conversion and Costs*, sharpened the Party's commitment to a European involvement. It declared 'an increased emphasis on alignment with other European countries . . . lies at the heart of our foreign policy.'[56] One example of that alignment and of a 'much more independent political role for the European countries' was the promise to increase cooperation 'between European NATO countries in reaching an independent assessment of Soviet capabilities and intentions.'[57]

On defence procurement, *Defence Conversion and Costs* likewise indicated support for 'some collaborative projects to be undertaken with our European

NATO partners.' In this way, 'Britain will be in less danger of over-reliance on US arms supplies.'[58]

In December 1986, the Party's publicity document, *Modern Britain in a Modern World: The Power to Defend our Country*, castigated the Conservative administration. It asserted that the government was siding 'slavishly with the Americans even if this has meant isolation from the rest of Europe. As a result real influence with our closest partners in Europe has been eroded whilst the illusory role in Washington has been obsessively pursued.'[59] In this way, Labour pursued a two-pronged approach of seeking a weakening in UK–US defence ties while aiming to get closer to European members of NATO. Thus *The Power to Defend our Country* promised: 'Everything we do will involve consultation with our allies.' While remaining silent about consultations with the United States, it stressed that, 'already discussions are underway with colleagues in Europe.'[60] That document made specific reference to the joint policy agreed between Labour and the West German Social Democratic Party in November 1986.

The two parties reached a common view on a number of issues, including the creation of a European pillar in the NATO alliance which should 'not be the embryo of a new military bloc.' Instead it should contribute 'towards defence, détente and disarmament.'[61] The European pillar should also become 'an instrument for developing and expressing a cohesive European policy.' The policy statement reiterated the demand that Europeans take greater responsibility for their own security and that they should be ready to 'participate in negotiations about conventional and nuclear weapons.'

In that regard, it was evident that, by itself, Britain had a very restricted capacity to shape East–West relations. However, if the Europeans formed a pillar within NATO, they would thereby enhance immensely their prospects for modifying relations between the alliances. Therefore if Britain wanted a major change in relations within NATO and between the blocs (i.e. NATO and Warsaw Pact), a dogmatic isolationism or unilateralism could offer little of substance.

For Labour, the achievement of a broad agreement with its sister socialist party in the key European NATO country (West Germany) was an immense shift in its attitudes and approach. In 1981, Labour was immersed in its own internal conflicts, and at the same time intensely hostile towards the US Reagan administration. It was determined to leave the EC and was profoundly at odds with NATO's leadership and strategy.

Five years later, in a climate of emerging international *détente*, much of the intensity of Labour's hostility to the United States had dissipated, although disagreements on policy persisted (e.g. on Central America). But now Labour was favourably disposed towards European institutions. The Party was engaged in a sustained effort to establish its support for a European identity, which was 'at the heart' of Labour's foreign and security policy. This European pillar, or identity, was central to Labour's ideas on alternative defence arrangements (e.g. on issues like threat assessment, weapons procurement, intelligence). To a large degree, it was considered a replacement for Britain's long-established close security relations with the United States.

By 1986, Labour's leadership was keen to highlight its policy agreement with the German SPD, which was the first such agreement on military security issues. Due to limited resources, Labour did not enjoy an extensive range of policy consultations with other non-British parties. The pact with perhaps the leading European socialist party had a number of potential benefits for the Party. It could confer legitimacy upon Labour's policy in the face of the fierce criticism of the Party's unilateralist non-nuclear approach by Conservative and alliance opponents.[62] Likewise, the Party leadership might use the agreement as a shield against Labour critics of the commitment to maintain the British Army on the Rhine.

The foregoing discussion of the convergence between Labour and the SPD is not meant to imply that the two Parties were at one on all major aspects of defence. First, the West German socialists were more concerned than Labour about retaining a US military presence in and a nuclear guarantee to Western Europe.

Second, the SPD attached less importance to unilateral action than Labour. Unilateralism had little appeal in Germany due to the disaster attending such a German foreign policy in the 1930s and 1940s. Moreover, German political leaders needed no reminder that war in Europe would devastate people in two German states. In addition, the SPD did not have to concern itself about a German nuclear force, while the Labour Party had no choice but to have a policy on Britain's nuclear capability.

Labour's policy on removing cruise missiles was therefore much more definite and precise than the posture of the SPD. The approach of the latter party was to make the removal of INF dependent on consultation with NATO. However, Labour modified its own position on cruise in the months preceding the 1987 General Election. Mr Kinnock's promise to withdraw British nuclear weapons from West Germany in December 1986 was not welcomed by the SPD, and later Labour backed away from any clear pledge to act unilaterally on the issue.[63]

Third, the SPD was, understandably, very interested in establishing a chemical weapon free zone in Europe and a nuclear weapon free corridor along the inner German border. To that end, it agreed plans for a chemical weapon free zone with the governing party in East Germany, the Socialist Unity Party (i.e. Communist Party). The SPD was also keen to avoid structures which it believed would entrench the division of Germany. Thus anti-tank barriers in the border areas of Germany were advocated by Labour,[64] but were rejected by the SPD.

Fourth, with regard to the potential military threat facing NATO, the SPD focused mainly upon the Central Front in Europe. By contrast, Labour tended towards a wider perspective which included the possibility of military conflict in the Atlantic and the Northern Waters, as well as on the Central Front.

Fifth, while Labour stridently repudiated any reliance on nuclear weapons, the SPD supported Franco-German military cooperation. That implied acquiescence in France's strong commitment to nuclear arms. Thus it conveyed an unclear message regarding the German socialists' attitude to nuclear weapons. Moreover, in all probability an SPD-led government would need to form a coalition with the Free Democrats. It seemed unlikely that such an administration would countenance major and rapid changes in the Federal Republic's foreign and defence policy in an anti-nuclear direction.

Turning to other perspectives on Labour's defence policy in the mid-1980s, the response of the European governments in NATO was not positive. A preliminary point should be noted in any consideration of this issue. Because European governments did not expect Labour to gain office in the 1983 General Election, they had little reason to concern themselves with the implications of the Party's policy.

Even some three years later, in 1986, when Labour appeared to have some prospect of acceding to office, the issue of the potential consequences of the Party's policy was unlikely to appear on the agenda of European administrations. Then much more urgent defence issues concerned European decision-makers, like the unity and the strategy of the NATO alliance following the Reykjavik summit of President Reagan and General Secretary Gorbachev. However, in December 1986, NATO's defence ministers did issue a communiqué rejecting unilateral disarmament in a gesture 'widely taken to be a deliberate rebuff of the non-nuclear policy of the Labour leader, Mr. Kinnock.'[65]

With regard to the general attitude of the European NATO countries to Labour's defence policy, few governments, except perhaps the Greek administration, sympathised with the Party's insistence on acting by itself. Even governments who refused to allow nuclear weapons on their own territory in peacetime, such as Norway and Denmark, were anxious to avoid measures which could severely disrupt the NATO alliance. The unilateral actions of a British Labour government might result in such a disruption.

On the substantive issue of Labour's non-nuclear policy, two broad tendencies could be identified among NATO governments. One group including West Germany, France and Italy saw no convincing reason to move away from NATO's mix of nuclear and conventional capabilities. For the Christian Democrat-led government of the Federal Republic, Labour's policies of denuclearising the British Army on the Rhine and RAF Germany were profoundly disturbing, unless their implementation was delayed to await NATO's agreement. French governments, whether composed of socialists or centre-right parties, attached great value to France's possession of nuclear arms. They appeared to have little understanding of the non-nuclear case made by the British Labour Party.[66] Thus while Labour believed nuclear confrontation between the blocs was the greatest threat to international peace and stability, French political leaders located the main danger in potential Soviet coercion.

On the other side, that of the nuclear sceptics, governments like those of Greece, Denmark and Norway, were not opposed to the general thrust of Labour's non-nuclear security policy. Given their own unease about the dominant role of nuclear weapons in NATO strategy, those countries could be expected to welcome broadly the advent of a Labour administration in the United Kingdom. Between the strongly pro-nuclear positions of France and Germany on the side of the United States, and the non-nuclear stance of some Scandinavians and Greece, were states like Spain and Holland. As the

Netherlands gave up two nuclear tasks in 1985, it might not oppose Britain going further along that route, and the Spanish government could be expected to adopt a similar position.

Labour's defence policy and the Soviet Union

As Labour was not in government throughout the period 1982–7, its pronouncements on defence policy as it related to the Soviet Union were composed of two elements. The Party's policy statements were devoted mainly to the perceived inadequacies and mistaken assumptions of NATO strategy, on the one side, and to outlining what Labour proposed, on the other. However, in their interviews, statements and comments, leading Labour politicians vehemently criticised both the substance and style of the defence policies pursued by the United Kingdom and the United States. The Party condemned both the prominent role of nuclear arms in Britain's defence and the UK government's behaviour within the NATO alliance. Labour attacked as well the United Kingdom's perceived negative stance on East–West relations and in the wider international community.

According to Labour, the very deep attachment of the Thatcher administration to Britain possessing a nuclear capability had many dimensions. One aspect was expressed in the decision to replace the Polaris nuclear force with the Trident D5 system which multiplied the strategic targeting capacity of the UK as much as eight times. Another was manifested by the UK government's success in persuading the United States to exclude Britain's strategic nuclear force from both the superpower negotiations on strategic nuclear arms and the discussions on reducing intermediate-range nuclear arms.[67] In Labour's view, such behaviour on the part of the United Kingdom, far from encouraging the Soviet Union to follow a constructive role in talks with the United States, added a further complication to those negotiations. Thus if the two superpowers could agree on equal ceilings or equal reductions for a category of nuclear weapon or delivery system, the United States would be perceived to retain a major advantage. That advantage derived from the fact that two of its allies, the United Kingdom and France, would still possess sizeable nuclear capabilities.

A third dimension of the UK government's devotion to its nuclear status was demonstrated in its apparent inconsistent attitude to nuclear arms reduction. For many years British governments had supported the Nuclear Non-Proliferation Treaty (NPT). But according to Labour, the Thatcher administration offered little evidence that it took seriously the promise (of article VI of the NPT) to negotiate the reduction of its nuclear capability. Similarly Britain had a prominent part in negotiating the Partial Test Ban Treaty (1963), but in the 1980s it showed little enthusiasm for reaching a Comprehensive Test Ban Treaty. In Labour's view, the UK government's evident determination to give the highest priority to remaining a nuclear power explained its ambiguous attitude to nuclear arms control. Moreover, it did nothing to sustain or strengthen the norms against the vertical and horizontal proliferation of nuclear weapons.

Within NATO, the UK government was viewed by Labour as an enthusiastic instigator or advocate of measures to modernise and enhance the alliance's nuclear armoury. Labour's leadership suggested that the British government was not genuine when it supported the NATO proposal for the removal of the NATO INF systems in return for the elimination of Soviet SS20 missiles. In fact, the UK assumed that the Soviet Union was very unlikely to entertain such an offer. In the early 1980s, the US Reagan administration rejected proposals for a freeze in both superpowers' strategic nuclear capability as a prelude to major cuts in their arsenals. Unlike Labour which supported a freeze, the Thatcher government endorsed that rejection. Labour also condemned the refusal of the UK government publicly to dissociate itself from the US administration's efforts to reinterpret the ABM Treaty. Such a reinterpretation would permit the deployment of space weapons and it might weaken or destroy the Treaty.

In sum, the UK Conservative administration was regarded by Labour as a most intransigent advocate of reliance upon nuclear weapons. Likewise, it was seen as a fierce opponent of efforts to establish trust and cooperative relations between East and West. It seemed to do everything it could to legitimise and enhance the role of nuclear weapons, claiming that such arms kept the peace in Europe since 1945. Therefore Labour believed that the United Kingdom was in effect giving maximum sustenance to those in the Soviet Union who stressed the value of military strength and nuclear arms. Such 'hawkish' elements placed little confidence in efforts to shift East–West relations to a cooperative basis.

By contrast, Labour's own defence proposals were designed in part to attract and strengthen Soviet proponents of *détente* and arms limitation agreements. The core concepts of Labour's approach to security, that is, common security and defensive deterrence, were examined in Chapter 3. Here the focus is on the Party's recommendations for limiting and reducing arms as they related to the Soviet Union.

Starting with issues which were the prerogative of the UK government, Labour's dominant concern had to do with nuclear arms. In the years 1982–7, the Party was pledged to remove nuclear weapons from Britain's arsenal at the earliest opportunity. During the 1983 General Election campaign, Labour was unclear as to whether Polaris would be decommissioned unilaterally or eliminated in return for the Soviet Union giving up some of its nuclear arms. Following the 1983 election defeat, Labour's new leader Neil Kinnock, accompanied by Denis Healey, discussed the issue with President Chernenko and his advisers in Moscow (in November 1984). According to Mr Healey:

> Labour's commitment to de-commission the Polaris force was matched by Chernenko's commitment to match the dismantling of every British missile by the dismantling of a Soviet missile. So what was once a unilateral commitment has now become a bilateral one. This increases the security of both sides and creates a precedent well worth pursuing.[68]

At that time, the Soviet Union seemed willing to contemplate the elimination of INF (SS20) missiles in return for the dismantling of UK Polaris missiles.

But following the start, in 1985–6, of US–Soviet negotiations on INF weapons, Labour leaders hoped for the removal of Soviet strategic missiles in return for giving up Polaris.[69]

It is questionable whether the claim made by Mr Healey regarding the meeting with Mr Chernenko was completely justified. That is to accept the point made by Mr Kinnock. The Labour leader noted: 'What you can't do in opposition, and what I refuse to do is to undertake any form of negotiation or to make policy contingent upon what may or may not happen because you haven't got the full hand of cards.'[70]

Prime Minister Thatcher often asserted that talk of unilateral disarmament by the United Kingdom was music to Soviet ears.[71] Nevertheless, a bilateral agreement would have considerable attractions for both a Labour-ruled Britain and the Soviet Union. On the Soviet side, a refusal to reciprocate the dismantling of Britain's nuclear weapons would undermine seriously the anti-nuclear movement in the United Kingdom and in other West European countries. It might be assumed that the Soviet Union would not welcome such a development. Moreover, Moscow would have no assurance that a successor British government would not restore the country's nuclear capability unless the decision was enshrined in an international agreement.

From the perspective of the British Labour Party, a bilateral reduction of nuclear arms could, as Denis Healey observed, be presented as enhancing the security of both Britain and the Soviet Union. Thus it would be much more likely to appeal to the British electorate than a unilateral measure of disarmament. Of course, Labour rivals would characterise a deal which stripped the UK of all strategic nuclear weapons and left the Soviet Union possessing thousands as in effect unilateral disarmament by Britain. At the same time, a bilateral agreement would probably mitigate the sharp divisions between unilateralists and multilateralists in the Labour Party.

With respect to Britain's conventional military capabilities, Labour was content to include them in the Mutual and Balanced Force Reduction Talks. It pledged to 'work to break the deadlock' in those discussions so as to achieve significant reductions on both sides and 'greater mutual confidence at a much lower level of armament'.[72] As the Party identified lack of mutual trust and political will as the principal obstacles to successful superpower arms reduction negotiations, it placed a high priority on the achievement of confidence-building agreements. These included facilities to improve East–West communication and new mechanisms for joint crisis management.[73] Labour expressed strong support for the efforts of the Conference on Confidence and Security Building Measures and Disarmament in Europe (CDE) which started in early 1984.

In the negotiations and measures mentioned, Labour believed that the United Kingdom should use its collective role in NATO to reorientate the alliance towards a defensive conventional posture. That non-provocative posture would be complemented by appropriate political and economic policies. If that course were followed, Britain could 'well have a profound influence in diminishing tension in Europe and improving relations between the blocs.'[74]

What undoubtedly did exert a profound influence on diminishing tension between the blocs was Mikhail Gorbachev's appointment to the leadership of the Soviet Union in March 1985. In Labour's view, that change did much to dissipate the entrenched pessimism about achieving major reductions in East–West arsenals. It also generated much optimism regarding the prospects for improved relations between the blocs. Many in the Labour Party thought that the Soviet proposal (of early 1986) for the elimination of all offensive nuclear weapons by the year 2000 offered a glimpse of 'the promised land', and they were encouraged by the Reykjavik meeting of President Reagan and General Secretary Gorbachev. At that meeting, in October 1986, the two leaders agreed, as part of a wider package, to eliminate INF weapons from Europe. If implemented, that proposal could affect NATO's strategy quite significantly, and in a manner that Labour favoured.

In 1985–6, Labour was strongly critical of the refusal by the UK and US governments to respond positively to the unilateral Soviet moratorium on nuclear tests. Similarly, during the early years of Gorbachev's leadership, the Party was deeply dissatisfied with the attitude of the UK government to the many Soviet proposals for the control and reduction of nuclear arms. In the words of one prominent Labour spokesperson, the 'Prime Minister's unholy passion for nuclear weapons' should not be 'allowed to overrule our clear national interests in playing a leading role in grasping the opportunity of ending the arms race and basing international security on some kind of world society.'[75] As for Labour's own response, Mr Kinnock welcomed the Gorbachev offer of an 'equivalent missile-for-missile reductions' for the dismantling of Polaris by Britain. But he indicated a preference for associating British–Soviet discussions with a broader disarmament conference.[76]

Notes and references

1 See Stanley R. Sloan, *NATO's Future: Towards a New Transatlantic Bargain* (Washington, DC, National Defense University Press, 1985), Chapter 5.
2 *Defence and Security for Britain* (London, Labour Party, 1984), p. 17.
3 Stanley R. Sloan, *NATO's Future*, op. cit., p. 82.
4 ibid.
5 In my interviews with US Congressional staff and specialists in December 1986, this point was strongly expressed by many.
6 The London *Economist* was mentioned by US interviewees (1986) as an important source on UK politics.
7 James B. Steinberg, 'Rethinking the debate on burden-sharing', *Survival* (Jan/Feb 1987), p. 60.
8 Professor Lawrence Freedman, 'Could NATO live with a Labour government?' *Independent*, 27 May 1987.
9 In his main address to Labour's Annual Conference in 1986, Mr Kinnock rejected vehemently any British reliance on nuclear weapons. He commented: 'I would, if necessary, fight or die, give my life for my country. But I could never let my country die for me.' *The Times*, 1 October 1986. In an interview on BBC Television on 18 September 1986, Neil Kinnock commented 'that there were "no circumstances" in which he would want nuclear weapons used on Britain's behalf.' In the same interview he noted that if the Soviet Union were to use nuclear

weapons first against NATO countries, 'they would have initiated a holocaust in which discussion was somewhat redundant.' See the *Independent*, 14 November 1986.

10 Denis Healey, 'A Labour Britain, NATO and the bomb', *Foreign Affairs*, vol. 65, no. 4 (1987), p. 727.

11 *Guardian*, 11 December 1986, and ITV, *TV Eye*, 2 October 1986.

12 See *Sunday Times*, 28 September 1986, and *Guardian*, 24 September 1986.

13 On 28 September 1986, Neil Kinnock suggested on BBC TV that Secretary Weinberger did not speak for the Reagan administration. See also *Sunday Times*, 28 September 1986. The rebuttal by the US Ambassador to Britain of Mr Kinnock's suggestion was reported in *The Times*, 1 October 1986.

14 *The Times*, 25 September 1986. Mr Perle's comments were even more vehement in a speech delivered in London on 5 February 1986. See *The Times*, 7 February 1986.

15 *The Times*, 6 December 1986.

16 *Guardian*, 5 December 1986.

17 Neil Kinnock, 'Components of security: defence, democracy and development', speech at the Kennedy School of Government, Boston, Mass., 2 December 1986.

18 ibid., p. 27.

19 *Guardian*, 5 December 1986.

20 One account of the British media treatment of Kinnock's visit is given by Alistair Campbell, 'You guys are the pits', *New Statesman*, 3 April 1987.

21 *The Times*, 28 March 1987, and *Guardian*, 18 March 1987.

22 David Butler and Dennis Kavanagh, *The British General Election of 1987*, op. cit., p. 105.

23 Neil Kinnock, 'Components of security', op. cit., p. 30.

24 Alexander M. Haig, Jr., *Caveat: Realism, Reagan and Foreign Policy* (London, Weidenfeld & Nicolson, 1984), p. 298. Mr Haig, who was US Secretary of State in 1982, went on to say that the United States would have behaved as it did no matter what party governed the United Kingdom.

25 In interviews in Washington in late 1986, this viewpoint was advanced by a number of assistants close to influential Senators and Congressmen.

26 *Guardian*, 2 February 1987.

27 Paul Anderson and Jamie Dettmer, interview with Denzil Davies, 'Labour defence policy: will it be all right on the night?' *END, Journal of European Nuclear Disarmament*, no.16/17, (Summer 1985), pp. 13–15.

28 *Guardian*, 11 December 1986.

29 This quotation comes from Mr Healey's Fabian Tract no. 501, *Labour and a World Society* (London, Fabian Society, January 1985), p. 7.

30 Denis Healey, 'A Labour Britain, NATO and the bomb', op. cit., p. 728.

31 During Labour's Annual Conference in 1986, Denis Healey responded in a BBC TV Panorama programme as follows: Question: 'So we could end up keeping America's weapons here if that is what the alliance wanted?' Answer: 'I would doubt it, but it's not inconceivable.' See *Guardian*, 30 September 1986.

32 Denis Healey, 'A Labour Britain, NATO and the bomb', op. cit., p. 726.

33 In December 1986, Mr Kinnock commented regarding UK nuclear arms in Germany: 'We are getting rid of those, obviously, in the course of discussions which will be conducted with the remainder of our allies in NATO.' See *Guardian*, 12 December 1986.

34 Mr Kinnock's interview in *Tribune*, 20 September 1985.

35 See *Britain Will Win, Labour's Manifesto*, June 1987 (London, Labour Party, 1987), p. 16.

36 Denis Healey, 'A Labour Britain, NATO and the bomb', op. cit., p. 728.
37 *Defence and Security for Britain*, op. cit., pp. 14, 22.
38 See, for example, Mary Kaldor, 'END can be a beginning', *The Bulletin of the Atomic Scientists*, vol. 37, no. 10 (December, 1981), pp. 42–8, and 'Bloc heads: getting Europe in on the act', *New Socialist*, no. 43, (November 1986), pp. 12–15.
39 Denis McShane, *French Lessons for Labour*, Fabian Society no. 512 (London, Fabian Society, 1986), p. 5. Writing in November 1986, Neil Kinnock indicated he was well aware of the lessons from France: 'It is vital that the European attack on unemployment is co-ordinated. If there is no co-ordination, expanding countries will suck in imports while failing to increase their exports sufficiently to pay for them. Expansionary policies will then be discredited, technological advance will falter and the whole European economy will be even more open to commercial colonisation by the producers from America and the Pacific.' See Neil Kinnock, 'Is there a European route to economic recovery?' *New Statesman*, 7 November 1986, p. 13.
40 *The New Hope for Britain: Labour's 1983 Manifesto* (London, Labour Party, 1983).
41 Quote from interview with Neil Kinnock in *Tribune*, 20 September 1985.
42 From Barbara Castle's (Labour Member of the European Parliament) article in *Tribune*, 4 July 1986.
43 ibid.
44 *The New Hope for Britain*, op. cit., p. 37.
45 ibid., p. 35.
46 *Defence and Security for Britain*, op. cit., p. 29.
47 ibid., p. 35.
48 Denis Healey, *Labour and a World Society*, Fabian Tract no. 501 (London, Fabian Society, 1985), p. 8.
49 Nikolaj Peterson, 'The Scandilux experiment: towards a transnational Social Democratic perspective?' *Cooperation and Conflict*, vol. XX (1985), pp. 1–22, 11.
50 ibid., p. 9.
51 ibid., p. 7.
52 Denis Healey, *Labour and a World Society*, op. cit., p. 7.
53 Interview of Denzil Davies in *END: Journal of European Nuclear Disarmament*, no. 16/17 (Summer, 1985), pp. 13–15.
54 *Defence and Security for Britain*, op. cit., p. 15.
55 ibid.
56 *Defence Conversion and Costs, Labour National Executive Statement to 85th Annual Conference 1986* (London, Labour Policy, 1986), p. 38.
57 ibid., p. 37.
58 ibid., p. 39.
59 *Modern Britain in a Modern World: The Power to Defend Our Country* (London, Labour Party, 1986), p. 4.
60 ibid., p. 7.
61 *Joint Communiqué of Meeting of the Joint Commission of the Labour Party and the SPD on Questions of Security and Foreign Policies* (Bonn, 14 November 1986), p. 2.
62 The potential role of the Labour–SPD agreement in legitimising the policy was noted in an interview with a well-informed Labour source in 1986.
63 See *Guardian*, 12 December 1986.
64 *Defence and Security for Britain*, op. cit., p. 29.
65 *Guardian*, 6 December 1986.
66 On 4 September 1986, President Mitterand, Prime Minister Chirac and other French ministers and politicians held discussions with David Owen and David

Steel, the leaders of the SDP–Liberal Alliance, on Anglo-French defence co-operation. No discussions of that kind occurred between the British Labour Party and French Ministers. See David Owen, 'European nuclear options', *Guardian*, 6 June 1986.

67 Stuart Croft, 'Britain and the nuclear arms control process in the 1990's', *Arms Control*, vol. 9, no. 3 (December 1988), pp. 265–76.

68 Denis Healey, *Labour and a World Society*, op. cit., p. 7.

69 See Denis Healey interview in *Tribune*, 26 March 1986, in *Marxism Today*, April 1986, and the article in the *Guardian*, 14 April 1986.

70 Interview with Neil Kinnock, 'Let's have the enemy in front of us', *New Statesman*, 13 February 1987, pp. 16–18, 18.

71 See *Hansard, House of Commons*, 3 November 1982, cols 24–6.

72 *Defence and Security for Britain*, op. cit., p. 41.

73 ibid.

74 ibid., p. 22.

75 Denis Healey, *Hansard, House of Commons*, 26 June 1987, col. 174.

76 See *Guardian*, 30 May 1986, and Mr Healey's interview in *Tribune*, 26 March 1986.

5 The review of Labour's defence policy, 1987–89

In his address to the Labour Party Conference some months after the General Election of June 1987, Neil Kinnock commented: 'The question of whether the policies were right or wrong in 1987 is of course a matter of some interest. But the question of whether the policies will be right or wrong for 1991 will be the matter of the most profound importance.'[1] Clearly, the 1987 General Election result, when Labour was defeated heavily for the third successive occasion, was a very severe setback for the Party. For the second time in the 1980s, the Party received less than one-third of the votes cast and the Conservative government enjoyed an impregnable overall Parliamentary majority of more than a hundred seats.

Labour gained Parliamentary seats in regions where it was already strong, such as Scotland and Wales. But it made no significant advance in the vital marginal seats in the Midlands, the North West and in Greater London. On the contrary, the Party lost some seats in London and the South East of England. In 1987 Labour was unable to attract the support of uncommitted and increasingly prosperous voters outside the big cities and the economically deprived regions of the United Kingdom. Voters perceived Labour as the Party of the deprived, of ethnic minorities, and of outdated notions of collective action. It was not viewed as an efficient organisation capable of providing strong leadership and economic competence in a changing society. This stark failure occurred despite the fact that Labour had recovered from its civil war of the early 1980s and had a leadership which conducted an effective election campaign.

As a consequence of the 1987 General Election, the centre-left Tribune section of the Party secured the leading position in the Parliamentary Labour Party for the first time. Thus it gained the leadership of the Shadow Cabinet, which is elected by the Parliamentary Party. Now all the key organs of the Party, that is Annual Conference, the National Executive Committee and the Shadow Cabinet, were controlled by the centre-left of the Labour Party in alliance with the Party's right wing. Only left-wing MPs belonging to the Campaign Group opposed the Kinnock leadership on issues of policy and presentation.

From 1987, centre-left politicians like Bryan Gould, Gordon Brown and Robin Cook shared leading parts in promoting Labour policies with right-wing figures like John Smith, Roy Hattersley, Gerald Kaufman and John Cunningham. Prominent right-wing figures Denis Healey and Peter Shore no longer held official leadership roles in the Party (the former by retiring from the Shadow Cabinet and the latter by losing in the Shadow Cabinet election).

In the autumn of 1987 the shift in the make-up of Labour's Shadow Cabinet, from centre-right to centre-left (which in turn meant a change from a multilateralist to a pragmatic unilateralist majority in that body) generated remarkably little public contention in the Party. Such a lack of reaction would have been unimaginable in the Labour Party of the early 1980s when contests for Party office were bitter and divisive processes. By 1987, most of the earlier sharp cleavages between different tendencies in the Party had virtually dissolved. That was due largely to the general realisation in the Party that any further acrimonious public Labour divisions would be fatal for its future prospects. It was accepted within the Party that henceforth Labour would have to espouse policies more attuned to the preferences of the British electorate, rather than offering policies close to the wishes of the active members of the Party. The minority right wing of the Party accepted its junior position, not least because it retained an influential position. At the same time, the ascendant and pragmatic centre-left Tribune group was anxious to attain maximum unity in the Labour Party.

Turning to Labour's defence debate following the heavy election defeat of June 1987, Party opposition to a nuclear-dependent policy reached its nadir in the weeks immediately after that event. This was illustrated by a vote at the biennial conference of the Transport and General Workers' Union (TGWU) in July 1987. There, a demand for a rethink of Labour's defence policy and for a referendum on defence by the next Labour government was defeated by 361 votes to 327. The relatively high level of support in Britain's largest union for a shift in its traditional policy was a manifestation of widespread unease about unilateralism. Leaders of that union from Frank Cousins onwards had strongly supported the unilateral renunciation of nuclear weapons by the United Kingdom. General Secretary Ron Todd maintained that 27 year tradition at the 1987 conference of the Transport and General Workers' Union. (In mid-1989, the union supported a unilateral non-nuclear policy, as it had in 1987 and again by a fairly small margin, thereby indicating unilateralism had not fully recovered its previously strong support within the TGWU.)

In the post-election assessment by analysts sympathetic to the Labour Party, there was unanimity concerning the negative electoral consequences of unilateral nuclear disarmament. Commentators such as John Lloyd (*Financial Times* and *New Statesman*), Peter Kellner (*Independent*, BBC and *New Statesman*), Ian Aitken (*Guardian*) and Hugh McPherson (*Tribune*) argued that Labour's defence policy diminished the Party's electoral support and would continue to do so until it was changed.[2] Similarly, at post-election conferences of the Fabian Society and the Labour Co-ordinating Committee, a centre-left group of Labour activists, a sizeable number of participants (including some Labour candidates in the recent General Election) demanded change. They suggested that it was essential to find some way of defusing the issue of unilateralism before the Party faced the electorate in 1991–2.[3] Except for Peter Shore (at the Fabian conference), very few participants demanded an unqualified return to a policy of UK dependence on nuclear arms. Some declared that a more gradual incremental approach to implementing the policy of unilateral nuclear disarmament would help the Party to regain the confidence of the electorate. Others asserted that this could be achieved by holding a national referendum on some key issue or issues (e.g. Trident), which they expected would result in a vote against change.

At Labour's Annual Conference in 1987, a motion to hold a referendum on the unilateral removal of Britain's nuclear force secured the support of a few major unions (e.g. the engineers and the electricians), but it was defeated decisively.[4] Thus the high tide of internal opposition to Labour's unilateral nuclear disarmament policy receded within months of the general election defeat. Instead, the Conference re-affirmed that policy by a very large majority.

The establishment of the policy review structure

In the weeks following the election defeat of 11 June 1987, prominent members of the Party offered various suggestions on how Labour should respond to that devastating outcome. Evidently the Party needed to avoid the extremely damaging divisions which followed the 1979 election defeat. But it faced a formidable task (even if united and disciplined) in sustaining its morale and effectiveness in the House of Commons, which had an over-whelming Conservative majority.

At the instigation of Tom Sawyer, Chair of the National Executive's Home Policy Committee, and with the keen support of Neil Kinnock, the 1987 Annual Conference of the Party initiated a process for the review of Labour policy. According to Mr Sawyer, the Party needed to ask four questions:

> First, how do we make our socialist values relevant to the majority of voters? Secondly, despite a superb national campaign, why do we still fail to get our message across so badly in June? Thirdly, how were our policies perceived by the people whose support we need to gain and what do we need to do in order to win them over next time? Fourthly, we have to look at the social and economic changes we can expect over the next four years.[5]

Clearly the dominant element in the Party was determined to get rid of Labour's image, which could be summed up as a paternalistic, bureaucratic and old-fashioned organisation committed to high taxation, controlled by the trade unions, and associated with providing remote and insensitive public services. Such a project would, in Neil Kinnock's words,

> daunt those who think that socialism has a vested interest in frozen attitudes. Those who want to go on ignoring realities and aspirations. Those who want socialism to form itself into a permanent movement for protests and condolences.[6]

Labour leaders believed it was essential to persuade the 'home owning, credit card carrying majority' who had not grown up in or experienced the solidarity of Labour's heartlands that the Party 'can act for them.'[7]

The most prominent Labour exponent of a contrary perspective was Tony Benn. He contended that Labour should not resort to opinion research and advertising experts in its efforts to attract voters, including those former Labour voters who had supported other parties in the elections since 1979. Rather, Labour should identify unequivocally with trade unions and others engaged in industrial and political struggle. It should endeavour as well to appeal to feminists, environmentalists and others who rejected existing modes of politics.

The mechanism employed to carry out the policy review was composed of seven joint groups, with members drawn from Labour's Shadow Cabinet and National Executive Committee. The inclusion of members from Labour's governing body, the National Executive Committee (which together with Annual Conference was the arbiter of Party policy) and its potential ministers was designed to produce a unified and coherent policy. That policy had to be acceptable to both the Party and the politicians who would have the responsibility for implementing it when in government. As Tom Sawyer and others were well aware, failures of communication and splits between a Labour government and sections of the Labour Party/movement could be disastrous for both. That was illustrated by the collapse of the Callaghan administration following the strikes and protests of low-paid, public-sector employees in 1979.[8]

The seven themes for examination by the policy groups were as follows: A Productive and Competitive Economy; People at Work, Economic Equality; Consumers and the Community; Democracy for the Individual and Community; The Physical and Social Environment; and Britain in the World. The latter group was to deal with international relations, common security, the European dimension, defence policy, and North–South issues of cooperation and development. These review groups were to start their work in November 1987 by considering the relevance of existing Party policy and identifying areas for further examination. They were to invite ordinary Party members and specialist professional and voluntary organisations to tell them about their concerns.

In the second phase, following the 1988 Annual Conference, the review groups were to write the new policy. This was supposed to draw upon opinion research, submissions by interested bodies and individuals, and other relevant evidence from the United Kingdom or overseas. The final policy statements, which were to include updates and refinements of the 1989 policy, would be submitted to the 1990 Annual Conference. Thus from October 1990, Labour planned to launch its new policies in good time for the General Election due in 1991 or early 1992.

The task facing the group reviewing Britain in the World, which included Labour's defence policy, was a formidable one. Ideally it would present the Party with a new policy attracting wide public support, which could be implemented in office and which did not alienate major sections of Labour's membership. Of course, the new policy had to be acceptable also to the leadership of the Party.

The membership of the Britain in the World review group, and particularly the choice of chairperson or chief convener, offered an indication of the likely outcome of its deliberations. The leader of the group (who wrote the new Party statement on defence) was Gerald Kaufman, the Party's chief spokesperson on foreign affairs (following the retirement of Denis Healey from the Front Bench in June 1987). Mr Kaufman had been associated with centre-right groups in the Party in the 1970s and 1980s, such as the Manifesto group of MPs and Solidarity. Accordingly, there was little reason to doubt his support for a multilateral approach to questions of arms control and disarmament. Other members of the group who were known to take that view included George Robertson (the Party's spokesperson on Europe), Gwyneth Dunwoody, and Tony Clarke (of the Union of Communication Workers), chairperson of the National Executive Committee's international committee. The unilateralist members of the group included Ron Todd, General Secretary of the Transport and General Workers' Union, Joan Lester, and Stuart Holland (who resigned from Parliament in mid-1989). Denzil Davies, Labour's chief spokesperson on defence, until his resignation in June 1988, was an important member of the review group. He did not have a record of outspoken adherence to a unilateralist or multilateralist perspective. Rather, he was concerned to make whatever defence policy the Party espoused as coherent and persuasive as possible. His successor Martin O'Neill could be termed a pragmatic unilateralist. Like his predecessor, he sought to present Labour policy in as logical and appealing a manner as possible.

Labour's comings and goings on defence, 1987–89

In compiling a defence policy for the Labour Party, the review group operated in a context of three major and partly conflicting pressures or influences. These were the policy sought by the Party leadership, the preferences of the majority of active members of the Party, and the course of relevant international processes and events. In an interview about one week after the 1987 election, Neil Kinnock commented that there was no need to alter the Party's defence policy. Soon it would look more practical and relevant to the voters. He observed:

> We are the only party which has accepted the speed of change in the international environment . . . We are the only party in Britain which can claim that our thinking is concurrent with the talks about reducing intermediate and strategic weapons.[9]

Yet that declaration of faith in the correctness of the Party's policy did not prevent Mr Kinnock from telling the Annual Conference (in late September 1987) that no area of policy would be excluded from the review process, including defence. He went on to welcome the improved relations between the superpowers. Mr Kinnock observed that he expected Labour would enter the next election with a defence policy 'capable of dealing with the changed conditions of the 1990's'.[10]

At a Conference fringe meeting in October 1987, Labour's foreign affairs spokesperson Gerald Kaufman praised the Kinnock leadership for linking the removal of cruise missiles from Britain with the international negotiations on INF weapons in the months leading up to the June 1987 elections.[11] That same week, Labour's defence spokesperson, Denzil Davies asserted:

There is no possibility that the Labour Party will go into the next election with a policy other than a non-nuclear defence policy. How we achieve that in the circumstances of four years' time . . . that could affect Trident.[12]

Almost two months later, at the time of the US–Soviet INF agreement, Gerald Kaufman expounded the view of the Labour leadership in a direct way. He noted:

We were proposing to make nuclear weapon reductions when no one else was doing so . . . [But now] The unilateralist nature of our [Labour's] non-nuclear defence policy has been overtaken by other countries doing what in the past we would do alone if necessary.[13]

The preferences of Labour's leaders regarding the outcome of the defence review seemed quite clear by the end of 1987, but they became confused by mid-1988. This confusion was a product of two apparently contradictory interviews given by Mr Kinnock in June 1988. In his BBC television interview of 5 June, Mr Kinnock referred to what he termed as the breakthrough in superpower arms reductions talks and he asserted:

There is no need now for a something-for-nothing unilateralism . . . [In the past, unilateralism] was very appropriate . . . because absolutely nothing was happening. Or rather, what was happening, was a perpetual build up and in those circumstances the effort to try to break the log-jam was very important. The logjam is broken.[14]

Mr Kinnock indicated that he expected the Soviet Union to match any reductions made in Britain's nuclear capability by a future Labour government. His comments in the TV interview carried particular weight. This was so because they were preceded by a private briefing given by the Labour leader to the political editor of the *Independent* newspaper. The resulting article in that newspaper suggested that Mr Kinnock now accepted that the Polaris/Trident force would be included in international negotiations.[15] It also indicated that his rejection of the presence of US nuclear weapons in Britain had become less clear-cut. Moreover, it signalled that Mr Kinnock was now more willing to go along with the notion of the US nuclear umbrella than previously.

Within ten days of Mr Kinnock's BBC television statement, Labour's defence spokesperson Denzil Davies resigned from his post. Apparently, Mr Davies felt that he had not been consulted about what he regarded as a change in the Party's policy. In addition, there were indications that he believed that the position articulated by Neil Kinnock lacked the coherence and consistency of a clear unilateralist or multilateralist stance.[16]

Some two weeks after his BBC TV appearance, Mr Kinnock seemed to retreat from the position he then expressed. In an interview with the *Independent* on 20 June 1988, he affirmed that 'Decommissioning is still our position' regarding Polaris and Trident. When asked how he would get 'something for something' from the Soviet Union if he intended to get on with decommissioning Polaris with such rapidity, he replied as follows: 'Because the Soviets want it at least as much [as we do] for very strong practical reasons.'[17] In Mr Kinnock's view these reasons included the intense pressure in the Soviet Union to transfer resources from the military to the civil sector. When challenged as to what he would do (as Prime Minister) if the Soviet Union did not disarm to an extent equivalent to the United Kingdom, he expressed the utmost confidence that that eventuality would not occur. He pointed to the scale and speed of the nuclear arms reduction process since 1986, and he noted that the Soviet Union had compelling reasons to reciprocate fully Britain's arms reductions.

According to the published account of the interview, Mr Kinnock was very reluctant to address the question as to how he would respond to a Soviet refusal to reciprocate a UK reduction of its nuclear arsenal. Finally he indicated that in such circumstances he would go ahead and decommission the Polaris force. Thus after a concerted effort by the Labour leadership to edge away from a mainly unilateralist approach to UK nuclear disarmament, Mr Kinnock thought it necessary to proffer an ambiguous retraction in June 1988.

The persistence and intensity of unilateralist sentiment in the Labour Party was demonstrated anew in June 1988 and at the Annual Conference in October 1988. In June, prominent unilateralist Labour Members of Parliament like David Blunkett (a leading member of the National Executive Committee) and Joan Ruddock (the former Chair of the Campaign for Nuclear Disarmament) expressed their concern about Mr Kinnock's attempts to move away from a unilateralist defence policy. According to Mr Blunkett, Neil Kinnock's 'something for something' comment produced confusion and anxiety throughout the Party. It risked causing 'an unnecessary and devastating split in the party.'[18] If such a split did occur, it could inflict immense damage upon the electoral appeal of the Party, given that memories of Labour divisions had not entirely dissipated.

At the Annual Conference in October 1988, the Labour leadership opposed a successful motion advocating unilateral nuclear disarmament. Concurrently it supported a motion proposing bilateral, multilateral and unilateral steps towards nuclear disarmament. The thrust of the latter motion, which was defeated, was to enlarge the options open to the Party in the policy review, and to avoid being constricted by a unilateral commitment and an inflexible timetable. Because of Labour unilateralists' suspicions of the Party leadership, they sought and succeeded in maintaining the Party's unilateralist stance in 1988. Their unease was generated in part by the behaviour of past Labour governments and by the signs that Mr Kinnock was increasingly uncomfortable with an unqualified unilateralist approach. Thus Ron Todd of the Transport and General Workers' Union warned: 'If we give an inch it will lead to a mile and another mile.'[19]

The Labour multilateralist case

In the months preceding the General Election of June 1987, the Labour leadership enunciated a major change in its defence policy concerning the removal of US cruise missiles from the United Kingdom. The shift in policy did not receive much attention during the election campaign, nor did it engender great controversy within the Party. This lack of contention was mainly due to the reluctance of Labour critics to damage the Party in the run-up to the General Election. The turn-round in policy concerned three interrelated issues: the method, domain and timing of achieving nuclear disarmament by Britain.

Britain Will Win, the Labour Manifesto for the 1987 General Election, stated the Party's position as follows:

> We have always recognised that a properly negotiated and monitored international agreement to remove nuclear weapons from European soil would provide the most effective guarantee against the horrors of nuclear war. It would be the most significant step towards an eventual worldwide renunciation of, and ban upon, nuclear weapons.[20]

The Party recognised that such an international agreement offered the best route to prevent the disaster of nuclear war. Therefore it promised to 'assist that process in every way possible'[21] by not demanding the earliest unilateral removal of cruise missiles from Britain. Thus it acknowledged that if a Labour government insisted upon the unilateral withdrawal of those weapons, it would not assist the INF international negotiations, and in fact it might disrupt them.

In this way, the Labour Party leadership asserted that negotiated and verified international pacts were more effective than unilateral measures. This was so because 'British independent action cannot rid the world of the nuclear threat',[22] and because, in the hyperbole of Labour's foreign affairs spokesperson Gerald Kaufman, 'a nuclear disarmament treaty signed on behalf of Britain by a Labour government can never be reversed.'[23] Moreover, it is assumed that the monitoring of agreements is likely to give states the confidence that what parties promised to do would in fact be implemented faithfully. Such assurance would not normally attach to an unverified unilateral decision, especially one dealing with the highly sensitive issue of nuclear weapons capability.

From the early part of 1987, if not before, Labour's leadership made clear that unilateral methods were applicable 'when nothing else is going on'.[24] According to Neil Kinnock, unilateralism is not an 'end in itself. To me it was always a tactic rather than a philosophy.'[25] Therefore when international negotiations to reduce nuclear arms show promise of achieving success, Britain's defence and disarmament policy 'will only be effective if it is of assistance to the much more significant international disarmament process.'[26]

From 1987, the Labour leadership made a concerted effort to persuade the Party that external developments, especially those between the superpowers, were of primary importance in promoting nuclear disarmament, and that Britain's decisions were of secondary significance. Thus at the 1987 Annual Conference that view was articulated by Labour's leader and deputy leader, along with the Party spokespersons on foreign affairs and on defence.

In mid-1989, defence spokesperson Martin O'Neill commented as follows on the Labour Party: 'It is time we recognised our relative insignificance on the world stage. We are the opposition party in a nation whose strategic importance is rapidly diminishing.'[27] Earlier, in 1988, Mr O'Neill observed that Britain was 'coming to terms with our diminished international status' and was moving towards 'a proper appreciation of our responsibilities in the Western European defence alliance.'[28] His sober perspective on Britain's influence suggested that Labour leaders no longer placed much faith in the capacity of the United Kingdom to break a logjam on disarmament. Now that the international logjam had given way to serious negotiations on reducing nuclear arms, Labour politicians could afford to be candid regarding Britain's international influence.

In the late 1980s, the objective of Labour's non-nuclear policy was identified as the reduction 'and the ultimate verified elimination of all nuclear weapons in the world by the year 2000.'[29] Therefore a Labour government could be expected to avoid measures which would retard the achievement of that aim and to play a full part in advancing it. Moreover, the Labour leadership's shift from a unilateral to a multilateral approach was associated with the aim of clearing the world of nuclear weapons. It was linked also with a change of attitude towards the implementation of the policy.

In late 1986, under intense pressure from US officials and politicians, and on the advice of Labour spokesperson Mr Healey, the Labour leadership adopted a more flexible attitude towards the method and timing of the removal of US nuclear weapons from Britain. That flexibility was extended when Mr Kinnock pledged not to expel US cruise missiles while awaiting the outcome of the INF negotiations.

From late 1987, Labour leaders like Mr Kinnock and Mr Kaufman promoted a policy which was much less urgent than previously about removing Britain's nuclear weapons. Now they had become more concerned about how such action would advance the overall objective of eliminating all nuclear weapons. Thus Gerald Kaufman observed that to 'speedily divest ourselves of nuclear weapons off our own bat . . . would mark the end of Britain's role in world nuclear disarmament.'[30] He advocated a 'more ambitious' approach of 'using the process of divesting Britain of nuclear weapons to participate in and hasten, world nuclear disarmament.'[31] Thus he 'specifically rejected a timetable for Britain getting rid of her nuclear weapons.' Mr Kaufman went on to accept that a Labour government would not be committed to eliminating all of its nuclear weapons while other states retained nuclear arms.[32]

Instead, as Neil Kinnock commented on nuclear arms, Britain 'can't afford them, we can never use them, why have them, is [sic] have them for the purposes of participation in the disarmament process securing verifiable agreements to clear the world of nuclear weapons.'[33] In this way Labour's leaders identified the contribution which the negotiated removal of Britain's nuclear arms could make to global nuclear disarmament as the primary objective of UK disarmament policy. This aim was now regarded as a more important and more worthwhile enterprise than the rather insular aim of rapidly and independently eliminating nuclear weapons from just one of the declared nuclear powers (i.e the United Kingdom).

The proposed shifts in Labour's nuclear disarmament policy in method, from unilateral to multilateral, in domain from one to all holders of nuclear arms, and in period from the earliest possible time to an uncertain date, had a number of attractions for the Party leadership. Chief among them was the

Party's need to offer the British electorate a defence policy which responded to their wishes and preferences. Commenting on the contributions of ordinary delegates at his own (previously unilateralist) union conference (in May 1989), Tom Sawyer, the architect of the policy review, made these observations: 'The overriding sentiment was that we need to change our policy in order to realign with where people are. If we are going to take people towards a non-nuclear defence policy, then unilateralism is a bridge too far.'[34] That is to say, the UK electorate might be persuaded to vote for a party advocating a non-nuclear defence policy pursued by multilateral means. It would be extremely unlikely to support the unilateral renunciation of Britain's nuclear arms.[35]

Neil Kinnock made a similar point in his address to the unilateralist Transport and General Workers' Union conference in June 1989. He noted:

> If our party was to go to the people of Britain after ten or 12 years of Thatcherism, and say we are going to disarm without negotiations, or that we are going to obey a deadline, regardless of all other considerations we would not be supported.[36]

In the period 1987–9, Labour leaders' speeches and interviews indicated their sense of relief about the change in international conditions. Now they could explain why a multilateralist approach to defence and disarmament was appropriate in conditions of fruitful international talks on nuclear arms. Much of that alleviation derived from the anxiety of the Party leadership to present an image of a responsible and effective team, well qualified to govern Britain. Labour leaders were acutely aware that the Party was perceived as not being serious about defence, that it was divided about the issue, and that unilateral nuclear disarmament would leave the country defenceless. The Labour leadership's proposed shift from early unilateral nuclear disarmament by Britain to a multilateral process embracing all nuclear weapon powers was immensely attractive. It matched the Party's electoral requirements quite well. This was so because the General Election campaigns of 1983 and 1987 had demonstrated in the clearest fashion that Labour's plans to give up Britain's nuclear weapons unilaterally inflicted heavy electoral damage upon the Party. Those plans also raised questions in the mind of the electorate about the fitness of the Party to govern.

For many electors, the proposal to give away an extremely intimidating weapon without getting any return seemed extreme, while negotiating 'something for something' appeared sensible and rational. Therefore if the proposed new policy enabled the Party to shift the defence debate on to the issues of multilateral nuclear disarmament, it would have removed one central obstacle in its efforts to secure election. A multilateral policy would be likely also to assist Labour's search for office because it might be seen as demonstrating the seriousness of the Party about defence by pursuing an approach which was in step 'with events and public opinion'.[37]

In addition to the probable electoral advantages, a multilateralist defence policy appeared as well to be more practical or feasible to implement than a policy of unilateral nuclear disarmament. A multilateral policy could be expected to enjoy substantially more support among the British electorate, the main political parties, the armed forces and senior civil servants than a unilateral approach. Therefore it seemed to have a much better prospect of success.

Much the same analysis applied to the international reception for a multilateral defence policy. Speaking in May 1989 (at the meeting of Labour's National Executive Committee which considered the report of the policy review group on the Party's new defence policy), Mr Kinnock offered this assessment:

> I have gone to the White House, the Kremlin and the Elysée and argued down the line for unilateral nuclear disarmament. I knew they would disagree with the policy, but above that they were totally uncomprehending that we should want to get rid of a nuclear weapon system without getting the elimination of nuclear weapons on other sides: without getting anything in return.[38]

He went on to say that he would not make that tactical argument for unilateral nuclear disarmament again: 'I will not do it. The majority of the party and the majority of the country do not expect me to do so.'[39] This stark assertion by Mr Kinnock indicated that he would refuse to lead the Party unless Labour adopted a multilateral policy on nuclear disarmament. It was not only a response to the incomprehension of those in government in other nuclear weapon countries; it had also 'been coloured by discussion with our European socialist partners.'[40]

Mr Kinnock may well have found the Elysée very short of sympathy and understanding for unilateral nuclear disarmament by Britain. He also probably received little support for unilateralism on his visit to Mr Chernenko in late 1984. But it would be odd if Mr Gorbachev had been equally conventional in approach. Given that the Soviet leader's new thinking embraced major unilateral initiatives for the reduction of Soviet military capability, it would be paradoxical if he excluded any role for unilateral measures by other states.[41] Of course, the Gorbachev leadership's aim of a nuclear-free world by the year 2000 could not be expected to be achieved without extensive negotiations and verification arrangements, if then.

With regard to the United States, Mr Kinnock learned in his contacts with its political leaders that it would do nothing to facilitate the implementation of Labour's policy of unilateral nuclear disarmament. On the contrary, from President Reagan down, US officials proclaimed that they regarded that policy as a serious threat to the proper functioning of the NATO alliance. They could be expected to use their best endeavours to thwart and frustrate unilateral nuclear disarmament by the United Kingdom.

Neither could Labour expect much support for its unilateral policy from other European socialist parties. Whether a UK Labour government was seeking to denuclearise Europe or to alter NATO strategy (in a non-nuclear direction), it would need the fullest support and cooperation from like-minded governments in countries like Germany. What had happened in Spain and in Greece in the 1980s demonstrated the limitations of a unilateral approach. In both instances, socialist governments came to reverse their earlier opposition to various aspects of NATO membership.

Thus a prudent British Labour administration would not treat the Europeans 'as if they did not exist or as if their opinions did not matter to us.'[42] On the contrary, those European socialist parties who shared Labour's antipathy to nuclear weapons (e.g. in Germany, Norway, Denmark, Belgium and the Netherlands) were uneasy about independent action by Britain which threatened to disrupt the NATO alliance. Therefore Labour could not look to them as a source of sustenance for unilateral nuclear disarmament. On the other hand, those same European parties, especially the German SPD which held consultations with Labour, would give greater support to a policy of multilateral nuclear disarmament. That course would be more compatible with their own approach.

The Labour unilateralist case

From June 1987 until the Labour policy review group reported to the Party Conference in October 1989, Labour unilateralists were suspicious and pessimistic about the direction the Party's defence policy would take. Their anxieties had to do with the expectation that a combination of domestic pressures and external constraints would lead the Party to acquiesce in Britain retaining nuclear weapons.

The concerns of Labour unilateralists were focused particularly on the process of multilateral negotiations regarding nuclear arms and the time-scale of such negotiations. Before the advent of Mr Gorbachev to the leadership of the Soviet Union (the time when Labour adopted its unilateral non-nuclear defence policy), few British Labour unilateralists expected US–Soviet talks on strategic nuclear weapons to result in the elimination of most or all of those countries' nuclear weapons. On the contrary, those talks were seen as instruments to regulate the superpowers' nuclear capabilities. Thus those negotiations did not prevent the United States and Soviet Union from updating and modernising their arsenals with the introduction of ever more sophisticated nuclear systems.

In the years from the start of the SALT talks in 1969 until the mid- to late 1980s, it was evident to British and other observers that the US–Soviet nuclear talks faced considerable problems. Prominent among those problems were the issues of verification and mutual lack of confidence, along with asymmetries in geography, nuclear weapons systems and strategic doctrine. Thus even the achievement of the limitation of Soviet and American strategic weapons proved an immensely difficult and drawn-out process.

Since the US–Soviet INF agreement of 1987, there was less scepticism in Britain about superpower negotiations on nuclear arms reductions. Yet few if any prominent UK unilateralists 'even at a best case analysis',[43] seriously expected the elimination of all nuclear weapons by the year 2000. The achievement of that aim would require not only the removal of all Soviet and United States nuclear arms. It would involve also the dismantling of British, Chinese and French nuclear systems, and the elimination of the nuclear weapon capabilities of undeclared nuclear powers. Clearly, the obstacles to reaching a nuclear-free world are so complex and formidable that no prudent analyst could proffer a persuasive account of when, if at all, that condition might be attained. For these and other reasons, Labour unilateralists have tended to identify British nuclear weapons (wherever they are located) as the primary domain for nuclear disarmament. In addition, they considered that Britain could exert a strong and effective influence to secure the elimination of nuclear arms based in the European NATO countries.

Labour unilateralists asserted that, unlike the proclaimed advocates of multilateral nuclear disarmament, they were the 'genuine' multilateralists. But most harboured strong misgivings about the process of international negotiations on nuclear weapons. Traditionally such negotiations have proceeded on the assumption that the nuclear capabilities of the participants are of immense value to their owners. As Labour's foreign affairs spokesperson Gerald Kaufman observed, for Britain to give up nuclear weapons speedily 'would mark the end of Britain's role in world nuclear disarmament.'[44]

A participant in such negotiations who signals they will surrender their nuclear arms whatever the outcome of multilateral talks risks destroying the incentive for other participants to make significant concessions. Likewise, a government of a nuclear weapon state which guarantees that it will never use its nuclear capability may lose much of its bargaining power. Again, the logic of international talks on reducing nuclear arms is for each participant to seek to maximise the concessions made by others, while retaining as many as possible of its own nuclear weapons.

Thus if a British Labour government participated in multilateral negotiations with a view to promoting global nuclear disarmament, it would in the meantime be unlikely explicitly to reject a posture of nuclear deterrence. For many Labour unilateralists, such a policy would be extremely disturbing. First, it could involve the United Kingdom in retaining weapons of mass destruction for a prolonged period. In their view, it would also violate the basic norms of the Party and might endanger the security of the British people.[45]

Given the uncertainties and multiple obstacles surrounding multilateral arms negotiations, the achievement of Labour's non-nuclear objective would depend predominantly upon the actions of other nuclear weapon states if a UK administration pursued an entirely multilateral approach. Thus a Labour government could have no assurance that its retention of nuclear weapons would not last indefinitely. Moreover, that government might find it quite difficult to resist pressures for modernising its nuclear capabilities. Such pressures would derive from that government's need to sustain its bargaining position in multilateral talks. It would probably find it essential also to retain the teams of engineers, scientists and technologists necessary to maintain its existing nuclear strength.

According to Labour unilateralists, the multilateral route to nuclear disarmament by Britain exhibits another profound defect. That relates to their view that, at source, support for Britain's nuclear status (whether in public opinion or among leading figures in politics and the armed forces) has more to do with notions of national identity than with concern for the United Kingdom's military security. As viewed by some unilateralists, 'Either you are in favour of Britain abandoning its status as an independent nuclear power in a world where others still retain nuclear weapons or you are not.'[46]

If Labour advocates a non-nuclear status for Britain it should, in the view of many unilateralists, clearly locate that objective in a cogent alternative foreign policy for the United Kingdom.[47] That alternative might emphasise common security, defensive defence, *détente* between rival ideologies, aid to developing countries, the promotion of human rights, and contributions to resolving global problems. Or it might stress close cooperation between a non-nuclear Britain and anti-nuclear political forces in Europe to build a non-nuclear European entity. A third option might focus on non-military ways of resolving international conflicts in Europe and elsewhere and ensure that Labour's policies on defence are consistent with its disarmament policies.

According to these Labour unilateralists, the vision of a nuclear-armed Britain, closely linked with the United States and playing a prominent role in a nuclear-orientated NATO, must be rejected. It should be countered with an attractive alternative vision of the United Kingdom. In their view, the advocacy of a non-nuclear status for Britain, to be achieved by multilateral methods and set in a context of a not very coherent foreign policy, did not add up to a credible alternative vision. Rather, it reflected a Party which, following two overwhelming election defeats of a unilateralist approach, had exhausted its determination to continue campaigning for the independent achievement of its non-nuclear objective. Thus Labour's leadership sought a middle course between the majority of British opinion, which remained attached to the belief that the United Kingdom was still a leading world power entitled to possess extremely sophisticated nuclear weapons on the one hand, and the demands of the anti-nuclear movement on the other.

That course was to eschew either an unambiguous reliance upon or a unilateral renunciation of nuclear weapons by the United Kingdom. Instead, Labour's leaders were hoping to make progress towards their non-nuclear aim by multilateral processes, thereby discarding the electoral albatross of unilateralism. The Party leadership was appealing for support on the following basis: elect us and we may, if international and domestic conditions permit, inch towards a non-nuclear Britain, some time in the future.

By contrast, many Labour unilateralists favoured what might be termed a campaign based on conviction. This would set the non-nuclear objective in the context of an alternative role for Britain, and it would seek to persuade public opinion to alter its perspective. Unless the Party engaged in such a daunting effort at persuasion, the obstacles to reaching a non-nuclear status for the United Kingdom, whether by unilateral or multilateral means, would be likely to persist. The core charge made by many Labour unilateralists against the leadership's move towards multilateralism was that it manifested a basic shortcoming. That is, it failed to work out how Labour's socialist values could best be applied in the international and domestic circumstances of the time. Instead, the leadership was seen as reacting to pressures and events without due regard for principle.

Labour unilateralists' recipe for the removal of nuclear weapons from Britain was not altered by the advent of Mr Gorbachev. As one exponent put it regarding unilateralism, 'Today it still offers the surest route'[48] to eliminating nuclear arms from Britain. For many unilateralists, Britain was the central domain of nuclear disarmament and the issue of nuclear disarmament deserved to be treated with the utmost urgency. Therefore despite the

formidable electoral and other impediments to achieving independent nuclear disarmament by Britain, the unilateral route still seemed the most
reliable and probably the only way of reaching that objective.

Despite the immense setbacks suffered at the General Elections of 1983
and 1987, some unilateralists remained convinced that Labour could have
managed its campaign much more effectively. TGWU Secretary Ron Todd
argued thus about the 1987 election: 'We should have had an aggressive
campaign on our non-nuclear defence policy which we never did. We reacted
to our opponents, we never went out and campaigned, and won our people
over to it.'[49]

Labour unilateralists recognised that from 1986 US–Soviet nuclear arms
negotiations had taken on a more positive character. But they observed that a
central ingredient of their own thinking had played a catalytic part in the
successes of those talks. Thus they rejected the view that unilateralism was
redundant because multilateralism works. That perspective 'fails to take
account of both the long history of failure in multilateral talks and of the
crucial role of Soviet unilateralism in bringing about the sole bilateral deal
[the INF] yet to remove nuclear weapons.'[50]

Beside the suspension of its nuclear testing, the core element in Soviet
'unilateralism' was Moscow's willingness to make asymmetrical or unreciprocated reductions in the 1987 INF agreement. It did likewise in the CFE
agreement on conventional forces in Europe (1990). Thus according to a
unilateralist analyst, 'Gorbachev learned from us . . . the principle that when
the Superpowers are . . . piling up weapons on both sides and creating
mutual threats',[51] it is entirely unnecessary to insist on numerical parity in
negotiated agreements. Therefore 'it is only because he has accepted it, that
arms reduction agreements are now possible.'[52] Unilateralists argued that if
the INF talks, had adhered to notions of reciprocity and balanced reductions,
they might well have failed to achieve a successful conclusion.

Labour unilateralists also suggested a way whereby the independent elimination of nuclear arms by Britain could promote nuclear disarmament
beyond the United Kingdom. They assumed that if a British government
unconditionally cancelled Trident and decommissioned Polaris, it would
evoke a substantial Soviet disarmament response. Consequently the two
countries could be expected to negotiate a verification agreement embracing
the affected nuclear weapons and facilities.[53] Without such verification,
other states might entertain doubts about the integrity of UK nuclear
disarmament.

Unilateralists were content to use the elimination of UK nuclear arms
politically (as against using it militarily by removing their threatened use) to
demand that other nuclear powers 'match our unilateral action.'[54] The
advantages deriving from the international verification of disarmament
measures, would, it was suggested, encourage other nuclear states to respond. Such reciprocal unilateralism by Britain, or unreciprocated if other
powers did not respond, would fulfil also the country's obligations under the
Nuclear Non-Proliferation Treaty (Article VI).

The revised Labour defence policy produced by the Britain in the World review group, 1989

Labour's principal defence statement of the 1980s, *Defence and Security for Britain* (1984) rested upon two quite separate pillars. These potentially incompatible assumptions were unconditional UK participation in NATO and a strong commitment to rid Britain of both UK and US nuclear weapons within a few years. In late 1986, as the proximity of a General Election increased, the Party leadership came under strong pressure to satisfy three diverse elements about its defence policy. The active members of the Party were predominantly committed to unilaterally removing nuclear arms, while the British electorate continued to perceive Labour as weak on defence. Simultaneously, US and other NATO members were quite disturbed by Labour's demand for the early expulsion of US nuclear weapons from the United Kingdom.

Labour's leaders did not respond to these conflicting demands by getting the Party conference to reverse the defence policy enshrined in *Defence and Security for Britain*, and in *Defence Conversion and Costs* (1986). Rather, it altered the presentation of defence policy (in its publication, *Modern Britain in a Modern World*, December 1986) to convey a new message. According to that message, Labour gave the highest priority to maintaining an effective non-nuclear defence for the United Kingdom within the NATO alliance.

The shifts in presentation and in policy did not succeed in neutralising defence as an electoral issue, and it cost Labour a highly significant quantity of votes and support in the General Election of June 1987. Labour's leadership interpreted that setback as a reason to eliminate, as far as possible, incompatibility between the Party's commitment to NATO and its dedication to a non-nuclear policy. This the review group Britain in the World did by inviting the Party (i.e. the National Executive Committee and the Party Conference) to modify the non-nuclear policy. Both the Labour leadership and review group argued that the changes to the non-nuclear policy were justified and required for two main reasons. First, the Party must take into account the consequences of the immense political changes in the Soviet Union and in Central/Eastern Europe. Second, Labour had to reassure Britain's voters about its defence policy.

The Britain in the World review group did not examine defence during the first year of its existence. Apparently, it decided to await the outcome of rapidly evolving international negotiations and events.[55] But during that time, members of the group collected information and advice at home and on visits overseas. Such information included findings from private polling in the United Kingdom on defence issues. In the early months of 1989, the review group carried out its examination and discussion of defence. The resulting report was written by the group leader Gerald Kaufman in collaboration with Martin O'Neill.[56]

Like *Defence and Security for Britain* (1984), the report on defence policy in *Meet the Challenge: Make the Change: A new Agenda for Britain: Final Report of Labour's Policy Review for the 1990s* (1989)[57] expressed a commitment to the objectives of a non-nuclear defence and to the concepts of common security and defensive defence. At the same time, it advocated moving NATO away from dependence upon nuclear weapons (e.g. abandoning the flexible response strategy, adopting a policy of 'No First Use' of nuclear weapons) and it opposed the modernisation and deployment of short-range and tactical nuclear arms by the alliance.

The 1989 review reiterated support for three (of the five) main UK defence roles mentioned in *Defence and Security for Britain*: defence of the United Kingdom itself, defence of the Eastern Atlantic and the Channel, and defence on the Central Front. It promised that the UK contribution to NATO, in the Atlantic and on the European mainland, would be maintained 'as long as NATO continued'. It noted that it looked forward to the simultaneous dissolution of NATO and the Warsaw Pact, when the elimination of East–West fear and suspicion permit.

The transformation of East–West relations in the half-decade from mid-1984 to mid-1989 is acknowledged by the review.[58] Thus it had little if anything to say about military tactics and weapons systems (e.g. employing barriers on the inner-German border, the role of precision-guided munitions, the case for cheaper weapons platforms), but it devoted much attention to the negotiation of international nuclear disarmament.

One of the most striking changes in Labour policy from 1984 to 1989 concerns the UK strategic force. In 1984, and again in the 1987 General Election, Labour pledged itself to decommission Polaris and to cancel Trident as soon as it came to office. The 1989 review comments that Labour was totally opposed to the acquisition of Trident and if it 'had won the 1987 general election we would have cancelled the Trident programme as wasteful, unnecessary and provocative.'[59] It goes on note that by 1991–2 there 'would be no financial savings available from halting the construction'[60] of three of the four Trident submarines. Thereby it seems to imply that the absence of savings constituted a coherent explanation of why Trident was not 'unnecessary and provocative' a few years later. The review promised to cancel the fourth Trident submarine which would generate savings,[61] and to limit the number of warheads on Trident to the total on the Polaris force. Concurrently the 1989 report pledged to place the Polaris and Trident systems in international nuclear disarmament negotiations.

Labour's change of policy on Britain's strategic nuclear force had one clear implication. Henceforth a Labour administration whose declaratory policy saw little military value in possessing such a capability would retain it as an instrument to promote international nuclear disarmament. The new policy appeared to raise difficult questions for Mr Kinnock, with regard to his willingness as Prime Minister to 'press the nuclear button.'[62] Given the fact that for decades he had rejected any dependence upon nuclear arms, an affirmative answer would lack credibility and would probably keenly disturb many members of the Labour Party. Yet if he indicated a refusal to contemplate such action, it would, according to conventional analysis, drain Britain's nuclear arms of deterrent value and thus greatly diminish their bargaining utility.

The leader of the Labour Party met the difficulty with the following statement: 'We will negotiate with Trident and with the policy line that comes with all that operational weaponry, the policy line that never says "yes" or "no" to the question, "Will you press the button?" ' He went on to observe that as long as nuclear weapons exist, 'The assumption by others will inevitably be that there may be circumstances in which those weapons might be used.'[63] Labour's defence spokesperson Martin O'Neill summed up the view of the Party leadership as follows: 'Whoever we are negotiating with is interested in our possession of nuclear arms, not our declarations about them.'[64]

Thus a Labour government, claiming to use its powerful nuclear capability as a means to promote a non-nuclear world, simultaneously deploys that capability in the military role of deterring a potential attack.[65] The sharp contradiction between the declaratory and the operational policy of such an administration would do little to enhance the credibility of either. If Mr O'Neill is correct in judging that what matters to other countries is the possession of nuclear arms, then such a situation would seem profoundly uncomfortable for an anti-nuclear Labour government.

In the 1989 review, it is noted that if the START-2 negotiations were long delayed and seemed unlikely to make progress, 'a Labour Government will reserve the option of initiating direct negotiations with the Soviet Union and/or with others in order to bring about the elimination of that capacity by negotiated and verified agreement.'[66] Although Mr Kinnock had supported a bilateral agreement with the Soviet Union from 1984 to 1988,[67] much of the Labour leadership had little enthusiasm for such an arrangement in 1989–90. A decisive objection to such an agreement concerned the expected response of the British electorate. It was expected to regard a pact which eliminated the UK strategic nuclear force, but which left the Soviet Union with most of its nuclear capability, as in effect unilateral nuclear disarmament by Britain. Accordingly such a deal would be unacceptable to British opinion. Moreover, it was not clear that the Soviet Union could offer the United Kingdom some alternative concession that would not be open to the objection of being covert unilateral nuclear disarmament by Britain.

What had become clear by 1989 was that the Labour leadership was determined to be seen as unwilling to eliminate Britain's nuclear capability while other countries retained their nuclear arms. Although not explicitly stated in the review, that determination was emphasised by Labour's refusal to accept any specific time-scale for the removal of Britain's nuclear weapons and by the linking of nuclear disarmament by Britain with that of all other nuclear powers.[68] Moreover, Mr Kaufman's account of the visit to Moscow in early 1989 by the Britain in the World review group gave the clear impression that he was reassured by what he learned from Soviet officials. Apparently they were interested principally in international negotiations embracing all nuclear powers. They showed little curiosity about a separate deal with Britain.[69]

The lack of enthusiasm by 1989 amongst most of Labour's leadership, especially Mr Kaufman and Mr O'Neill for a bilateral UK–Soviet agreement on nuclear disarmament, prompts the question as to why the review statement included the option. This query is reinforced in that the draft of the defence policy written by Mr Kaufman (the leading member of the review group) and presented to the National Executive Committee of the Party (on 9 May) did not mention it.[70] Rather, the option was proposed in an amendment by Robin Cook, a prominent anti-nuclear member of the National Executive Committee. Mr Cook viewed the possibility as a fall-back position to deal with Trident if multilateral negotiations were failing. In such circumstances a Labour government that took no action for some years, but continued to deploy the strategic nuclear force, would be regarded as virtually indistinguishable from a pro-nuclear UK administration. Such a possibility was quite unattractive for Labour's National Executive Committee and especially repugnant to its more committed anti-nuclear members.

In the 1989 review, one of the most important changes in Labour's nuclear disarmament policy concerned UK-based US nuclear weapons. From 1983 to 1987, the Party was pledged to remove unilaterally these weapons (i.e. nuclear weapons on F111 aircraft, US nuclear submarines) within the lifetime of a Parliament. The highly publicised criticism made by President Reagan, Defence Secretary Weinberger and others of Labour's plans for those weapons in 1986–87 had not been forgotten two years later.

Again the example of Spain, where the government's demand for the removal of US aircraft led to their relocation in Italy, suggested that unilateral action might not advance the cause of a nuclear-free Europe and thus 'was not an overall gain for disarmament'.[71] Therefore if the result of a UK request was that US nuclear weapons were 'simply moved to the Netherlands, the fallout from any nuclear attack on their bases would inevitably affect large parts of this country.'[72]

Thus the Party leadership and the Britain in the World review group left the issue of UK-based nuclear arms for multilateral negotiations. The review proposed the inclusion of US F111 aircraft in the Conventional Forces in Europe talks. It noted that successful negotiations would remove such weapons together with Soviet nuclear arms, and it disclosed: 'We were told in Washington that Holy Loch would be retired as a US nuclear submarine base by the mid-to-late-1990s.'[73]

The adoption of a multilateral process to deal with US nuclear arms was entirely consistent with the Party leadership's view. That perspective considered that the promotion of nuclear disarmament in Europe (or worldwide) by international agreement was much more significant and enduring than independent steps taken by the United Kingdom on its own. Moreover, that posture was identified with the Labour leadership's view that the United Kingdom should avoid disrupting the NATO alliance, a result which could well follow from the unilateral ejection of US nuclear arms from Britain.

Unlike *Defence and Security for Britain*, the 1989 review includes only a brief discussion about the level of Britain's defence effort, noting that 'the defence budget cannot and should not be increased.'[74] In 1987, Labour promised to use the substantial savings emanating from the cancellation of Trident to pay for improvements to Britain's conventional defence. By 1989 only limited savings were projected to be available from cancelling the fourth Trident submarine (if Labour won the General Election of 1991–2).

In 1989, Labour's shift from a mix of unilateral and multilateral measures to a predominantly multilateral approach to defence acknowledged that apparent short-cuts to a non-nuclear Britain were probably illusory. This was so because a Party offering the unconditional elimination of Britain's nuclear capability seemed unelectable. In addition, the early ejection of US nuclear arms from the United Kingdom threatened to sunder a vital alliance relationship and therefore was unsustainable.

The new multilateral approach made Labour's defence policy more coherent than it had been for some years. Now the policies on UK nuclear disarmament, UK-based US nuclear arms, and changing NATO strategy were broadly compatible with each other. Moreover, the recognition by the Party that the possession of nuclear weapons had a potential deterrent role suggested that Labour now accepted, albeit reluctantly, the concept of a US nuclear umbrella.[75]

But some tensions remained in the policy. In particular, these concerned the declaratory policy of a non-nuclear objective and Britain's likely retention of some nuclear arms for an indefinite period. Again the pledge of a 'No First Use' policy for UK nuclear weapons struck a jarring note for a Party which seemed unable to envisage any military use for nuclear weapons. The review's promise not to test UK nuclear devices was in line with Labour's long-standing support for a Comprehensive Test Ban. But there was reason to doubt whether a Labour administration possessing nuclear weapons would adhere strictly to that promise.

Explaining Labour's return to a multilateral defence policy

At the start of the 1980s, at a time of tense US–Soviet relations, fears of nuclear war were widespread and the influence of the British peace movement was at its zenith. Then the Labour Party adopted a defence policy which included a commitment to rid unconditionally the United Kingdom of all nuclear weapons at the earliest opportunity. By the end of the 1980s, superpower relations had been transformed, anxiety about nuclear war had virtually disappeared, and the impact of the peace movement had sharply declined. At that point the Party returned to a modified version of its earlier multilateral policy. By the autumn of 1989, Labour's declared policy was to retain nuclear weapons as a means to promote worldwide nuclear and conventional disarmament, while playing down any deterrent role for Britain's nuclear arms.

Three main factors may be adduced to account for Labour's shift to a multilateral defence policy. These were the disposition of the Party leadership, the attitude of the British electorate, and the change in international conditions. If the Labour leadership had not campaigned and manœuvred for the shift, it is highly improbable that the modification of a policy so deeply entrenched in the feelings and values of the Party would have occurred so soon.

The vehement refusal of the British electorate to countenance a unilateralist policy (as demonstrated in the General Elections of 1983 and 1987) presented Labour with a stark choice: either maintain fidelity to the unilateral policy and remain indefinitely in powerless opposition, or alter the policy to secure a prospect of office. Thirdly, the multilateral approach to nuclear disarmament gained considerable credibility following the signing of the INF Treaty (1987) and the inauguration of serious negotiations on strategic nuclear arms and conventional forces in Europe. These favourable conditions provided the Labour leadership with a plausible case for making the shift palatable to many within and outside the Labour Party.

In the three years before the shift of policy in 1989, Labour's leadership prepared the Party for the change. Initially this was done mainly by implication and hints regarding a multilateral policy. Later the full thrust of the change was spelt out. Thus even before the Britain in the World group turned its attention to defence in late 1988, statements and interviews by Neil Kinnock and Gerald Kaufman signalled, strongly, the adoption of a multilateral approach. Yet the review group had an important role in legitimising the shift in policy following its meetings with senior officials and politicians in Moscow, Washington and Bonn.

Virtually all sections of the Party supported the anti-nuclear language of the review. The leadership's acceptance of unilateralists' amendments to strengthen the statement's anti-nuclear thrust,[76] helped persuade some members of the National Executive Committee to support the review.

Probably a significant margin of the victory for the multilateral defence policy at the National Executive Committee (17 to 8) and subsequently at the Annual Conference (3.6 million to 2.4 million) was a result of the fact that Mr Kinnock made the issue into one of loyalty to the Party. He had declared that he would refuse to argue for the unilateral policy in future. Therefore a defeat for the multilateral course would almost certainly produce a divisive and highly damaging contest to replace a leader who had gained an overwhelming (i.e. 88 per cent of the electoral college) majority just a year before. The concern for the position of the leader, together with the public image of the Party, made it more difficult for some unilateralist members of the National Executive Committee to vote against the review. The same effect was engendered by the incorporation of some anti-nuclear amendments into the review statement. Given that a leader who was seen to have great difficulty in persuading his Party to support his policy would be seriously weakened in public perceptions, the pressures to support Mr Kinnock were quite strong.

In addition, solicitude for the unity of the Party and the integrity of majority decisions assisted the Labour leadership. Such concern meant that prominent unilateralist figures like Ron Todd of the TGWU and Joan Ruddock promised to abide by the decisions of the Annual Conference on defence, even if their preferred policy was defeated.[77]

Notes and references

1 *The Times*, 30 September 1987.
2 See John Lloyd, 'How to win in 1991', *New Statesman*, 19 June 1987, p. 3; Peter Kellner, 'Labour's future: decline or democratic revolution', *New Statesman*, 19 June 1987, p. 8–11; Ian Aitken, 'The double fudge on disarmament', *Guardian*, 22 June 1987; and Hugh McPherson, Parliamentary Column in *Tribune*, 26 June 1987.

3 See Labour Co-ordinating Committee, document, *Labour's Renewal: The Next Stage*, London, 4 July 1987. As an observer at those conferences, I was aware of participants' concern to get around what was perceived as the electoral albatross of unilateralism.
4 Consult article by Bill Jordan, President of the Amalgamated Engineering Union in *The Times*, 13 July 1987. In that article, Mr Jordan noted that, along with the leader of the electricians union Eric Hammond, he had an interview with Neil Kinnock shortly before the 1987 General Election. Their efforts to persuade Mr Kinnock to promise to hold a referendum on defence were unsuccessful.
5 See Tom Sawyer, 'Towards the listening Party', *Labour Party News*, no. 6 (November/December 1987), pp. 12–13, 12. See also interview with Tom Sawyer, 'The policy review is an opportunity for Labour to renew itself', *Tribune*, 11 December 1987.
6 Mr Kinnock's speech at a Fabian conference on 17 June 1988 quoted in *Guardian*, 18 June 1988.
7 Source is Tom Sawyer, 'Towards the listening Party', op. cit.
8 See Tom Sawyer's interview in *Tribune*, 11 December 1987.
9 *Observer*, 21 June 1987. Mr Kinnock repeated his support for the existing Labour defence policy on 2 July 1987. See *Independent*, 3 July 1987.
10 *Guardian*, 30 September 1987.
11 Mr Kaufman was speaking at a meeting sponsored by the Nuclear Freeze Campaign in Brighton on 30 September 1987. I was present at the meeting.
12 See 'Kinnock draws up formula on defence', *Guardian*, 2 October 1987.
13 *Guardian*, 28 November 1987.
14 See *Guardian*, 6 June 1988, for an account of the interviews.
15 The article by A. Bevins, 'Kinnock set to modify nuclear weapons policy', appeared in the *Independent*, 10 May 1988. See also John Lloyd, 'The wrong party', *New Statesman* 1 July 1988.
16 Mr Davies' commitment to a coherent and defensible defence policy was evident in my interview with him. For an interpretation of Denzil Davies' resignation, see J. Naughtie, 'Tea but not much sympathy', *Guardian*, 30 June 1988.
17 *Independent*, 21 June 1988.
18 See 'Benn rallies left to fight Labour "transformation" ', *Guardian*, 11 June 1988.
19 'Union votes block Kinnock on defence' in *Guardian* of 7th October 1988.
20 Labour Manifesto, *Britain Will Win* (London, Labour Party, 1987), p. 16. In March 1987, Mr Kinnock announced that if the INF talks ended with an agreement to keep a limited number of nuclear weapons on both sides, he would still delay the expulsion of Cruise missiles from Britain. See 'Kinnock defines position on cruise', *Guardian*, 20 March 1987.
21 *Britain Will Win*, op. cit., p. 16.
22 Martin O'Neill, 'Towards a nuclear-free future', *Labour Party News* (July/August 1988), p. 15.
23 Statement by Gerald Kaufman (Labour's Shadow Foreign Secretary) at the Annual Conference in 1989. See 'Arms spending cut backed', *Guardian*, 3 October 1989.
24 Neil Kinnock's interview with *Tribune* on 4 March 1988.
25 ibid.
26 Martin O'Neill, 'Towards a nuclear-free future', *Labour Party News*, op. cit., p. 15.
27 Martin O'Neill, 'Political realities change', *New Socialist*, no. 60 (April/May 1989), pp. 16–17, 17.
28 Interview with Martin O'Neill in *END: Journal of European Nuclear Disarmament*,

no. 31 (December/January 1987–8), p. 7.
29 See Labour defence background paper written mainly by Gerald Kaufman and published in *Tribune*, 21 July 1989. A shortened version appeared in *Labour Party News* (July/August 1989).
30 'Unilateralists win the day', *Guardian*, 7 October 1989.
31 ibid.
32 'The man who buried Labour's defence handicap', *Times*, 5 November 1990.
33 'Leading questions', *Labour Party News*, no. 17 (September/October 1989), pp. 8–10, 9.
34 Interview with Tom Sawyer, *Tribune*, 29 September 1989.
35 See account of debate at the National Union of Public Employees conference in 'NUPE switches 600,000 votes on defence policy', *Tribune*, 26 May 1989.
36 Quoted in Colin Hughes and Patrick Wintour, *Labour Rebuilt: The New Model Party* (London, Fourth Estate, 1990), pp. 123–6.
37 Note interview with Martin O'Neill, 'Labour "serious about defence" ', *END: Journal of European Nuclear Disarmament*, (31 December/January 1987–8). According to that interview, Mr O'Neill equated seriousness about defence with being in touch with public opinion.
38 'Kinnock gets way on defence', *Guardian*, 10 May 1989. See also Colin Hughes and Patrick Wintour, *Labour Rebuilt*, op. cit., Chapter 8
39 ibid.
40 See interview with Tom Sawyer, *Tribune*, 29 September 1989.
41 Mr Kinnock did not meet Mr Gorbachev in the Kremlin in the 1980s, although he did see him when the Soviet leader visited the United Kingdom in the second part of the decade. Ron Todd of the TGWU visited Moscow (as a member of the Britain in the World review group) in early 1989. He did not find 'blank incomprehension' of Labour's unilateralism in Moscow. See his interview in *Tribune*, 22 June 1989.
42 Calum MacDonald, MP, 'Changing times mean changes in the means to achieve disarmament', *Tribune*, 17 March 1989.
43 'Defence review's unfortunate results', letter from E.P. Thompson, *Guardian*, 27 May 1989.
44 See note 30 above.
45 'Labour's commitment to liberty, equality and justice at home is equally applicable to its relations with other nations and peoples . . . such values are incompatible with the use of nuclear weapons and arguably with their threatened use in the form of the nuclear deterrent', in Joan Ruddock, MP, 'The case for sticking with unilateralism', *Tribune*, 10 February 1989.
46 James Hinton, 'Keeping Trident: bilateral bargaining counter or appeal to knee-jerk nationalism?', *Tribune*, 9 June 1989.
47 See, for example, Joan Ruddock, MP, 'The case for sticking with unilateralism', *Tribune*, op. cit., Dan Smith, 'Relying on multilateralism is simply not enough', *Tribune*, 24 March 1989, and Mary Kaldor, 'Defending the indefensible', *New Socialist*, no. 63 (October/November 1989), pp. 15–17.
48 Joan Ruddock, MP, 'The case for sticking with unilateralism', op. cit.
49 Interview with Ron Todd, *Tribune*, 23 June 1989.
50 Joan Ruddock, MP, 'Postwar plans', *New Statesman and Society*, 18 August 1989.
51 Mary Kaldor, 'Defending the indefensible?', in *New Socialist*, no. 63 (October/November, 1989), pp. 15–17, 17.
52 ibid.
53 See Joan Ruddock, MP, 'The case for sticking with unilateralism', op. cit.

54 Consult letter from Joan Ruddock, MP, in *Tribune*, 23 October 1987, for discussion of the political uses of dismantling Trident.
55 Source: Hughes and Wintour, *Labour Rebuilt: The New Model Party*, op. cit.,
   Chapter 8.
56 ibid.
57 *Meet the Challenge: Make the Change: A New Agenda for Britain: Final Report of
   Labour's Policy Review for the 1990s* (London, Labour Party, 1989).
58 Given that the 1989 review is about one-third the length of *Defence and Security for
   Britain*, its treatment of many issues is necessarily much briefer than the 1984
   statement.
59 *Final Report of Labour's Policy Review for the 1990s*, op. cit. p. 87.
60 ibid.
61 During a House of Commons defence debate in November 1991, Labour's
   defence spokesperson Martin O'Neill indicated that the Party still considered that
   there was not a strong strategic case for a fourth Trident submarine. He noted: 'If
   we find, on reaching office, that the programme is sufficiently far advanced to
   render it foolish to go back on it, we shall review the matter carefully.' *Hansard,
   House of Commons, Official Report*, 22 November 1991, col. 555. Labour's 1992
   Election Manifesto was silent on the issue.
62 See discussion of this topic in Hughes and Wintour, *Labour Rebuilt: The New
   Model Party*, op. cit., pp. 123–4.
63 Source: *The Times*, 13 May 1989. See also the *Guardian* of that date.
64 Martin O'Neill, 'Political realities change', *New Socialist* no. 60 (April/May 1989),
   pp. 16–17, 17.
65 In the Labour defence background paper explaining the 1989 policy review, it is
   noted that because Trident has a longer range than Polaris, it will 'take less time to
   reach its patrol area' and 'will need fewer refits and less time for maintenance.'
   This is an indication of the military role envisaged for Trident. See *Tribune*, 21
   July 1989.
66 *Final Report of Labour's Policy Review for the 1990s*, op. cit., p. 87.
67 See Mr Kinnock's interview with the *Independent*, 21 June 1988.
68 Speaking at the launch of *Labour's Better Way for the 1990s* (1991), Neil Kinnock
   observed, 'We have at no stage, and this has been very clear throughout, made a
   commitment to get rid of all nuclear weapons for as long as others have them.
   Hence the process of negotiations.' See *Independent*, 17 April 1991. Consult also
   interview with Gerald Kaufman in *The Times*, 5 November 1990.
69 See Gerald Kaufman, 'Soviet ministers determined to deter "universal stupid-
   ity" ', *The Times*, 4 February 1989; 'Kaufman fires shell at unilateral policy',
   Guardian, 3 February 1989. Kaufman's view was strongly supported by Martin
   O'Neill. See *Hansard, House of Commons*, 22 November 1991, col. 551. Note also
   the interpretation, 'If there was a hidden agenda to the trip, it was to kill the third
   option of a bilateral deal, an approach which Kinnock still considered possible', in
   Hughes and Wintour, *Labour Rebuilt*, op. cit. p. 114.
70 ibid. pp. 116–23. At a Fabian conference in January 1989 (which I attended),
   Martin O'Neill rejected a missile-for-missile deal with the Soviet Union but
   indicated that he did not rule out Britain giving up Trident in return for cuts in
   Soviet conventional forces. See also P. Wintour, 'O'Neill rules out Labour missile
   for missile deal', *Guardian*, 9 January 1989.
71 Martin O'Neill, 'Political realities change', op. cit., pp. 16–17, 17.
72 ibid.
73 *Final Report of Labour's Policy Review for the 1990s*, op. cit., p. 87. The Holy
   Loch base was closed down in 1991–2.

74 ibid., p. 85.
75 See note 63 above. At a meeting of Labour's National Executive Committee on 17 May 1989, the members voted to accept Mr Kinnock's formula that possession of nuclear weapons could deter a potential attacker. See Hughes and Wintour, *Labour Rebuilt*, op. cit., pp. 124–5.
76 The changes accepted included the option for direct negotiations with the Soviet Union and/or others if international talks were stalled, the statement that the only relevant role for Britain's nuclear weapons was as an instrument to promote nuclear and conventional disarmament, and the expression of support for the elimination of all nuclear weapons by the year 2000 (originally proposed by Mr Gorbachev). See Hughes and Wintour, *Labour Rebuilt*, op. cit., pp. 117–21.
77 According to Phil Kelly's interview with Mr Todd, 'He is contemptuous of leading figures in the party who in the past have sought to over-ride conference decisions by public speeches.' Interview with Ron Todd in *Tribune*, 23 June 1989. At a Fabian/New Society conference in July 1989, Ms. Ruddock noted that because she did not want to be accused of causing splits in the Party, she felt inhibited from speaking. She made it clear that she would not disturb the public unity of the Party in the run-up to the next election. 'Ruddock breaks ranks on defence', *Independent*, 3 July 1989.

6 The changed European strategic context and Labour's defence policy, 1989–92

Speaking in September 1988, Professor Michael Howard commented as follows on Mikhail Gorbachev: 'Whatever the outcome of his regime, he will go down to history as one of the major figures of the twentieth century.'[1] President Gorbachev's claim to be regarded as a major figure in world politics rests upon his impact on Soviet politics and society, the politics of Eastern and Central Europe, and relations between East and West.

The Gorbachev leadership was a product of educational, social and technological change within the Soviet Union. It recognised that the Union faced immensely complex interrelated crises in the economy, the Communist Party and the political system. With regard to the economy, the new leadership promoted moves towards a market system and the devolution of decision-making. It assumed that the comparative isolation and insulation of the Soviet economy from the international economy had contributed to its stagnation and decline. Therefore it complemented proposals for domestic reform with plans to open up the economy to competition with the world's advanced economies and it hoped to gain credits, know-how and technology from those societies.[2]

Ideologically, the reform leadership retreated from a clear and strong adherence to Marxist–Leninist concepts and approaches. Instead, it adopted an instrumental pragmatic approach to domestic and international issues, emphasising the innovative character of its thinking. Thus it placed little stress on the key Marxist notion of the conflictual character of relations between states with different social systems. It underlined the interdependence of East and West in the global economy, in military security and in other areas. This was illustrated by the comment of Foreign Minister Eduard Shevardnadze in July 1988: 'The struggle between the two systems is no longer the prevailing trend of the present era.'[3]

In the political domain, Mr Gorbachev and his associates espoused open debate and discussion (until the shifts in attitude in 1990). These were seen as valuable in themselves and as a principal mechanism to attack corruption, abuse of power and inefficiency in the economy, the Communist Party and in other institutions. At the same time, most political prisoners in the Soviet Union were released, restrictions on religious practice were relaxed, and procedures for emigration from the Soviet Union were eased and codified.

Many changes were introduced affecting the character, role and function of

Soviet political institutions. For example, the advent of secret ballots and a choice of candidates in the 1989 elections to the Congress of Peoples' Deputies resulted in the defeat of senior members of the Communist Party. In the late 1980s, largely as a result of the political reforms introduced by Mr Gorbachev, the Communist Party lost its monopoly of power in the Soviet Union and it was deprived of its dominant position in the Baltic republics and some other states of the Union. The latter development reflected the intense and sustained demand by the majority in those republics for autonomy or full independence from Moscow.

By 1989–90, the failure of Gorbachev's attempts at reforming the centrally planned economy produced deep alienation among the population. So despite strong support for the democratic reforms especially among the intelligentsia (who contributed much in ideas and personnel to the reform programme), the collapse of the efforts at economic change and renewal gravely undermined Gorbachev's plans and prestige. Gorbachev's period in office coincided with changes which worsened the Soviet population's living standards and permitted the emergence of long-suppressed demands which threatened to destroy the territorial integrity of the Soviet Union.

The inability of the Gorbachev leadership to manage the multiple challenges to its position and policy led in August 1991 to a short-lived *coup* in the Soviet Union. Within weeks of the abortive *coup*, the three Baltic states broke away from the control of Moscow. By the end of 1991, eleven former Soviet Republics had become independent, and the Soviet Union had disintegrated. With the dissolution of the Soviet Union, Mr Gorbachev's role as President disappeared.

While the former Soviet Republics formed a loose group called the Commonwealth of Independent States (CIS), in mid 1992 the prospects for that association and for many of the new sovereign states seemed extremely uncertain. From the start of his period as General Secretary of the Communist Party, Mr Gorbachev recognised the strong relationship between new thinking and reform in domestic politics and in Soviet foreign policy. Along with colleagues like Mr Shevardnadze, he assumed that the international standing of the Soviet Union was measured mainly by the level of its technology and innovation, and by its capacity to sustain a high and rising standard of living for its people. Judged by those criteria, the Soviet Union has suffered a sharp decline in its international prestige since the early 1970s.

The Gorbachev reformers accepted that the allocation of a particularly high proportion of national income, along with highly skilled engineers, technologists and scientists for military purposes, had starved the civil Soviet economy of essential inputs. Moreover, they judged that the Soviet effort to maintain the military status of a superpower was bankrupting the Soviet Union. But it was failing to produce a stable and secure relationship with the United States. On the contrary, the cycle of intense US–Soviet military rivalry was accompanied frequently by relatively unfruitful superpower relations which in turn precluded Western technological and other assistance for the Soviet Union. Without such external support the Soviet Union was thought to have little prospect of reducing the gap between its own levels of productivity and technology and those of the West.

Accordingly, Mr Gorbachev and his associates sought cooperative relations with the United States and other Western countries and they advocated a Soviet military capability 'at a level of reasonable and dependable sufficiency'.[4] They considered that the Soviet Union should seek stability at the lowest possible level of nuclear capability. In addition, it should adopt a defensive military posture and seek to demilitarise international relations. If these objectives were to be attained, the Soviet Union would need to promote far-reaching measures of arms control and disarmament.

Changes in Central and Eastern Europe

In June 1988, Mr Gorbachev commented that the new Soviet thinking on international relations indicated that 'the imposition from outside by any means, not to mention military means, of a social system, way of life or policy constitutes the dangerous armour of past years.'[5] In the following two to three years, the Soviet Union explicitly rejected the Brezhnev doctrine. More significantly, it adhered to Mr Gorbachev's pledge in the particularly demanding circumstances obtaining in the Warsaw Pact states at that time.

Clearly, the Gorbachev reforms in the Soviet Union gave inspiration and encouragement to the advocates of change in Central and Eastern Europe. That was evident in the invocation of Gorbachev's name by demonstrators in East Germany and in Czechoslovakia during 1989. At that time the Soviet Union signalled that it no longer supported the neo-Stalinist rulers in those states. Thus when the regimes were challenged by immense popular demonstrations in 1989, the Soviet Union, in contrast with its actions in earlier decades, did not provide armed forces to suppress manifestations of discontent. Therefore the communist governments were forced to accommodate the demands of reformist communists and non-communist movements which led to the replacement of the old-style regimes.

The tumult of political change in Central and Eastern Europe in 1989–90 illuminated a reality which was previously obscured. Thus in the majority of those countries, the communist regimes enjoyed comparatively little legitimacy or popular support even after decades in government. Consequently, in free elections in Poland, Hungary, Czechoslovakia and East Germany, the communist parties, even when proffering a reformed leadership and policy, were unable to attract majority support or anything approaching thereto.

The most notable consequences of the revolutions in Central and Eastern Europe were the unification of Germany, the demise of the Warsaw Pact and of Comecon, and the adherence of most of the new governments to an independent stance in foreign policy.

The Federal Republic of Germany proposed that NATO should embrace the territory of the enlarged Germany because the electors of the former GDR supported that policy in the 1990 elections in East Germany. In addition, the Federal Republic believed that was the only practical option. Following strenuous objections by the Soviet Union, Moscow eventually accepted that the new enlarged Germany should be in the Atlantic alliance. In the agreement between Chancellor Kohl of West Germany and President Gorbachev (of 16 July 1990), it was settled that NATO troops or weapons would not be located in East Germany. The pact set the relatively low ceiling of 370,000 for the new Germany's armed forces.

With the advent of strongly anti-communist governments in Hungary, Poland and Czechoslovakia, and the inclusion of East Germany in the united Germany, the Warsaw pact lost its ideological and political coherence. By 1990 it had ceased to be a viable military organisation. As a result of those changes Soviet troops withdrew from Hungary and Czechoslovakia, and were due to leave Germany by 1994 at the latest.

The core expression of the post-war division of Europe, as reflected in the existence of two German states (adhering to rival ideologies, political-economic systems and military alliances), came to an end in 1990. So also did the military confrontation between NATO and the Warsaw Pact. In the early 1990s, the countries of Central Europe were moving at varying speeds towards pluralist political systems and market economies. They were also seeking close association with the European Community and with other Western countries. In this manner, the ideological, if not the economic cleavage between East and West died away.

Soviet accommodation of Western interests

For the four decades after 1945, governments and publics in the West shared a deeply negative perception of the Soviet Union. The Eastern bloc led by the Soviet Union was seen to be engaged in a fundamental and potentially disastrous ideological, military and economic competition with the West.

Within five years of Mikhail Gorbachev becoming leader of the Soviet Union, those perceptions had almost disappeared. By his statements and his actions, Mr Gorbachev reassured the West that he was willing to accommodate its interests. Thus he stressed the interdependence of communist and capitalist countries and promoted restructuring and glasnost domestically. Internationally he withdrew Soviet forces from Afghanistan and diminished Moscow's military involvement in Southern Africa, the Middle East and elsewhere. He also offered strong support for the United Nations in resolving international conflicts and facilitated Western military action in the Gulf War of 1991.

In the sensitive and important domain of arms control, the Soviet Union demonstrated the high priority it attached to reaching agreement with the West. It did this by accepting deeply asymmetrical reductions of its SS20 nuclear system in the INF Treaty of 1987. In December 1988, the Soviet Union announced its decision to recall and disband six tank divisions from the GDR, Czechoslovakia and Hungary and to withdraw landing-assault and landing-crossing units, with their arms and *matériel*, from those countries. The Soviet forces remaining in Central Europe were to adopt a defensive posture, thereby reducing sharply the Soviet capacity for surprise attack. These decisions, together with Mr Gorvachev's offer of a unilateral reduction of half a million men in the strength of Soviet armed forces, conveyed a clear message. They indicated that he recognised that past Soviet behaviour had contributed to negative Western perceptions of Moscow's intentions. Moreover, it demonstrated that he was now concerned to assuage NATO fears of a surprise attack.[6]

Soviet willingness to meet NATO anxieties was also evident in 1989–90, when the negotiations on conventional forces in Europe (CFE) were in progress. The subsequent Treaty enshrined Soviet reductions in tanks, artillery and armoured combat vehicles many times greater than those of any NATO country. In addition, it included unprecedentedly intrusive inspection arrangements (e.g. mandatory on-site inspections).

Cumulatively, the Soviet acceptance of non-communist governments in Central/Eastern Europe and of a united Germany as a member of NATO did much to assuage Western fears of the Soviet Union. So also did the prospective ending of the Soviet military presence in most or all of the former Warsaw Pact countries, and the emergence of glasnost within the Soviet Union. Paradoxically, the growing international acclaim of President Gorbachev demonstrated in Western public opinion polls, in the warm reception he attracted in foreign visits, and in the award of the Nobel Peace Prize in 1990 was not matched domestically. Rather, it coincided with the near collapse of his prestige in many parts of the Soviet Union.

NATO's response

Western responses to the reform policies of Mikhail Gorbachev from 1985 to 1989 might be viewed in terms of two stages. First, from 1985 to about 1987, Western public opinion and Western governments learned that the new Soviet leadership was decisively different from its predecessors. Second, from 1987 to 1989, much of Western public opinion expected their leaders to respond more positively to the improved international political climate and to the flow of the Soviet initiatives on arms reductions. But most NATO governments maintained an attitude of caution and scepticism. Thus in early 1987, Britain's Foreign Secretary Sir Geoffrey Howe noted 'that NATO's policy of hardheaded dialogue with the Soviet leadership, combined with firm defence of our national interests, is the right approach.'[7]

The conflicting pressures on NATO governments were evident in 1988–9 when the US and UK governments were pressing for the replacement of the Lance short-range nuclear missile, while German public opinion was vehemently opposed to such modernisation. By 1987, the frequent US–Soviet meetings at the highest level had done much to generate a convergence of East–West perspectives on conventional arms control. Furthermore, the INF Treaty was being implemented and the START negotiations were proceeding in a relatively favourable climate.

With the collapse of the communist regimes in Central/Eastern Europe in 1989–90, the emergence of new non-communist governments, and the unification of the two German states, NATO found itself in an immensely altered environment. Many of the long-established landmarks of the international order in Europe had disappeared. However, other challenges to a secure and stable Europe remained and new ones were emerging.

The Soviet Union continued to be a military superpower until its dissolution at the end of 1991. Thereafter there were indications of the disintegration of Soviet forces into the forces of the new republics. If those indications were confirmed, it would diminish the potential for the CIS states to offer a military threat to other European states. However, the turmoil experienced within and between the CIS states might still cause much anxiety on the rest of the European continent. With the removal of close Soviet control within the Soviet Union, and in Central/Eastern Europe, long suppressed ethnic, social, cultural and economic tensions threatened stability within and between those countries. As Germany united in 1990, initially much uneasiness was engendered among its neighbours with regard to the future behaviour of that country.

In response to the end of the Cold War and the other tumultuous changes in Europe in 1989–90, the NATO countries concluded that the alliance still had a major role to play in contributing to security and stability on the continent. The member-states assumed that although the United States would have a diminished involvement in Europe's security, the US political and military endowment remained an essential corner-stone for the alliance. Thus the United States was perceived as a necessary counterweight to the Soviet Union externally and to Germany internally. It was also regarded as a key actor in facilitating successful international negotiations on arms reductions.

In the London Declaration of July 1990,[8] the NATO governments set out their approach to the role of the alliance in the new international circumstances. They acknowledged that NATO and the Warsaw Pact were no longer adversaries and they arranged that the Soviet Union and others establish regular diplomatic ties with NATO. The alliance identified the Conference on Security and Cooperation in Europe (CSCE) as the appropriate framework to carry forward political dialogue throughout Europe. The CSCE established a Conflict Prevention Centre, and it was expected to foster many kinds of cooperative interactions including regular consultations between its many member states.

The London NATO Declaration noted that, with the departure of Soviet troops from Central and Eastern Europe, the alliance strategy 'will change fundamentally'. NATO would aim for smaller, mobile, mainly multinational forces and would want to move away from forward defence. The alliance remained loyal to its long-held perception of nuclear weapons as the ultimate deterrent to war in Europe, but it accepted that in less threatening conditions nuclear capability should be regarded as 'weapons of last resort'.[9]

At the Rome Summit of NATO Heads of State and Government in November 1991, the alliance emphasized two aspects of its response to the new strategic environment. First, it underlined its commitment to promoting cooperation and dialogue on security issues with the countries of Central and Eastern Europe. Thus the North Atlantic Cooperation Council, which embraces both the former European Soviet-bloc countries and the NATO member-states, was inaugurated by the end of 1991.

Second, in a context where potential threats to NATO's security are expected to emanate from instabilities in Central and in Eastern Europe and in the Commonwealth of Independent States, the alliance gives a high priority to the prevention and management of crises.[10] In early 1992, the NATO countries manifested considerable anxiety regarding the management (e.g. storage, transport and destruction) and control arrangements of nuclear weapons in the four former Soviet nuclear republics. They also indicated concern about the spread of nuclear arms, materials and expertise from the former Soviet Union to regimes elsewhere. By the middle of 1992, the causes and consequences of the conflicts within and between the former Yugoslav republics was causing NATO and other international organisations much anxiety.

The debate on Europe's defence

The recasting of NATO's role and strategy in 1990–1 overlapped with intense and sustained debate about Europe's defence arrangements and institutions. With the collapse of the Soviet military–ideological threat, and the sharply diminished role of the United States in the international economy, the extent of US involvement in Europe's defence seemed in question. This was so whatever American leaders promised in 1990–1. Already in October 1986, European governments had been disturbed greatly by two aspects of the Reykjavik summit meeting between President Reagan and General Secretary Gorbachev. First, Mr Reagan made proposals at the meeting which could well have a profound impact upon the defence arrangements of the European members of NATO if the latter were not first properly consulted. That failure to consult seemed to argue that the United States might be giving a higher priority to reaching arms reduction agreements with Moscow than to maintaining its fidelity with its European partners. Second, the US proposals for the removal of INF nuclear systems from Europe (later enshrined in the INF Treaty), and for the elimination of superpower ballistic missiles, raised sharp questions about the credibility of NATO's flexible response strategy.

European governments responded to the shock administered by the Reykjavik Summit by reviving the Western European Union (WEU). That body had long been regarded as a fall-back organisation in case the United States suddenly terminated its security pledge to Europe. In its Hague Platform on European Security Interests, of late 1987, the WEU emphasised its commitment to reliance on nuclear weapons. It noted that 'the construction of an integrated Europe will remain incomplete as long as it does not include security and defence.' But it made clear that the WEU contribution 'to the broader process of European unification'[11] should be seen in the context of a leading US role in NATO.

By 1990–1, Germany's partners were anxious to bind the newly united country at the centre of the continent into a larger European security entity, as were Germany's leaders. Thus proposals for a European Community with its own foreign policy and military security policy seemed like a culmination of EC plans for a single market in 1992 and economic and monetary union by the mid-1990s.

Plans to establish a European defence community, based on the fusion of the Western European Union (WEU) with the European Community, rested upon some favourable bases, but they also face daunting obstacles. Prominent among these impediments is the divergence of outlook and policy among member-states (in issues like the Gulf War of 1991 and European–US relations). Another derives from the absence of a single dominant leader. No member state seems capable of moulding the disparate EC states into a psychological unit, nor is one well qualified to provide a credible defence shield for the European countries.

The factors favourable for the establishment of an EC defence role include the general commitment of leading members thereto and the experience gained in coordinating EC countries' foreign policy in the process of European Political Cooperation. The favourable factors also include the perception that the 'European dream will inevitably fade' unless it creates the 'institutional tools it now lacks to act swiftly and decisively on foreign policy and security.'[12] Thus the creation of an EC foreign and defence policy is perceived by some as a mechanism to buttress its sense of identity by enabling the Community to act as one on important issues within and beyond Europe.

In practical operational terms, the existence of an extensive network of military institutions, structures and practices, within and outside NATO, such as WEU, Eurogroup, and the Independent European Programme, do much to facilitate European consultation. They also promote the development of standardised systems and the evolution of shared attitudes and expertise among member-states' armed forces.

Labour, NATO and European defence, 1989–92

When Labour produced its defence review statement in the first part of 1989, the unfolding political changes in Central and Eastern Europe were at a transitional stage. The German Democratic Republic was still a separate sovereign state and communist parties dominated government in most states of the region. Two years later, in mid-1991, the two German states had become one, and the previous communist rulers had been displaced in most countries in Eastern and Central Europe. In addition, the Warsaw Pact had been wound up as a military organisation. In response to the actual and planned withdrawal of Soviet forces from the former Warsaw Pact states (and the reduction of military forces agreed according to the Conventional Forces in Europe Treaty of 1990), NATO initiated major changes in its role and strategy.

In Britain, there was a limited and relatively superficial debate on the future of institutions protecting Europe's security. This reflected a very cautious approach by the Labour Party and the Conservative government in the period 1989–92. It could be summed up as seeking to conserve as much as possible of the existing arrangements for protecting the country's security, while adapting defence institutions where that was necessary and accepting new structures where it was unavoidable.

The Conservative Party had no wish to promote a wide-ranging debate on defence and Europe (such a debate could well exacerbate the existing divisions on Britain's relations with Europe, divisions which contributed to the resignation of Prime Minister Thatcher and Deputy Prime Minister Howe in 1990). Neither could Labour leaders see how their Party could benefit from such a discussion. It might divert attention from the Conservatives' disagreements on the EC and focus unwelcome scrutiny on Labour's low-key disputes on the Party's revised defence policy and the EC.

For some four decades, the twin pillars or assumptions of Britain's security framework were that Western Europe needed the American commitment to its defence and that the United States was able and willing to provide that pledge. Closely linked with those assumptions was the belief that Britain had a special intermediary role between Europe and the United States. The dissolution of the Soviet Union and the changes in Central and Eastern Europe undermined the assumptions on which NATO was founded. But the conclusion drawn by Labour leaders (like their Conservative counterparts) was that the alliance would endure for the foreseeable future, albeit in sharply modified form. Thus in a House of Commons debate in June 1990, Labour's defence spokesperson Martin O'Neill observed: 'NATO can continue for some time, but with different purposes and to different ends.'[13]

In May 1990, Labour's revised policy document *Looking to the Future* commented that the Party agreed with US Secretary of State James Baker that 'NATO's role should be political rather than military.' It went on to identify a positive and negative reason for NATO's survival. The first was the West's need for an organisation 'to negotiate, implement and verify disarmament agreements.' The second referred to NATO's existence making it 'unnecessary for the European Community to have any military role.'[14]

The approach of Labour's 1990 statement to NATO was notable in various ways. First, its declared policy supported NATO, not apparently as a result of the alliance's record or attributes but because NATO's survival was thought to reduce the likelihood of the emergence of a military role for the European Community. Second, it seemed that Labour perceived NATO's future role as being restricted to handling the process of arms control and disarmament in Europe. Third, Labour's statement employed terms quite akin to those of US Secretary of State Baker in late 1989 when he observed that NATO 'will become the forum . . . where Western nations cooperate to negotiate, to implement, to verify and to extend agreements between East and West.'[15] Thus Labour seemed entirely at ease with a formulation, albeit incomplete, quite akin to that used by the leading member of NATO.

Early in 1991, Mr Kinnock elaborated on Labour's approach to NATO's purpose and future.[16] He noted that it was 'in the interests of both Europe and the United States to avoid introversion in either continent. That's surely best done by retaining reduced but significant US links with European security.'[17] He emphasized the alliance's role in promoting disarmament and he stressed its potential contribution to the evolution of the Conference on Security and Cooperation in Europe (CSCE) in strengthening the new democracies in Eastern and Central Europe. Unlike the 1990 Party statement, the Labour leader listed defence as one of the functions of NATO, but he placed it as the last of three functions performed by the alliance.

The analysis made by Mr Kinnock reiterated Labour's commitment to gain 'maximum mutual disarmament' by negotiations resulting in verified agreements. It welcomed the shift in NATO's role from a mainly military–security function to a largely political–diplomatic part. This was happening in a context where European security is becoming increasingly defined in economic terms.

Labour's highlighting of NATO's shift of role from a predominant deterrent–defence function to a more political contribution was easy to understand given the Party's discomfort with most aspects of NATO's role in the earlier years of the 1980s. At the end of that decade, two closely related developments rendered the alliance a much more congenial organisation for Labour than it had been for some years. Force had become less significant in maintaining security in Europe, while NATO now described nuclear arms as weapons for last resort. As Labour had long been pressing for changes of precisely that type, this evolution of NATO was intensely welcome to Labour's leadership.

Since late 1986, the Party leadership had been engaged in a difficult effort to reconcile, as far as possible, Labour's non-nuclear policy with NATO's strategy and approach. Almost half a decade later, in the first part of 1991, Labour claimed that the 'objectives for NATO, which we set out in *Meet the Challenge, Make the Change* [of 1989] . . . [have] become, almost in their entirety, the programme adopted by NATO.'[18] It went on to list those objectives. They were NATO's abandonment of the policy, of flexible response and policy on the first-use of nuclear weapons, and the moves to eliminate such weapons by negotiations. Thus Labour claimed that NATO was undergoing a fundamental reassessment of its role.

The emphasis placed by Labour on its proximity to NATO's emerging position was partly a product of its political opponents claiming that Labour's defence policy could result in the break-up of the alliance. It was to be expected that the Party would seek to enhance the credibility and the respectability of its defence policy by stressing its compatibility with NATO's approach. The quite extensive narrowing of the divide between NATO's strategy and Labour's unilateral non-nuclear defence policy was a product of two major shifts. In Labour's policy review of 1989, the Party subordinated its non-nuclear policy to its commitment to NATO. Thus it explicitly placed the achievement of its aims in a multilateral process which no one state could fully control. By 1990–1, with the ending of the Cold War and the transformation of political security relations in Central Europe, NATO reduced decisively its reliance upon nuclear weapons. Thus with Labour adopting a flexible multilateral approach to reaching the aim of a non-nuclear world and NATO diminishing the place of nuclear weapons in its strategy, the once stark incompatibility of the two approaches was much reduced.

But one notable difference on nuclear arms separated Labour from NATO. That is to say, the Party still denied a legitimate deterrent role for nuclear arms. It contended that they could be retained only for purposes of promoting multilateral nuclear and conventional disarmament. By contrast, NATO's London Declaration (1990) commented that nuclear arms would be 'truly weapons of last resort', but they 'will continue to fulfil an essential role in the overall strategy of the alliance.'[19]

Returning to Labour's outlook on alternatives to NATO, the vehement refusal of the Party to contemplate supporting a military role for the European Community is in itself no surprise. Nevertheless, for much of the 1980s Labour was deeply alienated from what it perceived as a US-dominated and nuclear-reliant alliance. That experience might be expected to make it sympathetic to plans for any plausible alternative defence organisation such as an emerging EC defence community.

In the period 1987–92, Labour moved from a comparatively suspicious attitude towards the European Community to a stance of apparent near-enthusiasm for the EC. For example, Labour's 1987 General Election Manifesto *Britain Will Win* warned: 'We shall, like other member countries, reject EEC interference with our policy for national recovery and renewal.'[20]

The trends and pressures which led to the major shift in Labour policy towards the EC in 1988–9 are not difficult to elucidate. During the 1980s, British trade unions suffered an immense decline in their membership, role and influence. Some of that loss was due to the measures and attitude of the Conservative (Thatcher) administration. By contrast, the style of the European Commission, whereby it consulted with trade unions on social and economic matters, was profoundly welcome to UK trade unions. So also were its policies as made evident in the Social Charter to establish Community-wide minimum employment conditions on safety, training, wages and consultation. Accordingly in September 1988, the President of the EC Commission, M. Delors was welcomed at the Trades Union Congress. The following Annual Labour Conference, where trade unions have overwhelming voting power, formally accepted that Britain was integrated in to the Community. For UK trade unions, long excluded from national influence and with no assurance of when that might change, the prospect of using EC processes to promote their interests and policies seemed very attractive.

Second, in the June 1989 elections for the European Parliament, Labour claimed to be 'well-placed to make the most of European co-operation. Unlike the Tories, who are in any case hopelessly divided, we have many friends and allies in the Community.'[21] Labour's claim to have friends in Europe rested partly upon the participation of its Members of the European Parliament (MEP's) in the Socialist Group. In 1989, for the first time, Labour's Manifesto for the European elections was a joint statement with other European socialist parties. Labour's allegation of Conservative divisions on Europe pointed to public contention on the EC between Prime Minister Thatcher and ex-Prime Minister Heath.

In the aftermath of Prime Minister Thatcher's speech at Bruges (20 September 1988), which warned against a 'European super-state exercising a new dominance from Brussels',[22] Labour found it easy to portray the Conservatives as being negative about the EC. This was all the more so as the latter Party's election campaign was unenthusiastic about the Community. By contrast, Labour depicted itself as a 'European' party pursuing a 'communautaire' approach. Accordingly, the shift in votes and in seats (from 32 to 45) produced a substantial Labour win in the European elections, and it 'destroyed the nimbus of the invincibility of Mrs. Thatcher.'[23] That victory was associated with and partly a product of Labour's positive approach to cooperation in the EC, and of its relatively unified approach to the Community.[24]

Third, in 1988–9, the leadership of the Labour Party turned away from unilateral approaches to economic management in the United Kingdom. The influence of the Labour policy review, and the advice of Labour Members of the European Parliament, indicated the need for and value of coordinated and institutionalized cooperation with other EC members in dealing with issues like industrial regeneration and unemployment. The failure of the Mitterand government's experiment with 'Labour-type' economic policies some years earlier underlined the necessity for concerted EC-wide measures.

Fourth, the tumultuous changes transforming Central and Eastern Europe (in 1989/90), coupled with the preparation for the establishment of a single market in 1992, generated plans and initiatives for much greater European economic, monetary and political union. Labour had no choice but to respond to those initiatives. Two options were quite unattractive for the Party. Labour could not, with any conviction, adhere to a policy akin to that of Prime Minister Thatcher, having frequently criticised that approach for leaving Britain isolated in the Community. According to Roy Hattersley (Labour's deputy-leader), if Britain did not participate in talks about monetary and social union, the United Kingdom would be forced to join later on the Community's terms.[25]

On the opposite side, there was little possibility of Labour taking the lead in advocating rapid integration of the EC member states: given the keen hostility of much of the Party to the EC for many years, such a policy would also lack credibility. Therefore Labour followed the middle course of advocating that qualified majority decisions of the European Council of Ministers be extended from 'business and commercial matters to cover social and environmental affairs.'[26] Labour decided as well to support moves towards economic and monetary union in the EC on condition that it was preceded by a substantial narrowing of the gap in the member states' economic performance.[27] The bridging of that gap would, it was assumed, be much advanced by the implementation of intensive regional policies by the Community.

By 1991, Labour came to support greater powers for the European Parliament to initiate legislation, and to enable the Parliament to make the EC Commission more accountable. By now the Party accepted that UK membership of the European Monetary System could assist a Labour government to withstand pressures on the pound from financial markets and could be beneficial in other ways.

With regard to the particularly sensitive area of defence and security policies, Labour made the following analysis. Britain 'with a diminished role in world affairs' has to make maximum use 'of all organisations within which it' works, including the EC, to secure its objectives.[28] Labour's 1991 Statement, *Labour's Better Way for the 1990s*, noted that the implementation of common foreign and security policies will require the integration of political cooperation in the work of the EC institutions. It would need gradually to 'define priority subjects for joint action'.[29] These subjects included relations with other European countries and with the United States and Japan. Thus Labour views the EC as a major instrument for the United Kingdom and other member states to maximise their foreign policy aims by acting collectively upon the international stage.

Labour's approach to these issues is, however, somewhat paradoxical. The Party believes that defence policy must be determined by foreign policy[30] and is content to coordinate UK foreign policy within the EC. It accepts, with reservations, that Community institutions decide member-states' economic and monetary policy. Yet it advocates excluding defence from the competence of the Community.

A starting point in Labour's approach to an EC-based defence system assumed that the Community had to choose between two paths. One path depicted an inward-looking 'Euro-Gaullist' Community emerging in part from 'growing differences and tensions between West European countries and the USA.'[31] It was thought that such a Community could lead to a British–French–German military axis, possessing its own nuclear weapons.

That kind of Community would, it was believed, have many negative consequences. These included the entrenchment of the 'bloc division in Europe'[32] and the complication of international negotiations on arms reductions. It might also cause anxieties for the Soviet Union,[33] especially if (as seemed likely in 1991) former Warsaw Pact countries wanted to join the EC. According to Labour's 1990 Statement, *Looking to the Future*, a defence role for the EC would also generate other problems. It 'would make the position of Ireland as a neutral country very difficult—and make it impossible for Austria, Switzerland and Sweden, as neutral countries, to join.'[34]

The second option for the EC and the one which Labour strongly supports may be termed a 'Wider Europe'. The Party favours that course because it wants 'a majority of European countries to belong to the Community, so that it can begin to be a truly European Community.'[35] To promote the attainment of a wider Community, which the Party regards as a priority, Labour advocates 'speedy admission for Austria, Sweden, Finland and Cyprus, whose membership applications have been or are about to be lodged.'[36]

Labour's 1989 statement observed that given Austria and Norway's 'well-established and progressive social and environmental policies', 'they are likely to be natural partners at Council of Ministers meetings'[37] for a future Labour government. Moreover, their approach to defence issues and East–West cooperation 'are close to our own.'[38] Evidently Labour considered that enlargement of the EC could promote 'a sustained effort to establish durable alliances in the European Community so that a majority at the Council of Ministers will help protect and promote our interests.'[39]

Labour's declared support for giving the new regimes in Central/Eastern Europe 'realisable targets'[40] for full Community membership indicates that it welcomes countries whose political outlook and interests might not be close to those of a UK Labour administration. Labour's values and ideology with regard to the need to reduce international tensions and to diminish international economic and social inequalities predispose the Party towards the widest membership of the European Community.

For a variety of reasons Labour judges the EC 'should really have no competence in defence matters and will, in any case, have great difficulty in developing credibility in defence matters.'[41] Two issues are especially prominent among Labour's doubts about an EC defence role. First, the Party does not consider that without the United States the West Europeans possess the will or capacity to establish a viable defence system. In that regard, the Party has stated that a Labour administration could not participate in an EC force until it had a clear view as to whether military contributions thereto were voluntary or mandatory.[42] Second, Labour has expressed concern whether the force would have a nuclear capability and 'if so would any or all of the non-nuclear members of the Community be given a voice in nuclear strategy, targeting and use'.[43]

Many of Labour's objections to an EC-based European defence applied also to the Western European Union (WEU). That is to say, it was thought to possess many of the defects Labour perceives regarding a tight and exclusive European Community. In addition, the WEU's strong pro-nuclear outlook made it an unattractive organisation for states like Norway and Denmark. But prior to (and probably after) the Maastricht Treaty of 1992, Labour did envisage a role for the WEU as a 'forum for the exchange of ideas and, potentially, a way of providing the European Pillar'[44] in NATO. Thus while Labour is favourably disposed towards closer cooperation on defence with its European neighbours, it appears anxious to avoid undermining the link with the United States.

Besides the public reasons proffered by Labour for advocating 'retaining NATO as the functioning security structure',[45] the Party leadership was aware of other reasons for excluding defence from the competence of the EC. One such argument refers to the fact that even at the start of the 1990s, many active members of the Labour Party were suspicious of the EC, hostile to nuclear weapons, and uneasy about closer political union in Europe. Therefore the attractions of remaining in the long-established and now more congenial organisation of NATO were considerable. Moreover, Labour's painful electoral experience with defence in 1983 and 1987 made the leadership extremely wary of taking any new initiatives on these matters. So also did the knowledge that if the issue of an EC military role was raised, it would occasion vigorous internal Labour controversy. In the aftermath of the leadership's sustained and successful efforts to convert the Party to a multilateral defence approach in 1989, such a project had little to commend it.

Beyond the United Kingdom, Labour's leaders know that the support of US Secretary of State Baker for a 'strengthened set of institutional and consultative links'[46] between the United States and the EC does not embrace defence. In fact, the USA remains firmly opposed to the EC acquiring a military role.[47] This US opposition was presented by Washington as a rejection of European countries deciding on military issues in their own organisations, and then confronting the United States in NATO. Moreover, the record of the Community as a strong trade rival, challenging the United States in GATT and elsewhere, made the EC a deeply unpopular base for Europe's defence in the United States.

In 1987–89, a core reason for Labour to modify its defence policy was to remove commitments which deeply disturbed the United States. It was therefore to be expected that the Party would be sensitive to any action which might increase the likelihood of the departure of the United States from Europe. This was so largely because Britain remained especially vulnerable to the breakdown of European–US defence relations.

Thus on the one side, Britain is a 'small, medium-ranking nation state',[48] having fundamental shared interests in defence, politics and economics with its continental neighbours. This is indicated by UK participation in the European Community, the Western European Union and many other organisations. On the other side, Britain remains open (for years) to potential American influence over its military strategy due to its reliance on the United States for the strategic nuclear force together with related materials and facilities. A Labour administration, committed to including the Trident system in multilateral negotiations, could not be certain that this dependence on the United States would be ended even by the year 2000.

In addition, the United Kingdom is tied to, or closely associated with the United States in culture and international outlook, and in the extensive sharing of military bases and intelligence. The two countries share the legacy of relatively successful political and military collaboration, and the United States remains a leading destination for UK exports and overseas investment. Thus the Labour Party identifies a battery of international, national and internal pressures against supporting a European defence community, although many of those influences may be expected to decline over time.

Labour's perspective on Britain's defence role and expenditure

For most of the post-war era, including the 1980s, the level of Britain's military responsibilities and expenditure has been a deeply contentious issue in the Labour Party. When the principal perceived threat to Britain's security subsided with the end of the Cold War, the case for considering large reductions in UK military spending came to the top of the Labour Party defence agenda. In this way, the 1989 Labour Conference voted (against the recommendation of the leadership) to reduce UK defence spending to the average level of other West European countries. That view was confirmed at the Annual Conferences in 1990 and 1991. The successful resolutions indicated that the savings arising from defence cuts should be used to improve services like housing, health and employment.

The Labour leadership responded to these Party demands in an extremely cautious manner, although it did promise to seek 'orderly reductions in arms spending'.[49] In July 1990, the Conservative government announced proposals for substantial reductions in Britain's armed forces in July 1990.[50] Even after that statement, Labour offered few specific indications about the shape of Britain's defence effort under their administration.

In the years 1989–92, Labour leaders concentrated on attacking the Conservative government for not planning for the many consequences of reducing Britain's military capabilities following the immense political and military changes in Europe. They noted also that to a considerable extent the future level of NATO military strength depended upon the outcome of the CFE negotiations. Added to that, they sought major shifts in NATO's military doctrine and strategy towards a defensive stance (related to the concept of common security) which would facilitate large reductions in NATO's military forces.[51]

According to the Party's 1991 policy statement:

> Labour in government will take full account of international developments in determining what long-term defence commitments are needed to defend Britain properly. We will then be able to decide the size and type of armed forces needed to fulfil these commitments. The scale and nature of the British defence industry needed to equip and supply these forces will then become clear.[52]

Labour coupled its promise to review the country's defence commitments with a clear emphasis on internationally negotiated cuts in military strength, rather than unilateral reductions in Britain's military capability. Thus the 1990 Labour policy document observed that international negotiations can make possible reductions in UK defence spending far beyond anything envisaged at the Labour Party Conference of 1989.[53]

In October 1990, the majority section of the Labour leadership[54] resisted the decision of Conference on reducing defence spending, ostensibly because of the imprecise character of the resolution. Thus Labour's defence spokesperson Martin O'Neill noted that there were 'three different ways of measuring the average level of defence spending in other West European countries—per capita expenditure, total defence expenditure, and percentage of gross domestic product.'[55] He went on to warn: 'I don't want to send candidates into the next general election with an unspecified millstone round their necks.'[56] Although Mr O'Neill did not mention it, he was aware that as Labour was still perceived as weak on defence by much of the UK electorate, promises to cut defence spending would enable its opponents to exploit that weakness.

From the viewpoint of the Labour leadership, the successful 1989 Conference motions to cut UK defence spending were clearly inadequate in that they did not explicitly link such reductions with multilateral negotiations. The 1989 revision of Labour's defence policy was, above all else, a shift from a unilateral to a multilateral approach to reducing military capability. Therefore a proposal which displayed the signs of a unilateral outlook was unacceptable to the Labour leadership. As Martin O'Neill commented, the motion 'places less significance on negotiated disarmament than we want.'[57] Moreover, in the eyes of Labour's leaders, the Conference demand was premature in that it sought to determine the level of UK defence spending before a Labour government had conducted its proposed wide-ranging defence review.

In 1990–1 and thereafter, the most striking characteristic of Labour's approach to defence spending was the prominent part assigned to describing the Party's policy for defence diversification. A dominant concern of that policy was to reassure those likely to be affected by defence cuts. Thus the Party statements in both those years devote very considerable detailed attention to diversification.[58] This is not to forget the major statement on the issue in *Defence Conversion and Costs* (1986). But by the turn of the 1990s, Labour's analysis expressed a new theme and indicated a less confident assessment about the speed of implementing a policy of defence conversion. In 1992, the central theme of Labour's Election Manifesto, *It's Time to Get Britain Working Again*, was the building of a strong economy. Within that context, Labour acknowledged that 'The defence sector is a key part of the manufacturing base with around one in ten manufacturing jobs dependent on defence.'[59]

The immense importance of the defence industry in UK manufacturing stemmed not just from its contribution to employment. More significantly, it related to the leading place of British military technology (in sectors like electronics, naval shipyards, aircraft) in world markets. Due largely to heavy investments by leading corporations in the military sector, the United Kingdom is one of the world's largest defence exporters. By contrast, UK civil high-technology sectors (e.g. telecommunications and semiconductors) display relatively little capacity to compete effectively in international markets. As one analyst observed, 'Chemicals apart, most of Britain's key manufacturing corporations are highly or significantly dependent on defence work.'[60] Moreover, particular communities, employers and urban centres remain especially vulnerable to major reductions in demand for military equipment. Accordingly, very rapid changes in the level of military spending by the United Kingdom and by other customers for UK weaponry would drain some communities of their economic lifeblood. A Labour administration, concerned to expand rapidly an efficient UK manufacturing capacity, could not start such a process by hastily running down the most competitive part of that base, namely the defence-related sector. To do so would run counter to its declared objective of taking 'Britain out of recession and into sustainable growth.'[61]

Such considerations were reinforced by the strong voice of trade unions and by compelling electoral pressures. Unions such as the TGWU, which are influential in Labour policy-making, have been prominent in suggesting conversion plans and in demanding urgent government action to contain the 'tide of defence redundancies' announced since mid-1990.[62] In addition, the Labour leadership appreciated the need not to offend or ignore the many communities and constituencies dependent on arms production and military bases. As Martin O'Neill noted in October 1991, seventy of the parliamentary seats Labour needed to win (to form a government) were suffering from spiralling defence-related unemployment.[63]

Labour's wide-ranging conversion strategy placed the Defence Diversification Agency at its core, but it emphasised the coordinating role of the agency with government departments, local government, employers, trade unions and the proposed Enterprise Training Councils. To ensure that the 'diversification process happens as smoothly and effectively as possible',[64] the Agency was supposed to provide, on its own or in collaboration with other agencies, funds, research, information and retraining packages. It was expected also to supply advice on the best practices 'in arms diversification both nationally and internationally.'[65] According to Labour's 1992 Election Manifesto, the Agency would ensure that resources arising from reduced defence spending, would be used 'in the first instance for rebuilding and investing in our manufacturing base.'[66]

Labour's changed perception of the Soviet Union

As with other UK observers, Labour's perception of the Soviet Union altered quite sharply following the emergence of the Gorbachev leadership in the mid-1980s. For more than a decade before that, the Soviet Union was seen to have shrivelled as a serious ideological rival for the West except in some strife-torn Third World countries. Whatever credibility the Soviet Union enjoyed as a supposedly revolutionary superpower was eliminated by the disclosures regarding the Soviet polity and economy after the reform leadership introduced the policy of glasnost. (In the late 1970s and the 1980s, the Labour Party received official observers from the Communist Party of the Soviet Union, and other East European Communist Parties at its Annual Conferences, and it reciprocated by sending representatives to make contact with those parties. The majority in the Party regarded these contacts as a way to promote better relations with the Eastern bloc, not as a sign of approval for Communist Parties.)

In the very important domain of military strength, Labour had until the late 1980s taken the view 'that the Soviet Union and its Warsaw Pact allies have a large military capability which could pose a potential military threat to Western Europe.'[67] Labour acknowledged that NATO required quite large conventional military forces to counter that potential threat, but it strongly opposed most aspects of the alliance's strategy.

By the early 1990s, Labour statements noted that 'However problematic the future of the Soviet Union and some of its former satellites, there can be no return to the Cold War. The Iron Curtain is gone for good.'[68] But the Party leadership was insistent that the ending of any 'realistic threat of invasion from the East'[69] did not mean that Western relations with a 'volatile economically destitute and politically fragile USSR'[70] would be quite stable. On the contrary, in early 1991, Mr Kinnock's address to the Royal United Services Institute was full of expressions of anxiety about the direction the Soviet Union seemed to be taking. He noted the complications for international security arrangements 'especially when the political and economic plumbing is as bad as it is in the Soviet Union.'[71]

In the early 1990s, Labour statements articulated keen concern about the internal stability of the Soviet Union, the capacity of President Gorbachev to sustain his commitment to a policy of reform, and the use of repression to contain the Baltic Republics and other dissidents.[72] Given that the Soviet Union retained 'prodigious . . . conventional, nuclear and chemical might'[73] (even after the force reductions already agreed), Mr Kinnock commented that such might was in itself a reason to retain NATO. More generally he counselled circumspection by the West: 'Care must be taken because the Soviet Union is an unstable giant not because it is a stable monolith.'[74]

Thus the Labour leadership recognised that the ending of the Cold War and the winding up of the Warsaw Pact did not mean that Western countries like Britain could ignore entirely the immense military strength of the Soviet Union. The Party now emphasised the vital contribution a New Marshall Plan could make in saving the former communist countries of Eastern and Central Europe and the Soviet Union from economic collapse and political disaster. With the replacement of the Soviet Union by the CIS, including four nuclear republics, Labour's 1992 Manifesto identified a new set of potential threats emanating from those countries. It noted the danger arising from the further proliferation of nuclear arms in the CIS, and it went on to assert that the instability in the former Warsaw Pact countries 'could be as great a threat to world peace as the armed communism that has now disappeared.'[75]

Notes and references

1 Michael Howard, 'The Gorbachev challenge and the defence of the West', *Survival*, vol. XXX, no. 6 (November–December 1988), p. 483.
2 See T. Hasegawa and A. Pravda (eds), *Perestroika: Soviet Domestic and Foreign Policies* (London, Royal Institute of International Affairs/Sage Publications, 1990), especially Chapter 1.
3 ibid., p. 213.
4 See extracts from the notable speech by Mikhail Gorbachev at the UN General Assembly on 7 December 1988 quoted in *Survival*, vol. XXXI, no. 2 (March/April 1989), *Documentation*, pp. 171–6, 174.
5 See extract from Mr Gorbachev's Report to the 19 All-Union CPSU Conference on 18 June 1988 quoted in *Survival*, vol. XXX, no. 5 (September/October 1988), *Documentation*, pp. 465–8, 467.
6 For details of President Gorbachev's address to the UN General Assembly on 7 December 1988, see *Survival*, vol. XXXI, no. 2 (March/April, 1989), *Documentation*, pp. 171–6, 174.
7 Quoted in *NATO Review*, vol. 35, no. 2 (April 1987), p. 2.
8 See London Declaration on a Transformed North Atlantic Alliance of 6 July 1990 in *Survival*, vol. XXXII, no. 5 (September/October 1990), pp. 469–72.
9 ibid.
10 See Michael Legge, 'The making of NATO's new strategy', *NATO Review*, vol. 39, no. 6 (December 1991), pp. 9–13.
11 Western European Union, *Platform on European Security Interests*, The Hague, 17th October 1987.
12 See Jacques Delors' Alistair Buchan Memorial Lecture to the International Institute for Strategic Studies in 'European integration and security', *Survival*, vol. XXXIII, no. 2 (March/April 1991), pp. 99–109.
13 *Hansard, House of Commons*, 19 June 1990, col. 883.
14 *Looking to the Future* (London, Labour Party, 1990), p. 46.
15 Speech by US Secretary of State James A. Baker to the Berlin Press Club (excerpts), 14 December 1989, *Documentation, Survival*, vol. XXXII, no. 1 (January/February 1990), pp. 88–9.
16 Consult *Address by Rt. Hon. Neil Kinnock MP to the Royal United Services Institute*, Whitehall, London, 13 January 1991.
17 ibid.
18 Source: *Labour's Better Way for the 1990s* (London, Labour Party, 1991), p. 51.
19 See London Declaration, note 8 above, p. 472.

20 *Britain Will Win, Labour Manifesto June 1987* (London, Labour Party, 1987), p. 15.
21 *Meeting the Challenge of Europe: Labour's Manifesto for the European Elections 1989* (London, Labour Party, 1989), p. 3.
22 *The Future of Europe According to Margaret Thatcher, Europe Documents*, no. 1527, 12 October 1988.
23 Oskar Niedermayer, 'The 1989 European elections: campaign and results', *European Journal of Political Research*, vol. 19, no. 1 (January 1991), pp. 3–66, 9.
24 Labour's success in the European elections was principally due to discontent with the Conservative government regarding high inflation and high interest rates.
25 'Madness to buck EC integration trend, says Hattersley', *Guardian*, 4 December 1990.
26 *Labour's Better Way for the 1990s*, op. cit., p. 53.
27 Consult 'Campaigning on the economy and Europe', *Labour Party News*, no. 23 (January/February, 1991), pp. 24–5.
28 *Final Report of Labour's Policy Review for the 1990s* (London, Labour Party, 1989), p. 80.
29 *Labour's Better Way for the 1990s*, op. cit, p. 53. Labour leaders distinguished clearly between EC member-states acting collectively on selected issues and the establishment of a collective European foreign policy. Mr Kinnock's comment on a collective European foreign policy was 'Forget it'. See interview with Neil Kinnock in the *Independent on Sunday*, 3 March 1991.
30 See *Defence and Security for Britain* (London, Labour Party, 1984), p. 14.
31 *Defence and Security for Britain*, op. cit. p. 16.
32 ibid.
33 *Address by Rt. Hon. Neil Kinnock to the Royal United Services Institute*, op. cit, p. 4.
34 *Looking to the Future*, op. cit., p. 46.
35 ibid., p. 45.
36 *It's Time to Get Britain Working Again: Labour's Election Manifesto, 1992* (London, Labour Party, 1992).
37 *Final Report of Labour's Policy Review for the 1990s*, op. cit. p. 79. No doubt Labour's favourable reference to Austria and Norway applies also to Sweden.
38 ibid.
39 ibid., p. 80.
40 *Labour's Better Way for the 1990s*, op. cit., p. 53.
41 *Address by Rt. Hon. Neil Kinnock to the Royal United Services Institute*, op. cit., p. 4.
42 *Policy Document on European Political Union Agreed by National Executive Committee of the Labour Party*, 27 November 1991 (London, Labour Party, 1991).
43 ibid.
44 Neil Kinnock, 'International security in a changing world: the Labour Party perspective', *The RUSI Journal*, vol. 136, no. 2 (Summer 1991), pp. 1–6, 3. This is a slightly expanded version of Mr Kinnock's address to the RUSI in January 1991.
45 ibid.
46 Speech by US Secretary of State James Baker to the Berlin Press Club, note 15 above, pp. 88–9.
47 According to W.H. Taft IV, US Ambassador to NATO, the United States 'cannot support a European defence role which does not allow for full participation in policy making by those European countries who are not members of the WEU or the EC.' See *A Vision for a New Europe*, text of Mr Taft's address in Frankfurt, Germany, 21 February 1991 (US Information Service, US Embassy, London).

48 Interview with Glyn Ford, MEP, in *Tribune*, 20 July 1990.
49 See 'Arms spending cut backed', *Guardian*, 3 October 1989. It reports statement by Martin O'Neill, the Party's Defence spokesperson in the debate on defence at the Labour Conference in October 1989.
50 The 'Options for change' study by the UK government announced (on 25 July 1990) proposed cuts of about 40,000 (about one-quarter) in the British Army, about 14,000 in the Royal Air Force, and a few thousand in the Navy. The suggested reductions in UK forces in Germany were substantial, from four divisions to two, with sizeable cuts in aircraft also.
51 See 'No rapid military cuts, warns Labour Defence spokesman', *Tribune*, 9 March 1990.
52 *Labour's Better Way for the 1990s*, op. cit., p. 57.
53 *Looking to the Future*, op. cit., p. 46.
54 At a meeting of Labour's National Executive Committee in October 1990, Mr Kinnock's opposition to the resolution for reducing UK defence spending to the West European average had a majority of only one (i.e. 14 to 13). Prominent Labour figures who usually agreed with Mr Kinnock, like Bryan Gould, Robin Cook, Margaret Beckett and others, voted against his approach on that occasion.
55 Paul Anderson, 'Defence cuts defeat for Mr Kinnock', *Tribune*, 5 October 1990.
56 ibid.
57 ibid.
58 See *Look to the Future*, op. cit., pp. 47–8, and *Labour's Better Way for the 1990s*, op. cit., pp. 57–8.
59 *Labour's Better Way for the 1990s*, op. cit., p. 58.
60 Bernard Harbor, 'Tanks into tractors', *New Socialist* (June/July, 1990), pp. 8–9, 8. See also Jack Dromey, 'Time to bury the arms race', *Tribune*, 30 August 1991.
61 *Labour's Better Way for the Future*, op. cit., p. 5.
62 Jack Dromey, 'Time to bury the arms race', op. cit. Mr Dromey, a national secretary of the TGWU, leads for the industrial unions in negotiations with the Ministry of Defence and other defence employers. That union, which is the largest union affiliated to the Labour Party, has been prominent in pressing for defence conversion plans by government. The TGWU together with two other unions published *The New Industrial Challenge* (London, Transport and General Workers' Union) in 1990.
63 See report of defence debate at 1991 Labour Conference, *Guardian*, 4 October 1991.
64 *Looking to the Future*, op. cit., p. 46.
65 ibid., p. 47.
66 *It's Time to Get Britain Working Again*, op. cit., p. 27.
67 *Defence and Security for Britain*, op. cit., p. 6.
68 *Labour's Better Way for the 1990s*, op. cit., pp. 51–2.
69 *Looking to the Future*, op. cit., p. 46.
70 Neil Kinnock, 'International security in a changing world: the Labour Party Perspective', op. cit., pp. 1–5, 3.
71 ibid., p. 2.
72 See Mr Kinnock's address to the RUSI, *Looking to the Future*, op. cit., p. 46, and *Labour's Better Way for the 1990s*, op. cit., pp. 51–2.
73 'International security in a changing world', op. cit., p. 3.
74 ibid., p. 4.
75 *It's Time to Get Britain Working Again*, op. cit., p. 27.

Conclusion

In this concluding chapter, the coherence and feasibility of Labour's defence policy as it evolved in the 1980s is assessed. So also is the role of the Party leadership in shaping the policy. The chapter concludes with a review of Labour's response to the changed strategic environment of the 1990s.

Before the assessment is made, one important consideration should be noted about Labour's defence policy. An effective and successful policy must satisfy, concurrently, the requirements of three quite separate but interacting domains: the international environment (e.g. NATO and other security organisations), the British political system, and the Labour Party. Each of these spheres has its own set of players, ways of doing things and objectives. Each domain has some capability to initiate policy demands which affects the other two. Yet it is evident that the main opposition party in a medium-sized West European state (i.e. Labour) has much less capacity to influence the behaviour of the British political system and the international society than those systems have of constraining its actions. Similarly, the United Kingdom is, in general, more likely to find itself reacting to pressures from the international environment than to have the means to shape international decisions.

The logic of this situation is that in relation to defence issues any British political party which fails to reconcile the demands of the three domains has little prospect of securing its declared aims. In the early 1980s, Labour did not always try to take due account of the requirements of the other spheres. Instead, it ignored the fact that foreign and defence policy is largely about international relationships. At the same time it concentrated on what the United Kingdom should do without persuading the British people about the wisdom of the means it advocated (i.e. unilateral nuclear disarmament).

At the end of the 1980s, Labour adopted a revised policy which was relatively acceptable to UK opinion and consonant with international negotiations on nuclear arms. However, this impressive effort to accommodate the demands of the three domains was secured at a substantial price. That price included the reconciling of irreconcilables (i.e. retaining nuclear weapons while rejecting any role for them except the promotion of disarmament), the genuine unease of many in the Party, and the placing of Labour nuclear disarmament objectives almost entirely at the mercy of international processes.

The events of the early 1980s suggests that Labour finds it especially difficult to hold on to a balanced, well-rounded and feasible defence policy in the face of the urgent and intense demands of its members. Such demands, themselves a reflection of the fear of nuclear war, push aside the wider requirements of the Party. Conversely, the events of the early 1990s indicate that the very absence of demands from the Party or British opinion is leading to an inadequate response to the immense changes in the European strategic context. Such a failure could likewise prevent the Party from responding effectively to the altered environment of the 1990s.

One important test in evaluating a key policy of a major political party, such as Labour's defence policy, is whether that policy is contradictory on major issues. If that is so, it is likely to produce much confusion and uncertainty as to how a Labour administration would act on defence. In such circumstances neither the electorate, nor the armed forces, nor Britain's NATO allies could be very confident about the direction of defence policy under a Labour government. Even that government itself might be unsure about its policy on those issues marked by serious inconsistencies. Therefore the need for a coherent non-contradictory policy is undeniable.

From 1980 until 1989, Labour was committed to full membership of NATO while simultaneously being pledged to a non-nuclear defence policy. As NATO had been a nuclear reliant alliance for decades, the tension between the two strands of the Party's defence policy was evident. It was well illustrated during the general elections of 1983 and 1987 when Labour promised to remove US nuclear weapons from the United Kingdom. NATO and the United States might well be able to accommodate that demand without inflicting grave damage on NATO's military strategy. But that did not carry over into the political relations which held the alliance together. In other words, it seemed probable that the US Congress would react very negatively (perhaps by withdrawing a large portion of its forces from Europe) if it perceived that a Labour-governed Britain was unwilling to share the potential risks of a nuclear alliance.

Labour's political rivals contended, as did a few of its own Members of Parliament like Tony Benn and Eric Heffer, that the Party could advocate either full participation in NATO or a non-nuclear defence policy. But, they argued, it could not consistently support both positions simultaneously. As one proponent of a non-nuclear defence policy asserted:

> NATO membership is wholly inconsistent with a policy designed to reduce tension and to bring peace to Europe and elsewhere. A policy of active non-alignment . . . would make it possible to eliminate Britain's relations of dependence and to establish foreign relations suited to world peace and security and the country's own long-term interests.[1]

For most of the 1980s, the Labour leadership was acutely aware of, but unable to eliminate the core contradiction in its defence policy. If it sought to return to a nuclear reliant policy, it could not secure majority support in most sections of the Party, including the Annual Conference. On the other hand, if it advocated leaving NATO, it was expected to make the Party unelectable and to precipitate the disastrous resignation of many senior Atlanticist figures from the Party.

In these circumstances the leadership of the divided Labour Party followed the course of gradually removing some of the more glaring inconsistencies from the policy. Thus in the 1983 General Election Manifesto, Labour promised to provide 'effective defence through collective security' while pledging to 'reduce the proportion of the nation's resources devoted to defence.'² In this way, the UK defence burden would be brought into line with that of other major European NATO states. But in *Defence and Security for Britain* (1984), the pledge to reduce UK defence spending was made conditional on a number of variables. Moreover, it was not to be implemented by a Labour administration in the lifetime of a single Parliament.³

At the end of 1986 and in the early part of 1987, the Labour leadership reduced further the contradiction between its commitment to NATO and to a non-nuclear defence. This was effected by the relaxation of the promise to remove US nuclear weapons from Britain. Thus Labour emphasised that such a decision would be preceded by full consultation with the United States and other allies and would not be implemented according to a strict time-table. Moreover, the Party acknowledged that it would acquiesce in existing NATO strategy until it was changed, thereby indicating that it would not remove nuclear weapons from the British Army on the Rhine which would cause immense complications for the alliance. Similarly, the Labour leadership agreed not to eliminate unilaterally cruise missiles from Britain as long as superpower negotiations gave some promise of success.

Cumulatively, Labour's subordination in 1986–7 of the non-nuclear commitment to that of NATO's requirements pointed the way forward. That approach was extended to embrace virtually all relevant aspects of the Party's defence policy in the Policy Review which was completed in 1989. But even then, the Party's defence policy was not free from serious contradictions. Thus Labour's operational policy regarding Britain's nuclear weapons expresses a clear potential value in, and a possible use of that capability in the future. At the same time, Labour's rhetoric remains anti-nuclear in tone, and the Party asserts that it wants to retain the nuclear force as an instrument to promote nuclear and conventional disarmament.

The leadership asserts that its plans to maintain that nuclear capability until international negotiations 'are successfully and finally concluded with an agreement by all thermo-nuclear powers to completely eliminate those weapons.'⁴ Therefore the gap between the operational and declaratory Labour policy seems likely to persist for quite some time. Until that gap is eliminated, it has a strong potential to generate much confusion and embarrassment for the operational and declaratory strands of the policy of any future Labour administration. For example, the role of armed forces personnel engaged in sustaining Britain's nuclear force under a Labour government, such as the crews of Trident submarines, would be rather ambiguous.

Another central question concerning Labour's defence policy adverts to how well or ill based were its assumptions and how satisfactorily it was designed to achieve its stated objectives. The most striking example of a prescient analysis by Labour concerns its interpretation of how the Cold War might be eased. *Defence and Security for Britain*, the Party's 1984 statement on defence, observed: 'It is time for a new internationalist initiative to transform relations within NATO and the Warsaw Pact which could assist the phasing out of the cold war politics into which Europe is currently frozen.'⁵ It went on to assert that 'One consequence of new relationships within the blocs could be greater contact, communication and confidence building measures between the blocs' which might result in changes within 'the two alliances towards the long standing goal of their mutual dissolution.'[6] Developments within the Warsaw Pact and between East and West in the years 1986–90 suggest that that view was well founded. In particular, three changes initiated or permitted by President Gorbachev contributed decisively to establishing Western confidence in the Soviet Union and thereby to transforming East–West relations. They were the introduction of glasnost and perestroika within the Soviet Union, the unilateral Soviet withdrawal of offensive forces from Central and Eastern Europe, and Moscow's acceptance of non-communist governments in Warsaw Pact countries during 1989-90.

On the other side, Labour's vehement criticism of the strategy of nuclear deterrence asserted that it constituted a near inpenetrable barrier in the way of establishing normal relationships between East and West. Yet within half a decade of Labour characterising 'Nuclear "deterrence" as it has developed is therefore a dangerous or even suicidal approach to defending our society',[7] that threat-dominated relationship had been replaced by a normal pattern of relations between the blocs.

A much more serious criticism of Labour's defence policy has less to do with the accuracy of its assumptions and is more concerned with its failure to take due account of the circumstances wherein it would be implemented. For most of the 1980s, Labour defence policy can be seen as seriously deficient in four areas. Starting in the United Kingdom, the Party failed to persuade the British electorate that its defence policy merited their support. In the early 1980s, the Party was handicapped immensely in its efforts because of internecine divisions on defence and other issues. That handicap was reinforced by the resignation of senior Labour figures from the Party in 1981 and by the entrenched antagonism of the Conservative Party, the newly formed Social Democratic Party, and much of the UK media to a non-nuclear defence for the United Kingdom and NATO. But it was the passionate preference of Labour activists for ridding the UK unilaterally of nuclear weapons which proved the irresistible obstacle in the Party's efforts to gain the confidence of the electorate.

Second, for the first part of the 1980s Labour ignored the granite-like opposition of the United States to its non-nuclear objective. That hostility was directed especially at the pursuit of such an aim by unilateral UK action. Given that the United States was the dominant superpower and the hegemonic leader of NATO, Labour's neglect was remarkable for a Party which was committed to altering the strategy of the alliance.

Third, and related to the second point, the insular mood of the Labour Party in the first half of the 1980s meant that it took comparatively little interest in, or notice of the attitude of European countries towards a non-nuclear defence. From 1984 Labour came to realise that if NATO strategy was to be moved towards a reduced reliance on nuclear weapons, it would need the maximum support of other Europeans and especially that of West Germany. Accordingly the Party adopted a more outward-looking approach, especially towards other European socialist parties.

Fourth, and of most significance, Labour's defence policy contained grave defects in failing to accommodate complex and contradictory demands: that the policy should be able to satisfy the demands of the different strands of opinion within the Party and to attract the support of the British electorate. At the same time, it should be capable of implementation in an international environment where Britain could not guarantee its preferences would be accepted by other major powers.

In the period 1980–4, Labour's creation of a defence policy focused mainly on reconciling, not always successfully, the disparate perspectives of the anti-nuclear peace movement and the nuclear-reliant, pro-NATO Atlanticist sections of the Party. Thus Labour issued a defence policy which bore profound contradictions. It did not appeal to British voters and had little prospect of attaining its stated aims. Not least this was because it sought to implement in the lifetime of one (UK) Parliament an extensive programme which, if it could be realised, might take many years to implement.

In the General Elections of 1983 and 1987, Labour's defence policy challenged powerful interests within the United Kingdom and NATO. That is to say, it opposed NATO strategy and sought to break with a core element in British foreign policy, namely the commitment to working closely with the United States in the defence of Europe. It also demanded a shift from the practice whereby a small group of very senior officials, scientists and ministers decided Britain's nuclear weapon policy in private. Finally, the policy was sharply opposed to a prominent strand in English nationalism. That belief assumed that Britain's international status and history entitled the United Kingdom to possess the most advanced weapons, namely nuclear arms.

An astute Labour Party would have arranged the various parts of its formidable programme in sequence, so that it could endeavour to implement the less difficult elements at an appropriate stage and leave the more daunting issues until later. In other words, prudence would suggest that, while remaining true to its ultimate or strategic objective, it should follow a pragmatic incremental approach towards the achievement of sections of the policy. Evidently such an approach would take full account of the balance of favourable and hostile forces and pressures when deciding the order of implementing the defence policy. But mainly as a result of the deep legacy of mistrust by Labour members and activists regarding the Party leadership, and due to the sense of urgency generated by fear of nuclear war, the Party found itself committed to sweeping changes which were supposed to be achieved within a few years.

By early 1989, Labour's defence policy did take account of international conditions and it was comparatively acceptable to, if not popular with, the British electorate. Moreover, the policy was now shorn of timetables for the implementation of particular measures of nuclear disarmament, and the language of the 1989 revised policy was gradualist in tone.

Thus largely due to the prodding and persuasion of the leadership, Labour defence policy underwent an immense shift in the 1980s. By the end of that decade, Labour's policy manifested a pragmatic stage-by-stage approach. Then it accommodated both domestic pressures and international circum-stances such as the US central role in influencing NATO strategy and international negotiations on arms reductions. Therefore when Mr Kinnock visited the United States in 1990, he received a warm welcome from President Bush and other officials, in contrast with the politically cool reception he received on his visits in 1986 and 1987.

The success of Labour's leadership in reshaping defence policy was not achieved without raising serious doubts about the integrity of the revised policy. This is not to suggest that a Party seeking to widen its appeal should not modify some of its policies. Neither is it being argued that there is anything reprehensible in adapting policies so that they are easier to implement.

What is being contended is that a Labour Party which sought to maintain fidelity to its objectives faced severe tensions in reconciling those aims with the demands of domestic British politics and the international arena. Labour's leadership found that the combination of three powerful sets of pressures greatly strained adherence to its commitments. Thus Labour had shifted from its passionate commitment (of the early 1980s) to dismantle UK-owned and based nuclear arms at the earliest date. By 1991, Mr Kaufman was pledging that the United Kingdom would retain nuclear arms until all other nuclear states had agreed to eliminate completely their nuclear weapons. It was an enormous retreat by a Party which sometimes challenged successfully established policies and attitudes.

It marked also a major change of tone, from the 1989 Policy Review report, which asserted that the Party regarded it as essential for the United Kingdom to participate in 'international nuclear disarmament negotiations at the earliest possible moment.'[8] As a result of that change, Labour's sense of urgency about nuclear disarmament has been removed. Likewise the Party's declared support for the objective of eliminating all nuclear weapons by the year 2000 has lost whatever significance it may have possessed.

That shift derived firstly from opinion polling by Labour which confirmed that British voters adamantly refused to countenance the unilateral renunciation of UK nuclear arms. Second, it was a product of the relentless efforts by Conservative and other politicians to portray Labour as being weak, unreliable and irresponsible on defence and on nuclear weapons. Third, it was due to the clear communication by US officials in 1986–7 that they would deploy their immense resources to obstruct and defeat Labour's policy of unilateral nuclear disarmament.

When Mr Kinnock became Labour's leader in 1983, the Party espoused an inward-looking defence policy focusing almost entirely on eliminating nuclear weapons in Britain. Six years later, Labour had replaced a policy characteristic of an opposition party with a more or less worked-out defence strategy capable of implementation in government. The task of persuading the Labour Party to be less dogmatic about nuclear arms and about many other issues was entirely beyond the capacity of the leadership in the early 1980s. Then fear of nuclear war was quite intense in Britain, and the divisions within the Party were deep. Even in the late 1980s when such conditions no longer obtained, the transformation of the Party's defence policy was a highly significant achievement.

It resulted from the Kinnock leadership's special authority within the

Party which enabled it to promote the changes it considered necessary for Labour's survival and welfare. Mr Kinnock's authority was based upon the fact that he was the first leader to be elected by all sections of the Party, and his margin of victory was overwhelming. In addition, following the Labour 'civil war' of the early 1980s and the consequent election disaster of 1983, the Party was anxious to make every effort to support the leadership and to appear united even on contentious issues. Thus the leadership gradually secured a dominant position in the key organs of the Party, namely the National Executive Committee, the Annual Conference and the Shadow Cabinet. In this way Mr Kinnock achieved a more authoritative position within the Party as a whole than had any of his predecessors for two decades.

In the aftermath of the 1987 election defeat, the leadership responded by supporting the Policy Review which was designed to adapt and renew policy in the changing domestic and international circumstances of the late 1980s. The Review produced major changes in many policy fields, which brought the Party's position much closer to the outlook of the UK electorate. In this altered context many established policies, such as a unilateral approach to managing the UK economy, were seen as appropriate no longer. Thus the leadership used its influence and authority to persuade the Party to shift from a unilateral to a multilateral defence policy. As a long-time and eloquent advocate of unilateral nuclear disarmament, Mr Kinnock was particularly well placed to persuade those of a like mind that the Party could, with good faith, put its unilateralism on one side. Thus the unilateralist commitment, which for many Party members remained immensely important, gave way to another course.

Turning to the future for Labour's defence policy, two kinds of issue merit consideration. One concerns the Party's attitude to a European-centred defence system, while the other has to do with familiar issues such as defence expenditure and nuclear weapons. For a Party like Labour whose egalitarian values require support for and enhancement of services like health, social welfare, education and housing, the demands of defence are usually difficult to accommodate. In part this arises from the instinctive feeling of many in the Party that defence spending contradicts their principles, and if anything encourages rather than deters war and conflict. In that regard, it is notable that the Labour leadership was unable at successive Annual Conferences (1989, 1990 and 1991) to prevent strong majority votes calling for the reduction of UK defence spending to the average of other West European countries. Thus, at a time when the leadership enjoyed great influence within the Party, it could not secure an acceptable compromise, and it responded by disregarding the Conference vote in an ostentatious manner.

A somewhat contrary pressure on the Party is likely to stem from the demands of employees, communities and industries suffering from the decline in the size of the armed forces and of defence-related sectors. They seek to manage that process in a way which minimises unemployment and waste of resources. Therefore in the mid-1990s, the level of the UK defence budget and the issue of defence conversion are likely to be contentious topics in the Labour Party.

Labour's handling of nuclear weapons issues in the mid- to late 1990s

depend substantially upon two factors. Clearly, successful international negotiations for the reduction of nuclear weapons would do much to enhance
Labour's multilateral approach. On the other hand, a conjunction of international events which revived fears of nuclear war with domestic decisions for
the introduction of new nuclear arms could well generate intense Party
conflicts on nuclear weapons.

With regard to Labour's perspective on the altered strategic context of the
1990s, the Party's position seems to be influenced overly by past circumstances. In large measure, the approach to defence espoused by the Party in
the mid-1980s, involving support for common security, defensive deterrence,
and a reduced role for nuclear weapons, is much better suited to the Europe
of the 1990s. With the ending of the relationship dominated by the East–
West threat, the enhanced function for the Conference on Security and
Cooperation in Europe, and the emergence of the North Atlantic Cooperation
Council, the conditions are relatively favourable for the development of
diverse cooperative relations in Europe.

Since 1987–8, Labour has developed and updated its policy towards the
economic, social and environmental aspects of EC integration. It has done so
in response to changes in the European Community and as an expression of
the Party's increasingly European outlook. In the early to mid-1990s, the
European orientation of the Party is very likely to grow stronger as Labour
remains out of power in the United Kingdom. In these conditions, Britain's
trade unions, the European Parliamentary Labour and other elements of the
Labour Party can be expected to look to EC institutions for opportunities to
influence Britain's policies.

However, since the late 1980s, as the strategic context across Europe has
been transformed, Labour has not updated and reshaped its defence policy.
Many of the objections offered by the Party to an EC-based defence system
have lost their validity. Thus Labour's concern about such a system exacer-
bating Soviet fears and entrenching bloc divisions in Europe apply no longer.
Similarly, the enthusiastic efforts of the new democracies in Central and
Eastern Europe to get closer to the EC and to NATO, indicates they are not
averse to the Community developing a defence identity. At the same time,
the application for EC membership by Sweden and Austria argues that the
enlargement of the Community may not be impeded by the development of a
European defence community.

Of course, Labour's doubts about the capacity of the EC to develop a
strong political identity (as distinct from the identities of its individual
member states), and its concerns about the management of nuclear weapons
by a European defence community, are well based. Nevertheless, the history
of Britain's refusal to participate in EC institutions at an early formative
stage, only to join them later on extremely disadvantageous terms, offers a
message. On the other hand, in the uncertain and difficult international
conditions of the mid- to late 1940s, the Labour government played a seminal
part in establishing NATO, and the United Kingdom enjoyed a privileged
place therein for decades afterwards. These experiences suggest that it is
extremely unwise for Labour and for Britain to play a reactive and backward-

looking role in the debate about the evolution of the future defence organisation of the United Kingdom and its European neighbours.

Notes and references

1 Ben Lowe, *Peace Through Non-alignment: The Case for British Withdrawal from NATO* (London, Verso Books, 1986), p. 34. This pamphlet was sponsored by the Campaign Group of Labour MPs and has a foreword by Tony Benn, MP, and Jeremy Corbyn, MP.
2 *The New Hope for Britain* (London, Labour Party, 1983), pp. 36–7.
3 *Defence and Security for Britain* (London, Labour Party, 1984), p. 35.
4 Gerald Kaufman (Labour's foreign affairs spokesperson), 'Leading the way to peace', *Guardian*, 10 July 1991.
5 *Defence and Security for Britain*, op. cit, p. 15.
6 ibid., p. 20.
7 *Defence and Security for Britain*, op. cit., Appendix, pp. 43–4.
8 *Meet the Challenge: Make the Change: A New Agenda for Britain: Final Report of Labour Policy Review for the 1990s* (London, Labour Party, 1989) p. 87.

Select bibliography

Books and articles

Anderson, Paul and Detmer, Jamie, 'Interview with Denzil Davies: Labour's defence policy: will it be all right on the night?' *END: Journal of European Nuclear Disarmament*, no. 16/17 (Summer 1985).

Barnaby, Frank and Boeker, Egbert, *Defence Without Offence: Non-Nuclear Defence for Europe* (Bradford, Bradford University School of Peace Studies, 1982).

Booth, Ken and Baylis, John, *Britain, NATO and Nuclear Weapons: Alternative Defence Versus Alliance Reform*, (London, Macmillan, 1989).

Bullock, Alan, *Ernest Bevin: Foreign Secretary 1945–1951* (Oxford, Oxford University Press, 1985).

Butler, Nick *et al.*, *Working for Common Security*, Fabian Tract 533 (London, Fabian Society, 1989).

Chalmers, Malcolm, *Paying for Defence: Military Spending and British Decline* (London, Pluto Press, 1985).

Cook, Robin and Smith, Dan, *What Future in NATO*, Fabian Research Series 33 (London, Fabian Society, 1978).

Foot, Michael, *Aneurin Bevan 1945–1960: Volume 2* (London, Paladin, Granada Publishing, 1975).

Gapes, Mike, 'The evolution of Labour's defence and security policy', in Gordon Burt (ed.), *Alternative Defence Policy* (London, Croom Helm, 1988).

Gapes, Mike, *After the Cold War: Building on the Alliances*, Fabian Tract 540 (London, Fabian Society, 1990).

Gordon, Michael R., *Conflict and Consensus in Labour's Foreign Policy 1914–1965* (Stanford, Calif., Stanford University Press, 1969).

Harbor, Bernard, 'Tanks into tractors', *New Socialist* (June/July 1990).

Healey, Denis, *Labour and a World Society*, Fabian Tract 501 (London, Fabian Society, 1985).

Healey, Denis, *Beyond Nuclear Deterrence*, Fabian Tract 510 (London, Fabian Society, 1985).

Healey, Denis, 'A Labour Britain, NATO and the bomb', *Foreign Affairs*, vol. 65, no. 4 (1987).

Healey, Denis, *The Time of My Life* (London, Michael Joseph, 1989).

Hughes, Colin and Wintour, Patrick, *Labour Rebuilt: The New Model Party* (London, Fourth Estate, 1990).

Kaldor, Mary, 'END can be a beginning', *The Bulletin of the Atomic Scientists*, vol. 37, no. 10 (1981).

Kaldor, Mary, 'Block-heads: Getting Europe in on the act', *New Socialist*, no. 43 (November 1986).

Kinnock, Neil, 'Components of security: defence, democracy and development', speech delivered at Kennedy School of Government, Harvard University, 2 December 1986.

Kinnock, Neil, 'International security in a changing world: the Labour Party perspective', *The RUSI Journal*, vol. 136, no. 2 (Summer 1991).

McLean, Scilla, *Who Decides? Accountability and Nuclear Weapons Decision-Making in Britain* (Oxford, Oxford Research Group, 1986).

Morgan, Kenneth, *Labour in Power: 1945–51* (Oxford, Clarendon Press, 1984).

Neild, Robert, *How to Make Up Your Mind About the Bomb* (London, André Deutsch, 1981).

O'Neill, Martin, 'Political realities change', *New Socialist*, no. 60 (April–May 1989).

Prins, Gwyn (ed.), *The Choice: Nuclear Weapons Versus Security* (London, Chatto & Windus, The Hogarth Press, 1984).

Prins, Gwyn (ed.), *Defended to Death: A Study of the Nuclear Arms Race* (Harmondsworth, Mddx., Penguin Books, 1983).

Report of the Alternative Defence Commission, *Defence Without the Bomb* (London, Taylor & Francis, 1983).

Report of the Independent Commission on Disarmament and Security Issues under the Chairmanship of Olof Palme: *Common Security: A Programme for Disarmament* (London, Pan Books, 1982).

Rogers, Paul *et al.*, *As Lambs to the Slaughter: The Facts About Nuclear War* (London, Arrow Books, 1981).

Schneer, Jonathan, *Labour's Conscience: The Labour Left 1945–51* (Boston, Unwin Hyman, 1988).

Sloan, Stanley R., *NATO's Future: Towards a New Transatlantic Bargain* (Washington, DC, National Defence University Press, 1985).

Smith, Dan, *The Defence of the Realm in the 1980s* (London, Croom Helm, 1980).

Thompson, Edward, 'Deterrence and addiction', in C.F. Barnaby and G.P. Thomas (eds), *The Nuclear Arms Race: Control or Catastrophe* (London, Frances Pinter, 1982).

Thompson, E.P. and Smith, Dan (eds), *Protest and Survive* (Harmondsworth, Mddx., Penguin Books, 1982).

Labour Party publications

(These deal entirely or in part with defence and foreign policy. They are listed according to the date of publication.)

Sense about Defence: The Report of the Labour Party Defence Study Group (London, Quartet Books, 1977).

Democratic Socialism and the Cost of Defence: The Report and Papers of the Labour Party Defence Study Group, edited by Mary Kaldor, Dan Smith and Steve Vines (London, Croom Helm, 1979).

The New Hope for Britain: Labour's Manifesto 1983 (1983).

Defence and Security for Britain: Statement to Annual Conference 1984 by the National Executive Committee (1984).

Defence Conversion and Costs: Statements by the National Executive Committee to Eighty-fifth Annual Conference (1986).

Modern Britain in a Modern World: A Power for Good (1986).

Modern Britain in a Modern World: New Détente (1986).

Modern Britain in a Modern World: The Power to Defend Our Country (1986).

Britain Will Win: Labour Manifesto June 1987 (1987).

Meet the Challenge: Make the Change: A New Agenda for Britain: Final Report of Labour's Policy Review for the 1990s (1989).

Meeting the Challenge in Europe: Labour's Manifesto for the European Elections 1989 (1989).
Looking to the Future: A Dynamic Economy, A Decent Society, Strong in Europe (1990).
Opportunity Britain: Labour's Better Way for the 1990s (1991).
Policy Document on European Political Union Agreed by the National Executive Committee on 17th November 1991 (1991).
It's time to Get Britain Working Again: Labour's Election Manifesto April 1992 (1992).

Newspapers and periodicals

END: Journal of European Nuclear Disarmament
Guardian
Independent
Independent on Sunday
Labour Party News
Marxism Today
NATO Review
New Socialist
New Statesman
Observer
Sanity
The Times
Tribune

Index